"If You Don't Buy This Book, We'll Kill This Dog!"

—NATIONAL LAMPOON magazine cover lines by Ed Bluestone

"If You Don't Buy This Book, We'll Kill This Dog!"

LIFE, LAUGHS, LOVE, AND DEATH AT THE NATIONAL LAMPOON

MATTY SIMMONS

BARRICADE BOOKS INC. / New York

TO PATTI
whose love and persistence and wisdom
got me to write this book.

Published by Barricade Books Inc.
61 Fourth Avenue
New York, NY 10003

Copyright © 1994 by Matty Simmons

Printed in the United States of America

Simmons, Matty.
If you don't buy this book we'll kill this dog/by Matty Simmons.
p. cm.
ISBN 1-56980-002-2: $22.00
1. National lampoon—History. I. Title.
PN4900.N324S56   1994
051—dc20
93-42213
CIP

First Printing

CAST OF CHARACTERS

ACT ONE
The Early Years: What's so funny about that?

Me, MATTY SIMMONS: chairman, producer—Twenty First Century Communications, later National Lampoon, Inc.

LEE SIMMONS: my first wife

LEN MOGEL: president, Twenty First Century Communications, Inc.

HAROLD CHAMBERLAIN: president of Independent News Corporation, later Warner Publishing

ROB HOFFMAN: the *Lampoon's* first managing editor

HENRY BEARD and
DOUG KENNEY: the founding editors of the *Lampoon*

JOHN WEIDMAN: *Lampoon* editor

BILL JILER: investor, Twenty First Century Communications

GRAHAM LOVING: investor and underwriter

GEORGE TROW and
CHRIS CERF: early *Lampoon* contributors

7

MICHAEL O'DONOGHUE: a *Lampoon* editor

BILL SKURSKI
PETER BROMLEY and
MICHAEL O'SULLIVAN: the first *Lampoon* art directors

GERALD TAYLOR: advertising director, later publisher
of the *Lampoon*

BILL LIPPE: who followed Taylor as advertising director

SEENA HARRIS: who followed Lippe as advertising director

MICHEL CHOQUETTE
ANNE BEATTS and
SHARY FLENNIKEN: *Lampoon* contributors

SEAN KELLY: a *Lampoon* editor

MICHAEL GROSS: the *Lampoon*'s second art director

ESTHER BARRETT: bookkeeper, Twenty First Century
Communications, Inc.

CHRIS MILLER: a contributing editor

TONY HENDRA: a *Lampoon* editor

ALEX GARCIAMATA: Mrs. Doug Kenney

"MARY MARSHMALLOW": a *Lampoon* associate editor

LUCY FISHER and PETER IVERS: Kenney's closest friends

P. J. O'ROURKE: A *Lampoon* editor, later editor-in-chief

BRIAN McCONNACHIE: a *Lampoon* editor

ED BLUESTONE: a *Lampoon* contributor

GERALD SUSSMAN: a *Lampoon* editor

LOUISE GIKOW: copy editor, mother hen

MARY TRAVERS: singer and Gerry Taylor's wife

JERRY WEINTRAUB: deal-maker

MELISSA MANCHESTER: singer

BOB TISCHLER: sound engineer, producer,
"National Lampoon Radio Hour"

DANIELLE: a woman with exceedingly large breasts,
the *Lampoon* "Foto Funnies" queen

AMY EPHRON: writer and former friend of O'Donoghue's

DAVID KAESTLE: *Lampoon* art director of special projects

MARIO SAVIO: litigant

LIZA MINNELLI: litigant

WALT DISNEY: litigant

CHARLES SCHULZ: litigant

A MIDGET in Columbia, South Carolina: litigant

ALFRED BLOOMINGDALE: member of the *Lampoon* board

LEO VAN MUNCHING: the Heineken Beer baron

GEORGE SCHLATTER: television producer

* CHEVY CHASE: actor

* JOHN BELUSHI: actor

* ALICE PLAYTEN: actress

* MARY-JENIFER MITCHELL: actress

* GARY GOODROW: actor

* CHRISTOPHER GUEST: actor

* PAUL JACOBS: actor and musical director

*—the original cast of *National Lampoon's Lemmings*

EMILY PRAGER: a *Lampoon* contributor

PETER LAVERY: company manager *Lemmings*

DALE ANGLUND: his assistant

ART D' LUGOFF: proprietor of the Village Gate

JUDY BELUSHI: *Lampoon* staffer and John's wife

MICHAEL SIMMONS: musician and *Lampoon* columnist

JULIE SIMMONS: editor, *Heavy Metal* magazine

BOB MICHAELSON: *Lampoon* radio syndicator

POLLY BIER: producer of the radio hour

BRUCE McCALL: a *Lampoon* contributor

STEVE ROSS: chairman of Time-Warner

JANIS HIRSCH: a *Lampoon* staff assistant

GILDA RADNER
BILL MURRAY
HAROLD RAMIS
BRIAN DOYLE-MURRAY
JOE FLAHERTY
MEAT LOAF
PAUL SHAFFER
and

JIM STEINMAN—some of the actors and musicians in various *Lampoon* projects, including *The National Lampoon Show*

BARBARA SABATINO: my right arm for more years than either of us will admit

IVAN REITMAN: coproducer of *The National Lampoon Show* and *Animal House*

ACT TWO
The Middle Years: Hey kids, let's make a movie!

PETER KLEINMAN: Michael Gross' successor as art director

JAY EMMETT: president of Time-Warner

JERRY MILLER: assistant to the president of Universal Pictures

NED TANEN: president of Universal Pictures

BOB LEVINE: *Lampoon* entertainment attorney

MEL SATTLER: head of business affairs, Universal

ALAN KING
RUPERT HITZIG and
HOWARD COSELL—producers and star of ABC's "Prime Time Live"

LORNE MICHAELS: producer of NBC's "Saturday Night Live"

THOM MOUNT: Ned Tanen's assistant

SEAN DANIEL: Thom Mount's assistant

JOHN LANDIS: director, *Animal House*

TED MANN
JEFF GREENFIELD
PETER KAMINSKY
JOHN HUGHES
DANNY ABELSON
ELLIS WEINER
TOD CARROLL
FRED GRAVER
KEVIN CURRAN
MICHAEL GROSSMAN—some of the *Lampoon* editors
and art directors in the late seventies, and, in some cases,
early eighties

MICHAEL CHINICH: casting director, *Animal House*

DONALD SUTHERLAND
TIM MATHESON
PETER RIEGERT
BRUCE McGILL
STEPHEN FURST
TOM HULCE
JAMIE WIDDOES
KAREN ALLEN
SARAH HOLCOMB
JOHN VERNON
KEVIN BACON—some of the stars of *Animal House*

CHARLIE POWELL
BUDDY YOUNG: marketing bosses at Universal

BOB WILKINSON: head of distribution, Universal

SID SHEINBERG: president MCA

WENDY GOLDMAN and
RODGER BUMPASS: two members of the cast of *That's Not Funny,
That's Sick!*

JERRY ADLER: director of that show

DAVID BROWN and
RICHARD ZANUCK: executive producers, *National Lampoon's
Jaws 3–People 0*, the "biggest hit" that was never made.

JOE DANTE: director, *Jaws 3–People 0*

BO DEREK: that film's leading lady

GEORGE AGOGLIA: executive vice-president, Twenty First
Century Communications

HOWARD JUROFSKY: vice-president Twenty First Century
Communications

WALTER GARIBALDI: comptroller, *National Lampoon*

LEW WASSERMAN: chairman, MCA

DAVID BRENNER: litigant

JULIAN WEBER: counsel, then president of *National Lampoon*

MICHAEL FUCHS: president HBO

MICHAEL AND STEPHEN TOLKEN: story editors,
"Delta House"

MICHELLE PFEIFFER: an actress in "Delta House"

MARCY CARSEY: director of comedy, ABC

DAVID POLLACK AND ELIAS DAVID, coproducers
of "Delta House"

STEVEN SPIELBERG: a director

KATHRYN WALKER: an actress

HENRY JAGLOM and
BOB GIRALDI: directors, *National Lampoon Goes to the Movies*

HENNY YOUNGMAN: an actor

HARRY UFLAND: an agent

STEPHEN BACH: president United Artists

PAULA WEINSTEIN: Bach's successor

BRANDON TARTIKOFF: president NBC

MICHAEL MILLER: director *Class Reunion*

JACK KLUGMAN and
TONY RANDALL: actors

DON SIMPSON: president of production,
Paramount Pictures

BOB ZEMECKIS: a director

PENNY MARSHALL: a director

GARY NARDINO: president Paramount Television

MICHAEL EISNER: chairman Paramount Pictures

JEFF KATZENBERG: a Paramount movie mogul

FRANK MANCUSO: Eisner's replacement at Paramount

MARK CANTON: a Warner Bros. production executive

BOB DALY and
TERRY SEMEL: Warner Bros.; the folks in charge

FREDDIE FIELDS: president MGM

ROBERT ALTMAN: director, *O. C. & Stiggs*

BEVERLY D'ANGELO: Ellen Griswold in *Vacation*

ANTHONY MICHAEL HALL
DANA BARRON: the kids in *Vacation*

RANDY QUAID: Cousin Eddie in *Vacation*

CHRISTIE BRINKLEY: the girl in the red Ferrari in *Vacation*

IMOGENE COCA: the aunt in *Vacation*

BOB GRAND: production manager, *Vacation*

AMY HECKERLING: director, *European Vacation*

ACT THREE
The Later Years: We're out! We're back!
We're down! We're up! We're gone!

ANDY SIMMONS
LARRY "RATSO" SLOMAN and
DAVE HANSON: *Lampoon* editors 1985-1989

DONALD WILDMON: guardian of America's conscience

JERRY FALWELL: same job

CHARLES KEATING, JR.: a colleague of Wildmon's
and a well-known crook

MICHAEL WOLFF: a writer

AUSTIN FURST: chairman, Vestron

STRAUSS ZELNICK: his lieutenant

ANTHONY CASSARA: would-be humor baron

MARK SHANKER: same ambition

GEORGE VANDEMAN: Cassara's lawyer, partner

MICHEL ROY: president, FilmAccord

BERNIE BRILLSTEIN: president, Lorimar

ALAN PARSOW: a *Lampoon* stockholder

DAN GRODNIK and
TIM MATHESON: co-acquirers of the controlling shares
of *Lampoon* stock

DAVID BATCHELDER: their guru

BOB BECKER: broker, Drexel-Burnham

TOM JACOBSON: coproducer, *Christmas Vacation*

JEREMIAH CHECHIK: director, *Christman Vacation*

BRUCE BERMAN: president, film production, Warner Bros.

MICHAEL CARR: publisher *National Lampoon*

BILLY KIMBALL: never-quite *Lampoon*'s editor-in-chief

JIM JIMIRRO: whose J-2 company acquired the
National Lampoon

KEVIN EASTMAN: creator of Ninja Turtles

PATTI BROWNE-SIMMONS: my wife, my associate, my partner

KATE SIMMONS: noted: "The most beautiful baby in the whole goddamn world!" By the above referred to partnership

Many names have been omitted from this cast of characters that appear in the body of the book. Many names have not been included in the book itself, not because there weren't important *Lampoon* editors and contributors and actors and others who might well have been included but because my publisher urged me to keep this volume down under the weight of *War and Peace*. If I have offended anyone by omitting them, I apologize, but, after all, being offensive is the *Lampoon* way.

M.S.

FOREWORD

An elderly woman stands at the oceanside in Miami Beach watching her five-year-old grandson frolic in the surf. Suddenly, a huge wave rolls in, swallows the child and pulls him out to the open sea. She's frantic. In desperation, she lifts her eyes to the sky. "God!" she implores. "Do this one thing for me! Bring him back! If you do, I'll never ask for anything else as long as I live!" Another wave rolls thunderously into shore and deposits the sputtering child at her feet. She checks him to make sure all is well then looks back up to the sky. A pause, then, "You know," she says mildly, "he had a hat."

THAT'S A JOKE that appeared in my column in *Signature*, the Diners' Club magazine, in the early sixties.

If it had been a *National Lampoon* joke, only the hat would have come back.

This is what I had to learn late in 1969 when I first decided to publish the *Lampoon*. It was a kind of humor I was unaccustomed to, and I had to get used to the idea that among the many things people, particularly young people, would laugh at were war, death, sickness, depravity, deformity, deception, and grand larceny.

Brooklyn, where I was born, was a spawning ground for comedians and comedy writers, but it was a comedy of mother-in-law jokes, of Milton Berle and Henny Youngman, of Buddy Hackett and of my Uncle Danny who, hat snapped down over his forehead, cigar clenched tightly in his teeth, spewed one-liners in assembly-line fashion at the middle-aged matrons he sold shoes to. My first professional relationship with the joke was writing one-liners for the columnist Walter Winchell. Then came *Signature*.

After Len Mogel and I left the Diners' Club to start Twenty First Century Communications, our first magazine was *Cheetah*, a slick, humorless, hip culture publication that took itself very seriously while chronicling the happenings of a generation that probably took *itself* too seriously.

Being the only one connected with the magazine who could smile, I came up with the one idea that got laughs and the only one that the properly short-lived venture is remembered for, a parody of the *Playboy* centerfold featuring Mama Cass, quite chubby and quite nude.

> **Line from the National Lampoon stage review, Class of '86 while discussing Cass's untimely death: "If Mama Cass had shared her sandwich with Karen Carpenter, they'd both be alive today."**

Our second venture was *Weight Watchers Magazine*. For it, I edited a humor column which was simple, funny, and kind of sweet.

> **JOKE IN WEIGHT WATCHERS MAGAZINE: Jesus decides to relieve St. Peter at the pearly gates for a while. After a day or so, he looks up to see a bewildered old man standing in front of him.**

"I'm a simple carpenter," says the man. "Once I had a son. He was born in a miraculous way and was unlike anyone else in the world. He went through a great transformation even though he had holes in his hands and feet. He was taken from me many years ago, but his spirit lives on forever, and people all over the world tell his story."

Listening to this, Jesus is stunned. Tears stream from his eyes, and he reaches out and embraces the old man.

"Father," he sobs, "it's been so long!"

The old man squints, stares, and then, unsure, says, "Pinocchio?"

In some small way, all this prepared me for the *National Lampoon*. But no one was really prepared for the *Lampoon*. No one really planned it. No one was schooled for it. It just sort of happened. Books and articles have been written, trying to explain the philosophy behind the *Lampoon*. Hopefully this is the last time the word philosophy will appear on these pages. What was done was simply created to make people laugh. Everyone wrote for themselves. If most of the rest of the team thought it was funny, it was published.

Lenny Bruce probably started contemporary black humor and died doing it. But Lenny, at his most vicious, played to hundreds in nightclubs. His occasional appearances on television were heavily censored. On the tube he was funny but relatively sterile.

It was the *Lampoon* that first took its brand of take-no-prisoners humor to millions, that spawned the most popular comedy films of two generations and introduced many of the best known writers, directors, and actors in comedy today.

The three most popular movie comedies of our time were created by *Lampoon* people, *Home Alone*, *Ghostbusters*, and *Animal*

House. Former *Lampoon* editors and writers are all over such TV shows as "Cheers," "Seinfeld," "Married With Children," "Empty Nest," "The Simpsons," and perhaps a dozen or so more now on the air. "Saturday Night Live" was created by *Lampoon* writers and actors plucked from such *Lampoon* shows as *Lemmings* and *The National Lampoon Show* and from "The National Lampoon Radio Hour" which had exactly the same format.

And what was the basic formula that made the *Lampoon* work? First, an unprecedented gathering of talent. Second, a willingness on the part of management to let that talent have their way, no matter what the consequences. Third, the secret ingredient.

HOARY JOKE FOUND IN A 1936 BOOK OF HUMOR:
This old cowboy is teaching a tenderfoot how to ride a horse for the first time. The horse is old and cranky and is being difficult. "First," says the cowboy, "you smack him across the head, then you tell him to giddyup." "Why the smack?" "Once you get his attention," was the explanation, "the rest is easy."

The audacity and unexpectedness of *Lampoon* humor usually got the reader's attention. The rest was not easy but history.

There were three rules at the *Lampoon*. The first two were mine:

1. Say anything you want as long as it's redeemably funny.
2. Spread your targets. Pick on everybody.

The third was: Don't pay any attention to Matty's rules.

MATTY SIMMONS

CHAPTER ONE

HAROLD CHAMBERLAIN was the man who brought those of us who created the *National Lampoon* together.

Len Mogel and I left the Diners' Club in 1967. There, Mogel was the publisher of *Signature*, and I had been its editor-in-chief as well as executive vice-president of the Diners' Club.

I was a young press agent in 1950 when I reluctantly took on the Diners' Club account. Barely in my twenties, I'd been a newspaper reporter for the now long-defunct *New York World Telegram and Sun* when I was seventeen, then, after a blink in college, served time in the U.S. Army Corps for less than two years. There I produced shows for the troops at Fort Monmouth, New Jersey, and wrote a column for the camp newspaper.

When I was discharged in 1946, I was offered a job with a small publicity company, took it, and three months later, went out on my own. My first account was Lilliana's, an Italian restaurant on lower Fifth Avenue. My fee was thirty-five dollars a week, plus dinner. Soon, I graduated to the upper East Side and a swanky supper club called El Borracho. The proprietor was an elegant Sicilian named Nickie Quattrociocci who, at times, featured a talking myna bird and a "mad" guitarist who was locked in a cage during performances. At this point my brother Don left the Merchant Marine and joined me. We split the fifty-dollar-a-week fee, but since I was the so-called "front man," I got to eat the free dinners.

By 1949, we were also handling such clubs and restaurants as the Embassy, the Bagatelle, Jimmy Kelly's, Tavern on the Green, and the Chambord (then New York's classiest and most expensive restaurant), as well as celebrities such as Josh White and Artie Shaw and a newly imported beer from Holland, Heineken.

In 1950, we took on the Diners' Club as an account despite my firm belief that nobody really wanted to charge anything. Several years later when I was proven somewhat incorrect, I left the publicity business to join the Diners' Club and direct its sales, marketing, and publishing. My brother then ran the company on his own. He died in 1962.

In 1952, I married a beautiful young chorus girl by the name of Lee Easton and soon Michael, Julie, and Andrew joined the group.

In 1962, while at the Diners' Club, I became the major stockholder in the group that purchased the Philadelphia Warriors. After moving the basketball team to San Francisco, it managed to set the league record for consecutive losses. I sold the team the following year for $850,000, a $25,000 profit and approximately $140,000,000 less than its current value. I also owned a string of harness horses, wrote a number of books, put on thirty pounds that I didn't lose until the mid-1980s, smoked twleve cigars a day, made a lot of money on Diners' Club stock, and decided to leave after seventeen years simply because I was getting bored. The creation of the world's first credit card system, once a challenge, was now, with the company having been acquired by a major insurance conglomerate, immersed in red tape, know-nothing consultants, efficiency experts, and parental guidance. It was not what I wanted to do. So despite having three kids in private school, a ten-room apartment on Park Avenue with two in help, I left the security of the Diners' Club for a first year's salary of fifteen thousand dollars.

Len Mogel and I started a company called Twenty First Century Communications. Our first magazine, *Cheetah*, failed quite quickly. Our, second, *Weight Watchers Magazine*, succeeded just as speedily. By the second year, my salary soared to twenty-five thousand dollars. Our savings, sharply reduced by the investment in the new company and by our sizeable living expenses, was dwindling rapidly.

One of my new friends in our new business was Harold Chamberlain, president of Independent News, a public company that owned D.C. Comics, publishers of *Superman*, and the biggest magazine distributorship in the country. A large, bald, rotund man, Harold looked like a nearsighted Buddha. We were regulars in a weekly poker game that was interrupted one night when Harold jumped to his feet and announced that his glasses were missing and that he couldn't see. For the next half hour, five of us searched every corner of the room. Finally, someone noticed the glasses dangling from the chandelier that hung over the poker table. Lost in thought while contemplating a wager, Harold had absentmindedly hooked them on the overhead fixture. There was no such absentmindedness when he did business.

"I just had these kids in my office," he phoned to tell me one day. "They're from the *Harvard Lampoon*, and they're putting together a parody of *Life* magazine. We're going to distribute it. They're pretty damn smart, but they're kids and they don't know anything about the magazine business. I think they need some help."

We were operating out of congested offices at 1790 Broadway in midtown Manhattan. My office, the largest in the tiny complex, was barely big enough to hold the five of us for our first meeting, Mogel and me and Rob Hoffman, Henry Beard, and Doug Kenney, the three "kids" from Harvard.

Rob Hoffman was about twenty-one, good-looking with alert eyes and a take-charge attitude. In all negotiations, he would do nearly all the talking for his group. My experiences with Rob were brief and unhappy. He was to epitomize for me what was to happen to young people in the eighties. He was the ultimate tough unrelenting yuppie.

When I met Henry Beard, I said to myself "George S. Kaufman." I thought he was a ringer for the legendary humorist with whom he'd be compared by others in later years for reasons other than his appearance. He was beyond slim. He was gaunt. His skin was blemished with adolescence. His hair was dry and bushy like Kaufman's, and you hoped he wouldn't shake it. He wore a grey tweed jacket draped loosely over his body. The jacket looked twice as old as Henry. We worked together for eight years after that meeting, and as I look back now, it seems as though he always wore that same jacket. In his mouth was a pipe which he toyed with throughout the meeting. He looked very wise. John Weidman, who was on the *Harvard Lampoon* staff and became one of the first contributors to the *National Lampoon*, remembers his first impression of Henry at Harvard in the mid-sixties. He compared him with someone other than Kaufman. "Henry was like Bernard Baruch, the guy who sat on the park bench and told you how it was. He was the resident genius. His hero was S. J. Perelman, and we thought of him like Perelman, too." So, Beard was Kaufman and Baruch and Perelman and he was twenty-three. Henry's wisdom and demeanor and the way he was perceived were not to change.

Kenney was harder to peg. He was extraordinarily good-looking with the features of a leading man and long flowing blond hair. He wore granny glasses and seemed very nervous. Never, in those early meetings, would one imagine that this twenty-two year old one day would be considered the foremost humorist of his time.

The meeting wasn't one of particular importance to Len and me. Any relationship agreed to would be for a one-shot publication. No one in the room that day envisioned the possibility of a monthly magazine.

In addition to editing *Weight Watchers Magazine*, I was in the midst of a massive direct mail campaign for subscriptions. It would prove very successful. By 1968, the circulation of the weight-loss magazine would be more than 500,000. A few years later, it would reach one million. We built the credit card business with direct mail and having learned on the job at the Diners' Club, I had it down pretty well. It was a skill that would prove almost useless when the *Lampoon* came along since there were few mailing lists available with the names and addresses of young men.

The meeting was pleasant and simple. We would provide whatever know-how was meaningful at this point (the magazine was scheduled to go to press in less than a month), and our advertising people would rush out and try to sell advertising. That's what happened. We gave them advice about production and distribution and sold some ads, taking a small commission on any we sold and nothing else.

The *Life* parody was not successful. It was only mildly funny and sold about half of a print run of 750,000. As is the custom with failure, everybody had a reason for why it lost money; the principal and most plausible theory being that doing a parody on a magazine that had long since lost its popularity had probably not been a very good idea. But there were other reasons. We had gotten into the act only weeks before the magazine went to press. Costs were already out of hand, printing and paper had been bought at top dollar. A 50 percent sale on a magazine with no overhead and virtually no editorial expenses should have made a lot of money, but Hoffman, smart as he was, knew nothing about publishing a magazine. Mogel and I were convinced that with the right target and the right management, it would have worked.

Later that year, we discussed publishing another parody, this one of *Time* magazine. We would run the business end and sell the advertising. We'd split any profits. The *Harvard Lampoon* had lost $75,000 on the *Life* parody, and its board of directors wasn't about to lose any more, so we agreed to underwrite any losses.

The results were very businesslike and very profitable. The parody of *Time*, with a sexy cover and more nudity than Harvard had ever seen before, was published in early 1969 and earned $250,000, a nice figure for a one-shot back when—as one wit has put it—$250,000 was a lot of money.

Mogel was big on statistics. He'd sit and doodle with numbers for hours at a time. When the early estimates on the *Time* parody came in, he went to work. He projected a 90-percent sale. Only one major magazine in the industry, *Cosmopolitan*, was selling in that stratosphere. We sat in my office, looked at his projections, and we agreed that there was money to be made in this *Lampoon* business.

That June we met again with the Harvard three to make a deal. Kenney and Beard were out of school and had decided they, too, liked the magazine business. The five of us agreed we wanted to publish a monthly magazine to be called the *National Lampoon*. It would have a cover price of seventy-five cents and would be a slick, good-looking publication much like the *Time* parody. Hoffman stipulated that no issue could be entirely a parody of another magazine. That would conflict with the *Harvard Lampoon*. Then, primarily negotiating with himself as the business manager of that venerable publication, he carved out a deal giving him and Beard and Kenney the right to license the *Lampoon* name for a royalty. The royalties earned by the *Harvard Lampoon* in twenty years would not equal Hoffman's eventual cut for about four or five months work.

By now, about to graduate from Harvard Business School and the son of a hugely successful Texas and Nevada bottler and distributor of Dr. Pepper, 7-Up, and other soft drinks, Hoffman was not overmatched in the negotiation that ensued. Ralph Schneider, the one man who perhaps had most to do with introducing the credit card to the world, had been my mentor at the Diners' Club. He had once said to me, "The best deals are made by the guy who's least hungry." I had spent years being the principal negotiator at the Diners' Club. I'd convinced the major restaurant and hotel chains and airlines to honor the card. I had the background and experience, but Rob Hoffman was the "least hungry." He could take or leave this new magazine idea. He'd already promised his father he'd join him in the soda pop business. He'd also hedged his bets by having discussions with other Harvard grads who suggested they were willing to back the venture if we didn't. We did bring more to the table than money. We'd proven with the *Time* parody and with *Signature* and *Weight Watchers* that we could run a magazine. Because of this, he preferred to make the deal with us, but it wasn't a must.

We, on the other hand, were indeed hungry. *Cheetah* had failed. *Weight Watchers Magazine* was doing very well, but we owned only half. We needed a flagship magazine if we were going to be a major force in the publishing business. Hoffman wanted a fifty-fifty deal, like the *Time* parody. I held out for an eighty-twenty split of the stock. If we owned 80 percent, we could combine 80 percent of the gross and of the revenues and earnings of the magazine with our own, and it would be far more meaningful in our company's growth. If we owned less, we could only take out dividends if and when the magazine made money. Furthermore, I thought we were bringing more to the deal than they were. The *Lampoon* name was not being given free, and our attorneys had questioned Harvard's ownership of the *Lampoon* name for a truly national magazine. Only the *Harvard Lampoon* parodies, published sporadically, sometimes not for years, had national distribution. The *Harvard Lampoon* itself was basically a college humor magazine, not unlike or particularly superior to those at Yale or Columbia or hundreds of other schools.

What was coming from the other side of the table, then, was Kenney and Beard. It turned out that this was one helluva contribution, but in June of 1969, their resume included only the *Life* and *Time* parodies and a paperback parody of Tolkien's *Lord of the Rings*. (Beard, with his customary modesty, has described the Tolkien parody as "a terrible piece of shit.") No one knew at that time whether they could come through with an original national magazine of satire and wit. We had a hunch they could. We were willing to back that hunch with time and money. But it was still only a hunch. They were not yet "S. J. Perelman" or "Kaufman"—or Lenny Bruce for that matter.

Hoffman insisted they'd only go for the fifty-fifty split. We anguished over that for another day. We were getting hungrier by the hour.

Finally, we carved out a plan which gave our company the eighty-twenty split we needed, but we agreed to buy them out at the end of five years as though they owned fifty percent.

The next arguing point was at what price we would purchase their shares. We suggested eight times earnings. Hoffman came up with a study of the value of publishing companies listed on the New York Stock Exchange. They were selling at an average of twelve times earnings. That's what he wanted. We wanted to think about it. The deal haunted us. The more successful the *Lampoon* might be in five years, the greater the amount of money that would be needed for the buyout. We could have a huge hit and lose the magazine. We made counter-offers, trying to get a calamity clause so that, if we couldn't raise the money, we could pay it out over a period of years. Hoffman said, *"No* deal."

"Did you ever get the feelin' that you wanted to stay? And then you get the feelin' that you wanted to go," Jimmy Durante used to sing. For days we couldn't decide whether to pass on the deal or take a chance.

Bill Jiler, who with his brothers, Harry and Milton, founded Commodity Line, a company they sold to Dun and Bradstreet for more than ten million dollars, was, as were his brothers, among our original investors. I discussed the deal with him. His reaction was that with *Weight Watchers Magazine* already being successful, an underwriting to raise the money needed to pay off the Harvard group five years down the road would not be difficult since, of course, the payoff would be sizeable only if *Lampoon* earnings were. He suggested I discuss the matter further with another of our investors, Graham Loving, who was running one of the successful little brokerage and underwriting firms that flourished during the hot stock market of 1969. Graham's firm would underwrite a small public offering for us in 1971.

Loving was a fascinating character. He was a handsome little man with blond hair drooped over his shoulders and a black patch over one eye. We met at his spectacular Fifth Avenue duplex. His girl friend, equally good-looking, poured drinks. Graham offered me some marijuana. I passed and we started talking business. I told him I was worried about sticking my neck out on this deal.

He shrugged. "Hey," he said, "it's a good gamble. Billy's right. If the *Lampoon* makes good money—I mean earnings in the millions—I guarantee an underwriting for whatever you need." He smiled and sucked on the joint dangling from his mouth. "I absolutely guarantee it."

The following week, Len and I met again with Hoffman, Beard, and Kenney. I told them I was worried about being able to raise the money if the magazine did well. I laughed. "This is incredible, I'm worried about the magazine being too successful."

Doug had the first reaction. It was one of the few times he said anything about business during these discussions. "Hey," he assured us, "we're partners. Whatever happens, we would never hurt you."

Hoffman and Beard said nothing. I turned to Mogel. We left the room and talked. We agreed we had to take a chance. "If we can't raise the money, we'll work something out with them," I said. "They're not barracudas. Let's make the deal."

Years later, reading the first rough draft of *Animal House*, I came across a line that Doug had written. Freshman pledge Kent Dorfman had just had his brother's car totaled by his fellow Deltas. He turns to Otter, the leader, for solace. Otter shrugs and says it all. "You fucked up! You trusted us!"

I smiled when I read the line. I never did quite recover from trusting them.

CHAPTER TWO

LATE IN 1969 we rented an entire floor in a handsome new building at Fifty-ninth Street and Madison Avenue in midtown Manhattan. We spent several months redoing the office so that the staffs of *Weight Watchers Magazine* and the *Lampoon*, which was to first reach newsstands in March of 1970, were as far away from each other as possible.

We moved into the new offices just after the first of the year. Meanwhile, Henry and Doug shared a tiny office at 1790 Broadway. Most of their time was spent meeting artists and writers. A number of their cohorts at the *Harvard Lampoon* were already in the mix. George Trow, a staffer at the *New Yorker*, was to be a contributor and their advisor. For the first year of the *Lampoon*, he put the name Tamara Gould on the masthead instead of his own, apparently unsure of what reaction his regular employers might have. Christopher Cerf, another former *Harvard Lampoon* editor, was also to be among the first contributors. Both men were responsible for introducing yet another key figure to the *Lampoon*.

Cerf was working at Random House, a company founded by his late father Bennett Cerf. There, he was pitched on a series of projects by a rather ragged, undernourished-looking individual named Michael O'Donoghue. O'Donoghue was writing for an underground newspaper called the *East Village Other*, which considered itself an alternative paper to the

Village Voice, which in those days was itself an alternative paper.

The *Other* was a newspaper for the alienated. No one was ever more alienated than Michael O'Donoghue. Among the properties he presented to Cerf was a small book called *The Adventures of the Rock*. This was not "the Rock" as in Sylvester Stallone or Rocky Marciano. This was a real rock. And it would just lie there, immobile as rocks are wont to be, while adventures went on around it.

Cerf, never one for traditional concepts himself, was intrigued by O'Donoghue and his weird ideas. "This guy is nuts," he told Trow. "But he's terrific. You should meet him." And he did. They eventually agreed to write a film together, *Savages*. It turned out to be an early forgettable offering from the director James Ivory, who is today, of course, an important film maker.

What else happened was that George introduced Michael to Doug and Henry. For the first years of the *Lampoon*, these three would be its most important writers and editors. There is no question that they set the tone that made the magazine popular. Michael, however, insisted that he didn't want a "job" and at first worked as a free-lancer.

I'd made another deal with Doug and Henry. We'd agreed that I would give them a free hand editorially and that they would stay away from every other phase of the business. Immediately, they hired a trio of art directors who called themselves Cloud Studio. Bill Skurski had a beard and long-flowing hair to his waist. Peter Bramley dressed in eighteenth-century knickers and stockings, a beaded jacket, and a scarf. Their partner was Michael O'Sullivan, a short round man who had a massive head of hair and a thick black beard. Their appearance, once they left their East Village environs, was, to say the least, startling, and it reflected their artwork which was, to say even less, weird.

Remembering the *Time* parody, which had no shortage of pictures of barely dressed women, the cover of the first issue of the magazine featured a sexy girl in a leather bathing suit. OK. So far. Next to her was what appeared to be a duck. This was supposed to be the *Lampoon* trademark like *Playboy's* bunny or *Mad's* Alfred E. Neuman. I'd suggested having such a symbol to Doug and Henry months earlier. It was a duck unworthy of being a symbol for a high school humor magazine, to which this issue unfortunately bore more than a faint physical resemblance.

Both girl and duck were set against a murky color which, after twenty-three years, I have still not been able to identify. There were no cover lines to give someone glancing at covers at a newsstand even a vague idea of what the magazine was about. The inside was equally disastrous. Layouts were disjointed, and color reproduction and production values were awful. Cloud Studio had brought to our new magazine the free-fall, undisciplined, helter-skelter look of the sixties.

Doug loved it.

Henry wouldn't say.

I hated it and I said it—over and over again.

While the look was horrendous, the words were wonderfully funny. Weidman wrote a parody of Dr. Seuss called "I, A Splurch," which remains one of the best pieces ever to appear in the magazine. O'Donoghue kicked off his years at the *Lampoon* with "Pornocopia," a takeoff on pornographic books. Kenney dreamed up a series of erotic Norman Rockwell paintings, a visual grouping which was to set the standard for future such parodies in the magazine in that the art was dead-on Rockwell, but the characters in the art, of course, were doing things that had the potential of driving the homespun artist to an early demise.

"A Day with Playboy's Playmate" recalled an earlier *Harvard Lampoon* parody of that magazine. Henry introduced "Letters to the Editor," which would be a *Lampoon* standby for twenty-three years and were really letters *from* the editor. One was ostensibly from the artist Hans Holbein notifying the editors that he would only subscribe to the magazine if they published dirty pictures.

Doug wrote the first regular feature that would really get people talking about the magazine, "Mrs. Agnew's Diary," a monthly column supposedly from the typewriter of the vice-president's wife in which she signed off as "Judy," affectionately called her husband "Spiggy," and basically complained that President Nixon treated him like an idiot—a suggestion so close to the truth that the column immediately earned a fandom that each month eagerly awaited her revelations.

Doug insisted on keeping Cloud, needling me in issue number two with an editorial that gloried in the art staff's incompetence. "Everytime we call Cloud for layouts," he wrote, "someone leaves the phone off the hook, mumbles, 'Oh,wow,' and walks into a wall. Typical. Skurski and Bramley couldn't draw a straight line with a ruler."

I stayed on his case.

By the fifth issue, the magazine was floundering. It was funny but haphazard. Circulation, after a first issue sale of 225,000, was now lingering around the 175,000 mark. Advertising was minimal. But some interesting things were happening. College bookstores were getting requests from students and placing orders for small quantities of the magazine. And we were getting reader mail. We were forming a hard-core readership base that didn't just like the magazine—they loved it. Apparently they weren't bothered by its uncombed look. They thought it was great! Subscriptions started coming in from the best of all places—advertisements in the magazine itself. It meant they had read the magazine and wanted to read more. The early mail revealed something else. Kenney and Mrs. Agnew and the letters column were stars, but they wanted more of O'Donoghue, too.

ITEM: CALL YOUR MOTHER

O'Donoghue was sitting in my office one day when his father called from their home in upstate New York. "Michael," he told him sadly, "I have terrible news. It's your mother. She lost her toe."

Without blinking, Michael asked, "Did you look behind the refrigerator?"

This was not your ordinary, run-of-the-mill sick humorist.

I was unhappy with the layouts in the magazine, and I was livid about the covers. We were basically a newsstand magazine, but our covers didn't interact with the potential purchaser. And the colors still weren't popping out so you could see the covers from a distance on a newsstand. I announced that I would come up with the cover for the September issue. What I concocted was bright yellow and red so you wouldn't miss it. It had big, blatant cover lines that highlighted features about John and Yoko, Raquel Welch, and Charles Manson, and it had a "sexy girl"—Minnie Mouse, dressed to the nines and revealing something that had never been revealed before.

Minnie flashed tiny little titties covered somewhat discreetly by flowery pasties.

Kenney and Beard actually liked it. For the first time Independent News approved of a *Lampoon* cover. Harold Chamberlain called me to say, "Christ. It's about time you had a cover you could see more than a foot away!"

We waited for reaction. It came two days after the issue went on sale. The Walt Disney Company sued us for eight million dollars.

Since that amount was close to eight million dollars more than we had in the bank at the time, we eventually settled by agreeing never to parody a Disney character in the magazine again.

Magazine sales now started inching up. Hoffman, who served as managing editor over the summer of 1970, had left to join his father's business in Texas. Years later I reflected that I should have urged him to stay—he would have been the perfect executive to help build the *Lampoon*. He was not an editor, but he would have made a terrific second-in-command of the company. We always had a serious executive shortage. Mogel's strength being in production and advertising. Besides the *Lampoon*, we were publishing *Weight Watchers Magazine* and a nostalgia magazine, *Liberty*, which did moderately well for a few years. I was running them all. I'd also signed a book deal with G. P. Putnam and Sons and was completing a novel called *The Card Castle*, which came out in 1971 and made a fleeting visit to a couple of best-seller lists. I needed help. Hoffman, so young and smart and tough, would have been perfect, but I never forgave him for refusing to budge during our negotiations, and I never asked him to join the company on a permanent basis. I don't know if he would have accepted, but I should have tried. I was wrong.

Other things were happening. When we'd started to publish *Liberty*, Mogel had hooked us up with an advertising sales rep in Chicago by the name of Gerry Taylor. He'd impressed us and now he was selling for the *Lampoon* as well. We'd always needed a strong advertising director. Len urged Taylor to move to New York and take the job. At the time he was dating Mary Travers of Peter, Paul, and Mary. She lived in New York. He liked what we were doing. That was enough. Over the next few years, he would bring in two strong associates, Bill Lippe and Seena Harris. Later, when Jerry would leave for upward mobility, first Bill and then Seena would replace him as advertising director.

From the very beginning of the magazine, Doug and Henry had been searching for contributors who could write with some of the same surgical madness that they'd found in O'Donoghue. A Canadian named Michel Choquette sent in material then showed up one day with his girl friend, Anne Beatts, who had been an advertising copywriter. Choquette had so many ideas that it took a week for him to fully discuss them. He also knew people who would become contributors, a Canadian college professor named Sean Kelly and a couple of cartoonists who lived and worked in Seattle, Bobby London and Shary Flenniken. We liked them immediately.

Bobby was being sued for ten million dollars by the same folks at Disney who had attacked us. Bobby had gone even further than showing Minnie in pasties, having published an entire magazine dealing with the sexual activities of Mickey and Minnie, genitalia and all. Humorists all over the country were contributing to the Bobby London Defense Fund. We made a donation, and eventually Bobby did a regular comic strip for the *Lampoon* called "Dirty Duck." "Dirty" in no way resembled Donald.

Bobby's wife, Shary, was the major discovery. From the early seventies until 1991, she was to become the most popular *Lampoon* cartoonist. Her "Trots and Bonnie" comic strip led all reader surveys in popularity. In 1979, she became the first female staff editor of the *Lampoon*, leaving that job in 1981 but remaining as a regular contributor. "This is baby seal hunter humor," Michael O'Donoghue once told me. "We leave everything covered with blood. Nice people are out of place around here." For the most part he was right. Shary was one of the exceptions. Sean Kelly was the only person I ever heard her complain about. "You'd sit in a room with Sean," she once told me, "someone would come in, and they'd exchange a few pleasant words about almost anything. The person would leave, and Sean would turn to you and say the most god-awful things about them. It happened all the time. He was so charming to your face, and then he'd destroy you when you weren't around. I got to wondering what he'd say about me." Almost everybody I spoke to when preparing this book, years after Sean had left the *Lampoon*, echoed that sentiment.

His contributions to the magazine were good but not remarkable. He was a poet more than a writer of prose, and his magazine humor was often mean without being redeemably funny. O'Donoghue was even meaner, but his stuff was so brilliantly funny that it didn't seem to offend anyone.

Kelly did find his niche when the *Lampoon* went into the entertainment business. His lyrics for various record albums and for the show *Lemmings* often combined his inherent nastiness with talent and humor much as O'Donoghue did in his prose.

"He's only really funny," someone said of Kelly, "when it rhymes."

He would rip people or institutions apart effortlessly. He'd frequently be quoted in other magazines, much to my amazement, saying something eloquent and vicious about the *Lampoon*, this while he was on staff.

When I'd call him on it, he'd shake his head in dismay and insist he was misquoted. He was "misquoted" perhaps two dozen times.

When Gerry Taylor left the magazine for the first time in 1976, Kelly said to him, "You're like a ship leaving a sinking rat."

Choquette was a unique character. Like nearly everybody connected with the *Lampoon*, except me, he was rail thin. He had eyes that seemed always to be darting around the room and a mind that was equally active. He created a board game called "Orgasm." If you won, you got to touch a jellylike substance on the board. He was assembling a book of comics drawn by famous people, and he'd gotten many celebrities to contribute, including John Lennon. But he never seemed to finish any of his many projects.

One day Henry came into my office with Michel in tow. They showed me pictures of a man Michel had met. The guy was a dead ringer for Adolf Hitler. At the time, he made a meager living posing for whomever would pay him to pose as Hitler. Michel's idea: "I take 'Hitler' and a photographer to an island in the Caribbean. We show him living the great life, basking in the sun, playing with the native girls, telling fireside stories of his past exploits. We never mention Germany, the Nazis, or the name Hitler." I looked at Henry. We smiled. Choquette said he could do the shoot in a week, that he'd budgeted it at five thousand dollars.

A week later, they left for their island. Seven days after that, I got a telegram. "Hitler being difficult, shoot not completed. Need additional $3,000." I sent the money. Three days later, another telegram came. "Hitler an impossible human being. Need more time. Need additional $2,000." I sent back a telegram. "No more money. No more time. No more Hitler. Return at once." Two days later, Choquette returned with photos and with "Hitler," a mild little man who was starting to get second thoughts about his chosen role in life and seemed neither "difficult" nor "impossible."

The piece ran in the magazine in February of 1972 and in three subsequent anthologies. It was sold to newspapers and magazines all over the world, and aside from being an outstanding feature for the *Lampoon*, earned more than a hundred thousand dollars on the sale of the reprint rights, money we shared with both Choquette and "Hitler."

Toward the end of the summer of 1970, I told Doug and Henry that we had to make a change in art directors. I'd tried not to interfere with their editorial decisions, but I had to insist on this. As usual, Doug argued. Henry shrugged. I interviewed art directors and selected Michael Gross, a redheaded and bearded young man in his mid-twenties who had created the posters for the Mexico City Olympics and had been art director of *Family Health* magazine.

Michael recalls now, "I'd seen the *Lampoon* on the newsstand when it first came out and fell in love with it. In my head I'd redesigned it before it ever entered my mind that I could be associated with it. When I was offered the job, I went home and discussed it with my wife. 'I've never said this to you before,' she said, 'but I don't think you should take this job. It's ... it's a crazy magazine!' I was too far gone. 'There's great stuff in it,' I insisted. 'I know I can fix it!'"

When I introduced him to Beard and Kenney, Beard was warm and chatted with him for an hour. Kenney left after saying hello. He remained pissed at me for firing Cloud until he saw what Gross could do.

Gross' first issue as art director was November 1970. The theme was nostalgia, and the cover was another Norman Rockwell parody, this one of a barber cutting a young hippie's long hair. There were many cover lines placed attractively around the art. Colors popped out and held the eye. Gross had spent two days at the printing company in Kansas supervising color reproductions as the magazine was being printed. The regular features were redesigned, everything was clear and simple—easy to read and easier to understand. Because of that, it was funnier.

Even Kenney agreed. Gross had hit a home run his first time at bat. He was to keep hitting them until he left five years later.

In 1974 the magazine received the annual Columbia School of Journalism Magazine Award, the magazine industry's version of the Pulitzer Prize. The award was given for visual excellence.

Eventually Gross and Kenney got to be good friends and worked together closely.

In later years, Gross remembers Doug musing, "We invented nostalgia. Everybody wanted to read about their high school, their college, their first sex, their pesky sister, and their first zit. We brought it back to them." It was another reason the *Lampoon* was so popular—besides the anger and ridicule, it was a mirror in which the reader could look and see his own absurdities.

Gross tells of having lunch in the early years with Beard and Harvey Kurtzman, creator of *Mad* magazine and a legend to young people, including Beard and Gross, who grew up reading *Mad*. They urged Kurtzman, who had left *Mad*, to do a comic strip for the *Lampoon*. "No," he said softly, "I wish you all the luck in the world, but I just don't *get* the *Lampoon*. I don't relate to it. That's you. I'm me."

Gross recalls Beard saying to him proudly when the *Lampoon* really started to surge in 1972, "This is a phenomenon, and we're living it." And with Beard-like pessimism, he added, "It won't last."

It had now become the magazine in America that young men read and talked about. "I majored in English Lit and the *National Lampoon*," screenwriter John Fasano told me recently, "and of the two, the *Lampoon* was more important to me."

In a sense, the *Lampoon* was the magazine young people read after they graduated from *Mad* (the average reader was twenty-two), but more than that, it conveyed a feeling of anger and mistrust and disgust with so many of the things that young people felt were wrong with the world, such as Vietnam and lying politicians and greed in business. It did so without wordy analysis or rambling preachings—it did it like you wanted to do it yourself, by being nasty and clever. It was funny and to the point. "Fuck you!" the *Lampoon* said to the pompous and prejudiced and phony.

"You remember Esther?" Gross asked me recently. Of course I did. Esther was the elderly woman who ran our bookkeeping department and sentineled every dime that filtered through the company coffers. "We came up with a cover on which we were going to burn a hundred-dollar bill. You approved it," he reminded me, "and I went to Esther. I wanted three one-hundred dollar bills that I might not return, two extras in case we didn't get the right shot the first time around. She looked at me like I was nuts. I explained that it was for a cover and that you'd OK'd it. 'You're gonna burn it?' she asked incredulously. I nodded. Finally, she came up with a good reason not to be a party to this ridiculous plan. 'How do *I* know,' she said, 'that you're really gonna burn it?' Eventually you convinced her to give me the money. After the issue came out we were visited by two Treasury Department guys who told us it was illegal to burn real money and warned us not to do it again. 'See,' Esther said when she heard about their visit. 'I knew it was a lousy idea!'"

The one-panel cartoons in the *Lampoon* were always funny and dark. Best known of all *Lampoon* cartoonists was Sam Gross. In 1970, Sam, who looks more like the accountant he once was than a "sick" humorist, sold the *Lampoon* the cartoon that would appear over and over again on its pages, be used as a cover illustration for a *Lampoon* album and cartoon book, and be sold as an engraving in limited edition. The scene is in a restaurant. A sign says "Today's Special—Frog's Legs." Emerging from the kitchen is a frog on a cart which he is powering with two irons in his webbed "hands." He is legless. No one cartoon in the history of the *Lampoon* or, to the best of my knowledge, any other magazine, has had similar reaction or popularity. The engraving sold out in days. "I wish," Sam Gross once told me, "I could remember what I was thinking of when I came up with that one."

"We were hitting young America dead on," Michael Gross says today. "Most older people would look at the magazine and say, what the hell is this about? I hoped back then, that in twenty or thirty years, I'd read the *Lampoon* and wouldn't understand a thing in it."

Around the office, O'Donoghue had not yet affected the dandy style of dress that he became noted for later on. In the early years of the *Lampoon* (and one presumes, before those years) his clothing looked like Salvation Army rejects. He wore faded military World War II issue. In the winter, he was invariably cloaked in a heavy olive-drab army coat which was equally ancient. His thinning red hair was usually covered by a hat, most often a tired grey cap. On his nose sat a pair of granny glasses. Stubbles of red beard dotted his jaw.

It was 1972 and the gems were rolling off Michael's typewriter. He had already crafted "How to Write Good," "Children's Letters to the Gestapo," a piece so sick it could make you violently ill and yet so funny that you had to wonder at both the mind that could conceive it and yourself for laughing at it, "The Floor of the Sistine Chapel," and "The Vietnamese Baby Book." Many consider the "Baby Book" the most remarkable work of satire written in our times. In six awesome pages, O'Donoghue traced a war-born baby's life from birth, weighing eight pounds, ten ounces, to his first birthday at which his weight was five pounds, twelve ounces. In one sick, shocking sweep, he said more with ridicule than a thousand protestors could with peace signs.

It was an amazing exhibit of black humor. No one who saw it was unmoved.

ITEM: THE SURPRISE!

One of the men in the mail room walked into my office to say that a package had just come in for Michael O'Donoghue. The thing about the package that bothered him, he explained, was—it was ticking. O'Donoghue was out to lunch so I went into the mail room and very carefully checked out the package.

It was wrapped in brown paper, tied not too neatly with cord and, indeed, it was ticking. I decided to open the package and did so very slowly. Under the paper was a cardboard box. I carefully removed its cover and there, attached to a ticking clock, were six sticks of dynamite. I leaned back to ponder my next move. As I did, I felt someone's breath on my neck. I turned slowly. Everything I was doing now was being done slowly. Michael, his normally pale face now even whiter, his eyes bugging, had arrived.

For long minutes we sat together and stared at the package. Then he called a friend, the writer George Plimpton, who, Michael informed me, was an expert on explosives. He described the condition of the dynamite to George. No, Plimpton told him. It's no longer dynamite. It had now crystallized and was nitroglycerin, which could go up with the slightest disturbance. I immediately ordered everybody out of the building and called the bomb squad. After the police cleared Madison Avenue from Fifty-seventh to Sixty-third Streets, the bomb squad removed the package. The police then interviewed Michael who was wearing his woolen cap and tattered army coat and a six-month beard. "Remember," I cautioned them, "he is the bombee, not the bomber!"

The event was all over the radio and television news. I suddenly remembered my aging mother who sat at home listening to the radio all day. I called her to tell her that everything was under control. "Sure," she snapped. "No wonder! That's what happens when you publish that dirty magazine."

Postal authorities traced the package to Salt Lake City where they found the young man who sent it. A postal worker, he was a Lampoon and O'Donoghue fan who thought the dynamite was no longer "live" and that it would be a great gag to pull on the master of sick humor.

We urged the postal people not to press charges, and the practical joker was released.

Things started looking good. Gross was really into it now. The covers were getting stronger as was the art in the magazine. Gross introduced "The Funny Pages," comic strips that were a strange and fascinating blend, ranging from Jeff Jones's "Idyll," the adventures of a naked nymph with no story line and no particular point, that was to be for years one of those features that you turned to as soon as you got the magazine, to "Nuts," nostalgia by Gahan Wilson, whose macabre cartoons for *Playboy* had made him, at that point, perhaps our most famous contributor.

There was Shary's "Trots and Bonnie," Rodriguez's variety of amazingly sick cartoon humor, and perhaps the most memorable of all the early works, Vaughn Bode's "Cheech Wizard." Cheech was a—I don't know what Cheech was. He seemed to be a crossbreed of man and hat. He walked around his cartoon kingdom uttering drugged-out words of wisdom and unloading a quick kick to the balls of anyone who offended him.

Gerry Taylor had come up with a plan. The magazine had so offended the establishment, particularly those prone to more conservative thinking, that selling major advertising was a hard road. In the history of the *Lampoon* only one auto advertiser, Jeep, appeared on its pages. National advertisers were basically cigarette and beer and liquor companies. Taylor looked at the demographics. The average reader was in his early twenties. What did he buy? Recordings. Taylor concentrated on sales to the music industry, and by 1972, the *Lampoon* outsold all monthly magazines in that category and actually outsold any twelve issues of the bimonthly *Rolling Stone* which was considered, then, to be primarily a music magazine.

Circulation was growing rapidly. The second issue of the *Lampoon* in 1970 had a paid circulation of 120,000. By the end of 1971 that figure was 250,000. By the end of 1972, it was 530,000.

Chris Miller, who would become the most popular writer of short stories in *Lampoon*'s history, arrived in 1971. His reminiscences of his fraternity days at Dartmouth would eventually become the basis for the movie *Animal House*. One of his earliest short stories was *"Remembering Mama,"* the tale of a young man who visits the past and falls in love with his mother as a young girl. Some years later, Bob Zemeckis and Bob Gale, who were avid *Lampoon* readers, wrote a remarkably similar movie called *Back To The Future*.

Also newly arrived was Tony Hendra, a British comic and TV writer who was down on his luck in Hollywood when Beard called to invite him to join the group.

Hendra was to provide a sizeable fund of funny and well-written materials to the magazine. His wordless comic strip parody of a spaghetti western, "Il Showdown A Rio Jawbone," was another *Lampoon* classic, as was his "Deteriorata," a parody of the poem "Desiderata" which was popular in the late sixties.

But throughout his nearly ten years at the *Lampoon*, he carried baggage that hurt him and the magazine—no one trusted him.

With Sean Kelly, he was to create an atmosphere that wasn't there before they arrived. O'Donoghue was truly mad, but you knew exactly what he was and who he was. If he didn't like you or was upset with something you did, you knew it. After Kelly and Hendra arrived, there were factions and long periods when people weren't talking to each other. And, of course, there was the Hendra-O'Donoghue episode which will be discussed later.

Probably, however, neither had anything to do with what would happen in the summer of 1971. Doug Kenney disappeared.

CHAPTER THREE

THE EXACT DATE of Kenney's disappearance and where he went and why, was, at the time, somewhat obscure. At any rate, we did know that Doug left that summer without a goodbye. He'd been married for a year or so to Alex Garciamata, daughter of a South American diplomat and Doug's principal girl friend during his later years at Harvard and hers at Radcliffe. Their wedding was the first big *Lampoon* social affair, taking place on the grounds of the bride's parents' Connecticut estate. *Lampoon* editors and writers mixed with diplomats and politicians in a patrician affair that was highlighted by the arrival of O'Donoghue in a white suit, white shoes, white Panama hat, and carrying a black walking stick. His beard was neatly trimmed, and he walked with the gait of someone bred to the manor, someone perhaps out of the Gatsby era.

The terms "married" and "principal girl friend" in no way suggest monogamy on Doug's part. Women loved him and he loved them right back with great ardor and frequency. For a year before he left, he'd been having an affair with a *Lampoon* editorial assistant whose name had somehow metamorphosed into "Mary Marshmallow." Doug, without mentioning it to me or Henry, had promoted Mary to managing editor. We first learned of it when we read the masthead. Her responsibilities remained the same as when she was an editorial assistant, and since he neglected to mention this new title to me, her salary remained the same. She was a lovely sixties hippie with dark eyes, long flowing black hair, and a smile that suggested she knew exactly what time it was at every moment. Neither his wife nor Mary Marshmallow knew where Doug had gone. Lucy Fisher did.

Lucy was one of Doug's closest friends. Her boyfriend, Peter Ivers, was at Harvard with Doug. Lucy and Peter lived together for a number of years in Cambridge and New York and Los Angeles and were very much a part of Doug's life in New York when the *Lampoon* started.

"I remember," she told me, "Doug was living in an East Side apartment he shared with Rob Hoffman and Henry Beard in 1970. He was lonely and, mostly, unsure of himself. He didn't know if he was good enough to be the editor of a national magazine. And he was going to be married. No one could figure out what his hurry to get married was. Even Doug didn't seem to feel they were well matched. She was—well— sensible. Doug, as always, was all over the place, haphazard, moody, changeable. They were kind of a strange couple.

"When Doug left the *Lampoon* in 1971—it was early summer—he came to L.A. without any cash or credit cards. We had moved there a year earlier. He called us but we were out of town for a couple of days. He hadn't even told us he was coming. He'd heard us talk about a friend—Howard Smith, a film editor. He looked him up and called. He told Howard he was a friend of Peter and Lucy's and asked if he had room for him to stay. So, this perfect stranger put Doug up for a week or so until we showed up. We'd given up the apartment we'd been living in so when we arrived, we all moved in with Howard for a while.

"Doug did absolutely nothing. At night I'd read to him or we'd all sit around and talk. Sometimes, he'd walk around to bookstores and ask if they had a copy of *Teenage Commies From Outer Space*, the book he'd dreamed about writing for years but, at that point, hadn't even started. A lot of the clerks would tell him they knew the book and that they'd sold out all their copies.

"After a couple of weeks, he still hadn't written to Alex or to you or Henry. Peter and I begged him to let you know where he was. I used to buy funny postcards for him to send. Finally, he sent a card to you. I remember that it had no return address on it. All it said was 'Next time, get a Yalie!'"

Doug returned to New York the following winter, never talked about where he'd been or why he left, moved out of his place with Alex and, for a while, worked on the magazine. Then he left. Again.

That fall we got reports that he had been seen with Mary Marshmallow, who this time had disappeared as well, and that they were living in a tent on the beach at Martha's Vineyard. Later, a postcard from Doug confirmed this sighting. In the card he mentioned that he was working on *Teenage Commies From Outer Space*, which he had always promised would be "the best recollection of youth ever written."

When Doug did come back in the late fall of 1972, Mary Marshmallow wasn't with him. If he mentioned her, I never heard about it. She was never seen again at the office. Lucy Fisher recalls that Mary had always said to her, "I don't want to be a home breaker."

Doug and Alex were divorced soon after he returned. He did bring with him his rough draft of *Teenage Commies*. He showed it to some of us. Henry shrugged. O'Donoghue shrugged. I shrugged. Doug picked the manuscript off my desk, and he shrugged, too. "Yeah," he said, "it sucks doesn't it?" He tossed it into my wastepaper basket.

The book was never mentioned again. In 1979, we did a comedy special for HBO. We called it "Disco Beaver From Outer Space."

O'Donoghue, however, still remembers a line that he cherished from the book. In describing an incredibly noisy scene, Doug had written, "It sounded like a gunfight in a bell factory."

When Doug left, Henry had taken sole command of the editorial side of the magazine. Unlike Kenney, he was calm at all times. Beard handled O'Donoghue with stoicism, always massaging his ego and encouraging him to do more. If Henry had been as unpredictable and volatile as many of the writers working for him, both he and the magazine would have been in shreds after Kenney's departure.

Beard listened a lot, spoke less than anyone else and, by doing this, earned everyone's respect. He was a solid editor, changing this, suggesting that, forever complimentary, even when rejecting an idea or article. He was also a damned good writer. Without the passion of O'Donoghue or Kenney, he didn't write pieces that shook you up and had you talking about them for months and years, but he wrote funny stuff and he wrote a lot of it.

"News on the March," a look at the people and happenings in the headlines, was Henry's baby. It would be the forerunner of the news as read by Chevy Chase in the first act of the first Lampoon show, and it would then reappear as a fixture on "Saturday Night Live." It was probably the one feature that most shaped Chevy's career. "My Gun Is Cute," the story of a female Mike Hammer, was a short story by Beard that, like the

Hitler article, was reprinted around the world. But it was as editor that Henry best served the *Lampoon*. He was, Kenney's particular brilliance aside, the best man for the job and for five years he did it with near perfection.

Henry introduced writers' dinners, held once or twice a month and paid for by the company. These might include eight or ten of the regular contributors. The ideas and one-liners would fill the air along with a lot of cigarette smoke, not to mention other varieties of smoke. The dinners proved fruitful and at these sessions writers would often pair up to develop ideas that had been discussed over the table.

In the early years of the magazine, it seemed that Henry had no personal life, that the magazine occupied his every thought. It was rumored furthermore that, now in his mid-twenties, Henry was still a virgin; a condition reportedly cured when an actress in a *Lampoon* stage production volunteered to introduce him to the mysteries of connubiality.

ITEM: COMPLAINT DEPARTMENT

Michael O'Donoghue was in his office screaming at the other end of the telephone. That was not unusual, but this particular tirade was classic O'Donoghue. He discovered obscenities not yet conceived. He had gone from loud to earsplitting. One by one, the staff gathered outside his door to listen in wonder. He was addressing a clerk at the Columbia Record Club, and he was now describing the individual's ancestors. It seemed they had sent him the wrong recording, one he did not order. The screams came louder and echoed throughout the floor. The staff of Weight Watchers Magazine joined the Lampoon group outside Michael's office. In a burst of venom, he told the clerk that the correct album would be sent or violence would follow. Finally, he viciously slammed down the receiver then—maiming his fourth phone in a month—ripped the offending equipment out of its socket and flung it against the wall. There was a moment or two of silence. The door opened slowly, and Michael looked out at the perhaps fifteen people now outside his office. Slowly, a sly smile crossed his face. His audience applauded. Michael beamed.

Kenney changed a great deal when he came back. He never wanted to be in charge again. He took the title senior editor and had billing on the masthead below Beard and Hendra, who was the managing editor. Henry was in charge, but all editors were on an equal basis, unless there was a decision they couldn't agree on. Then Henry had the last word. If it was something that affected company policy or could get us sued, I would overrule everybody. An issue editor, who was theoretically editor-in chief for the month, was the cohesive creative force for a given issue, with Beard and the others remaining closely involved with the selection, rewriting, editing of material.

Regular features like the "News" or "Mrs. Agnew's Diary" were not part of an issue editor's domain nor were the comic pages or cartoons which were selected by Gross. Ideas for covers were usually concocted at cover meetings. The right cover could mean a difference of twenty-five percent or more in newsstand sales, and we were primarily a newsstand magazine. I had to approve any cover.

An example of the variance in cover sales appeared most dramatically in 1974 when the Pubescence Issue featuring a cover with a beautiful teen-age girl holding a cherry in her hand sold just more than one million copies, the highest single copy sale in the history of the *Lampoon*. The next issue, Civics, featured a much more clever rendering of then-President Ford jamming an ice cream cone into his forehead. (Ford was becoming legendary for his inability to "chew gum and walk at the same time," a notion that Chevy Chase was to remind "Saturday Night Live" viewers of again and again.) Sales dropped to less than 600,000 with that issue, a dip of more than forty percent.

In a book he wrote some years ago, Hendra, who (well after he left the magazine) liked to tell people that I was a pornographer because I wanted attractive women on the cover, suggested that the drop-off occurred because the offending Girl With Cherry Issue was so bad that the readers didn't come back for the next one. He blamed P. J. O'Rourke who was issue editor that month for what he considered a serious decline in both quality and humor.

The theory was illogical since subsequent issues, many of which had good-looking women on the covers, all sold well in excess of the Ford and Ice Cream Issue. In 1985, we did a fifteen-year study on the sale of *Lampoon* issues. Almost every cover with an attractive woman on it sold better than covers with men or anything else during the same year. In 1977, I went for broke, conceiving a cover with a pretty woman, a dog, and a baby, those traditionally being the subjects that sold the most magazines. Under the picture was the legend "Give me a magazine cover with a pretty woman, a dog and a baby on it and I'll give you a magazine that sells." It was signed, "William Randolph Hearst." Hearst never, to anyone's recollection, ever said that—but he could have. The issue sold well.

CHAPTER FOUR

ITEM: BAD DAY ON THE BIG ROCK

Hendra decided that it would be good exercise for him to bike from his home in Greenwich Village to the midtown offices of the Lampoon each day. His first day out, he ran over a little old lady on Park Avenue, was given a summons, and later was hit with a personal injury suit. The second day, he chained his bike to a bus stop. When he came back in the evening, only the frame of the front of the bike remained. The staff chipped in and bought him a skate.

BY THE END of 1972, the magazine was soaring. Graham Loving had brought Twenty First Century Communications public the previous year, and in its first year as a public company, it had declared a dividend. The public issue was small and was to serve to set up the much bigger secondary one we anticipated needing in 1975. *Lampoon* circulation had gone from just under 200,000 at the beginning of 1971 to 550,000 in 1972. Company revenues had tripled and earnings had quadrupled. Newspapers and magazines were flooding us with requests for interviews. This was not an immodest group and such requests were readily honored. Frequently, they would turn from interview to Marx Brothers' movie with Beard snapping out one-liners, O'Donoghue and Kenney improvising a sketch, Kelly topping all with his cutting and very quotable wit, and the others competing not necessarily for ink but to see who could succeed best at getting his colleagues to laugh.

It wasn't difficult. This group didn't necessarily all like each other, but they liked to laugh. And they all respected each other's talents.

Harold Ramis, the actor-writer-director who is considered by many to be one of the most talented and intelligent people in Hollywood, came to the *Lampoon* in 1973 to work on the "National Lampoon Radio Hour." "I thought the editors," he recalls, "were the smartest, hippest guys I'd ever met and to be with them all in one room was devastating. When I arrived, the first thing I did was read every word of every issue of the magazine and listen to every tape of the radio hour. It was mind-boggling. To work with them in person was even more exciting. So much talent. So bright. So witty."

More than two decades later, Michael O'Donoghue would echo Ramis's thinking. "These were the brightest guys I ever met, before or after. [When he left the *Lampoon*, he became the first head writer of "Saturday Night Live."] Certainly, the group at "Saturday Night Live" was never as good as the one at the *Lampoon*. Doug, in particular, had an unparalleled gift for comedy," he remembers. "He could make anything funny. But he was deeply insecure. Within a few seconds, he could be 'superboy' and then the victim that superboy rescued.

"Henry was one of the smartest people alive. To be good at humor, you should know a lot about a lot of things. Henry did. Henry taught himself to be funny. He didn't have a funny bone in his body, but he figured out how to do it. Doug was naturally funny. Henry wasn't. He decided to become funny and did.

"P. J. was the same way. He studied humor. He took some of my style, some of Doug's, whatever he could learn from Henry (who was like a chameleon and had no one style), mixed them together and created P. J. the humorist.

"O'Rourke was like that," he mused. "Very ambitious. Very upwardly mobile. I always liked him.

"Doug and I used to compete. We thought of ourselves as the 'A-Team.' We liked each other, but each of us was always trying to show he was the funniest.

"Tony's problem was he always felt incredible pressure to compete with Doug and me. He wanted to be on the A-Team so bad, he was not beyond swiping or taking at least partial credit for good ideas he had nothing to do with. It became a joke around the office.

"Brian McConnachie was great. A terrific person and very funny. When he first came to the *Lampoon* as a cartoonist, he was OK but not exceptional. He just got better and better. I think management's policy of more or less leaving us alone had a lot to do with our ability to be funny frequently. We were never asked to conform. There was no one *Lampoon* voice. When you read *Playboy*, it was Hefner's voice. All magazines have one approach to writing and one basic result. Not the *Lampoon*. It was a lot of different voices.

"I never met anyone who could write poetry like Sean Kelly. Once, I gave him an idea, 'The Love Song of J. Edgar Hoover.' In one day he came up with a brilliant, biting poem that would have taken me a month to do half as well.

"Unfortunately, he had the backbone of an anchovy. He'd never be in fights, but he knew how to egg other people into having them."

The *Lampoon* was booming, *Weight Watchers Magazine* circulation was moving up toward the million mark. *Liberty*, which we sold by the end of that year, 1973, because we didn't think it was going anywhere, was showing small profit. And we'd purchased the teenage girl's magazine, *Ingenue*. We were making a noticeable dent in the publishing industry.

ITEM: MY 1972 CHRISTMAS GIFT

O'Donoghue and Michael Gross bought me a sled for Christmas. They blanked out the name "Flexible Flyer" and wrote in "Rosebud."

The *Lampoon* had now become a magnet for many of the most talented young writers and artists in the country—and from Canada, too. The Canadian influence on the *Lampoon* was already pronounced with Kelly and Choquette. It became even greater with the arrival of Bruce McCall, Ted Mann, Ivan Reitman, and others.

In 1971, smelling around for a buck as always, I had the staff put together a collection of the best articles and art of the first year. It was called simply "The Best of Number One." It was more profitable, without advertising, than any single issue had been during the first two years of publishing. Naturally, we followed up in subsequent years with similar collections including a 1972 edition called "The Breast of the National Lampoon" which with voluptuous girl on cover, sold almost 90 percent of a 350,000 distribution.

Brian McConnachie was the most whimsical of all the Lampooners. His sense of the odd never left him. He was strolling past the subscription department one day when he noticed a letter from an irate reader of *Weight Watchers Magazine* who had written to complain that she'd asked for a back issue of that magazine but had inadvertently been sent a copy of the *Lampoon* instead and that she had been offended by its contents. McConnachie assured the subscription clerk he'd handle the matter. He promptly wrapped another, even more abrasive issue of the *Lampoon*, and sent it to the person registering the complaint. "Sorry for the mistake," he wrote in a letter accompanying the issue. "Hope this is what you wanted." He signed it "B. McConnachie, Subscription Manager." Back promptly came another complaint, this one even angrier. Back, just as promptly, went still another copy of the *Lampoon*. This correspondence went on for more than a month and got more heated with each exchange. Finally, when the reader stopped writing, Brian sent her a bill for the last issue mailed to her.

Brian was particularly noteworthy in his savage send-up of violent kids' film cartoons in "Kit 'n' Kaboodle," in a collection of photographs called "Our Wonderful Bodies" which included a photo of an electric storm, the caption to which suggested that this was the inside of a Chinaman's brain while attempting to pronounce the letter "L," and with a send-up of the Studs Turkel man-in-the street interviews in which, in the mode of "Where were you the day John F. Kennedy died," he asked, "Where were you the day Ezio Pinza died?" Of course, nobody but Mrs. Pinza would have remembered.

In an article on the *Lampoon* in the *New York Times Sunday Magazine* in 1972, Mopsy Kennedy Strange quoted me as saying, "There is no one unassailable taboo, thing or attitude it [the Lampoon] holds sacred. I want [the staff] to pick on everyone—they shouldn't pick favorites. Part of our success is that we insult everyone."

In an essay, "Foreigners Around The World," P. J. O'Rourke didn't just "pick" on everybody, he savaged them. The article, published in 1976, signaled what was to come from O'Rourke. It was well written, as all his pieces were, but it was so vicious that you got the feeling that he meant it.

O'Rourke described Arabs thusly, "They bugger little boys and practice some stupid religion that they're trying to get all Negroes to believe in." Of the Chinese he said, "No one can possibly know what dark and grotesque things pass through the minds of this hydra-headed racial anomaly." In the article he took on everybody, English ("cold blooded queers"), everybody. It was O'Rourke against the world, and he hated all of its three billion inhabitants.

As in the case of earlier articles by Hendra and Kelly, advertisers started canceling schedules. Was I wrong in allowing the article to appear? Probably. Certainly it bothered me. Mainly because it was angrier than it was funny, violating the principal *Lampoon* rule. But humor is a very personal thing, and it would have been impossible for me to make the "is it funny enough?" distinction on every story that was controversial. The *Lampoon*, after all, was a magazine of hard-hitting satire. It's interesting to note that O'Rourke's commentaries in *Rolling Stone* have not been tempered or tampered with.

After he left the *Lampoon* in 1981, P. J. went on to *Rolling Stone* as their foreign correspondent and to write best-selling books. He has suggested in his books that "coon" and "shit-skin" were popular forms of address for Africans. He referred to Jews as "an American ethnic group who wear their jewelry in the pool." His success has been impressive. Even die-hard liberals read his stuff and laugh. He still exists on the *Lampoon* code, "You can say anything as long as it's funny."

Former *Lampoon* editor Peter Kaminsky once said of P. J., "A guy on the right wing with brains who's funny is so rare, it's something he can do for years."

O'Rourke's writing has been described by friends as an extension of his habit in the seventies of sitting directly in front of the television and shouting "bullshit!" each time a politician said anything.

O'Rourke first showed up at the *Lampoon* in 1972 wearing old army clothes and suggesting that he was evading the draft. His early articles showed promise although many on the staff weren't exactly enamored of him mostly because he was too sure of himself and they weren't. Later, Hendra wrote, "O'Rourke was a narc, a very good narc who hit all the right notes, but whose police-issue shoes showed beneath his bell-bottoms."

Another reason Hendra and Kelly, in particular, didn't like O'Rourke was that he and I were close. I made him my assistant in 1973, and he worked on *New Ingenue* magazine for me as well as the *Lampoon*. I liked P. J. He was smart and attractive and, unlike Hendra and Kelly, he battled with me when he thought I was wrong and he was right. I have always been more at ease with people who disagree with me to my face rather than my back. His work on both the "High School Yearbook" with Kenney and the "Sunday Newspaper Parody" convinced me that he was a major talent.

In 1978, I made O'Rourke editor-in-chief and he took charge. Kenney, the "editor," had been a best friend and Beard, his staff's wise old uncle. P. J. was the "boss." "He went from being Huckleberry Finn to Alex Keaton in twenty-four hours," Kelly recalled in an *Esquire* piece on O'Rourke in 1990. But, if he was a dictator, he worked hard at it, and he organized what had become a magazine that had little organization when he took charge. For the first time in two years, issues were on time. Assignments were given well in advance. It actually was being run like a real magazine. Between us, we had discovered the *Lampoon's* most important new talent in years, a Chicago copywriter by the name of John Hughes who would become one of the stars of the magazine before he left for the movie business.

Kelly, who can be counted on to contribute a clever sneer to anything written about the *Lampoon*, "Saturday Night Live," or virtually any other former employer or associate, has been quoted thusly on O'Rourke and what he thought he did to the magazine while editor-in-chief: "He's an upwardly aspiring, middle-American guttersnipe. Our enemies were wealth and religion. Their [O'Rourke and his staff] enemies were welfare and others." I disapproved of where O'Rourke wanted to take the *Lampoon* philosophically, but I always respected how hard he worked, how much he cared about producing a good magazine, and how very good he was and remains at his craft.

O'Rourke, in a 1978 *Time* magazine article, related his own, not unsimilar, theory on the *Lampoon* as he saw it. "It's just the opposite of the Woody Allen 'I'm defenseless-against-the-world-school-of-humor.' We take the stance of the white, educated, upper-middle class." And we pretty much did during O'Rourke's years as editor-in-chief.

The first woman to write for the *Lampoon* was Janet Maslin who was at Radcliffe when Doug and Henry were at Harvard and later became a film critic for the *New York Times*. Anne Beatts, never an actual employee, was the first woman contributing editor of the magazine. After Michel Choquette had left, she and O'Donoghue lived together for a number of years. "I got into the humor business on my back," Beatts often told people. She didn't do it without writing talent, however. The infamous Volkswagen ad parody was Anne's creation. At the time, Volkswagen prided itself in the unusual fact that their car actually floated on water. This was soon after the Ted Kennedy-Mary Jo Kopechne tragedy. Anne's ad had a picture of a Volkswagen—floating—and one of Teddy in an inset saying, "If I'd driven a Volkswagen, I'd be president today." Volkswagen sued for unauthorized use of their car and trademark and asked for twelve million dollars in punitive damages. It was settled instead by the *Lampoon* prominently displaying a notice in two issues that reminded all that Volkswagen was not a party to the parody. Nothing was ever heard from the Kennedy camp.

Beatts, after my break with O'Donoghue, went on with him to be one of the original writers of "Saturday Night Live," then moved to Hollywood where she created and produced "Square Pegs," a teenage comedy which had some success in the mid-eighties. Since then she's done well writing and producing.

Ed Bluestone was an enigma in *Lampoon* annals. A former stand-up comic, he had perhaps the perfect mind for black comedy. His ideas were, like all the good ones, simple, yet frequently rivaled even O'Donoghue in combining humor and repulsion. O'Donoghue was one of his biggest fans. "The man's sick," Michael, of all people, would mutter admiringly. Features Bluestone created, such as "How to Tell a Kid His Parents Are Dead" (Adult to kid doing his homework: "Stop sweating over those multiplication tables. You'll get straight A's when they hear about your parents."), "Famous Last Words" (Julius Caesar to his assassins: "Weren't those the daggers I gave you for Christmas?"), were among the best remembered in the magazine. He conceived the most popular magazine cover of all time (as picked by the Society of Art Directors), the infamous "If You Don't Buy This Magazine We'll Kill This

Dog" image which we (as so many others have) borrowed for this book.

Despite all this, Bluestone's name is not among those well remembered from the *Lampoon*. It should have been. Who else would have recorded that Michelangelo's dying words were, "Wh-what do you mean, they're repainting the ceiling?" or that among the "Nineteen Ways To Be Offensive at a Wedding," one could "propose a toast to the bride's nose-job" or "return a bra which the bride left in your car." In the "sequel," "Nineteen Ways To Be Offensive at a Funeral," Bluestone suggested, "tell the widow that the deceased's last wish was that she have sex with you" or "place a hardboiled egg in the mouth of the deceased."

They don't make humorists like that anymore.

It's hard to believe that such a gentle soul as Gerald Sussman would not only find his way to the *Lampoon* but would write some of its most memorable pieces and, along with Chris Miller and Shary Flenniken, would be with the *Lampoon* from its very early years until soon before it ceased regular publication.

Before he joined the *Lampoon* staff, Gerry was a copy-writer for several major advertising agencies. He seemed always to be short of money, frequently requesting and get-ting advances for articles not yet conceived much less written. Because, like most contributors, he was paid by the word, every piece he wrote would come in twice as long as neces-sary. The editors expected this from Gerry. Pencils would strike out a couple of thousand words, and the article would be quickly pared to size. In the later years of the *Lampoon*, I edited his stories myself, once trimming an eleven-thousand-word story to thirty-five hundred.

Gerry's most famous creation was "Bernie X," a New York cab driver with an imagination as wondrous as Baron Munchhausen's. He would regale his passengers and the readers with tales of his interludes with Sophia Loren or of his "other jobs" as a spy for the CIA or hit man for the Mafia. Gerry used to say that Bernie's voice "gave a Jew a chance to ridicule everybody else for a change." And he did just that. Bernie was a bigot, a loudmouth, and a liar who put down everybody—Catholics (the Cardinal of New York was a favorite target), Arabs, celebrities, politicians, and other Jews. He lambasted WASPs and blacks. He made fun of Chinese and Indians and cops in squad cars who frequently handed him traffic tickets. But, unlike O'Rourke's scathing writings on foreigners, Sussman's "Bernie X" was so broad, so preposterous, and so funny that nobody took it seriously.

The manner of Gerry's death in the late eighties was almost as hard to believe as his creation's tales. An asthmatic who was allergic to cats, he visited a friend in another city who had several of them. When he left the friend's house to check into a nearby motel, his throat swelled and he suffocated.

In his fifties, he left his wife, the *New York Times* writer Elaine Louie, an infant, and "Bernie X."

"Isn't Louise Gikow the nicest person in the whole world," everybody would say. And they were right. They particularly wondered how, like Sussman, anyone so nice, so warm, and so pleasant could cope not only with the vicissitudes of life at the *Lampoon* but with the infighting of the editors. She did. Louise replaced the "missing in action" Mary Marshmallow in 1972 and stayed until 1978. She was copy editor and mother hen combined.

"She was the first copy editor we had," Michael O'Donoghue recalls, "who wouldn't try to change the spelling of a word we intentionally misspelled. She always got the joke."

"When we hung out in the ladies' room," her pal Janis Hirsch would say in later years, "Louise was the only one who wasn't crying or smoking dope."

Today, Louise is the head of the book division of "Sesame Street." "Gee," someone said to me recently, "Louise went from manic-depressives to muppets."

More than a copy editor, Louise wrote, managed, mothered, and calmed. Louise's associate editor and eventual replacement was Susan Devins, an equally delightful young woman whose face would turn bright red as she edited some of the more colorful *Lampoon* prose.

Staff editorial meetings, like the writers' dinners, were wall-to-wall havoc. No one was ever serious. My presence at such meetings lent a mild form of reason to the proceedings, but while the staff treated me with as much respect as they were capable of mustering, they were still always "up," always anxious to ridicule something or somebody, always anxious to get the big laugh, and, with some reserve, always prepared to show that while I was the boss, I was more like a pesky, demanding older brother they neither feared nor, to a degree, obeyed.

"Getting around Matty's orders" was a game constantly in play. If I put a budget on a story or a spread or an issue, someone would figure out how to go overbudget by borrowing from a budget three issues down the road. If I was chary about paying an artist or writer too much, they would figure out ways to accommodate the demand and still not exceed their authority. If I was adamant about certain targets and wanted them to lay off for legal reasons or simply because I thought it was overkill, they'd bide their time and try again an issue or so later.

There is no question that some of them resented me because I was "authority," and the basic thrust of what we were doing was antiauthority. Over the years, however, I got along with most of the editors and other contributors. Down deep they knew damn well that I wasn't big on "authority" either. If I had been, I'd have never published the *Lampoon*.

By 1973 Gerry Taylor's dealings in the music industry were increasing *Lampoon* advertising sales sharply. One day he said to me, "Why don't we do a comedy record album? O'Donoghue and Hendra would love to put it together. It could get us airplay all over the country and promote the *Lampoon* name."

I asked for a budget, got one, and OK'd it. O'Donoghue and Hendra assured me it would not interfere with their work on the magazine. We were in motion.

CHAPTER FIVE

THE WORD THAT O'Donoghue and Hendra were going to produce a comedy album didn't please Henry Beard. Henry hated
show business. "We're literary people," he told me, "and we
should stay with that until we get it right." More importantly,
he didn't like the idea that O'Donoghue and Hendra would
have this distraction. But, I had been assured the album would
only take a month or so to put together, Kenney was back,
and we had added McConnachie and Kelly to the staff so we
could pursue other ways to market the *Lampoon* name and use
to advantage the constantly growing group of free-lance creative talent coming to our door. We proceeded with the
album which Michael immediately dubbed, "Radio Dinner."

Taylor got us off well. He had just married Mary Travers.
Her manager was Jerry Weintraub who had guided John
Denver's career and was a major force in the record industry.
Taylor brought in Weintraub as sort of an agent for our record
operations. Within days, he had a contract with RCA. I wasn't
happy with the advance of twenty-five thousand dollars, but
they agreed there would be no censorship, and Weintraub
assured us such freedom wasn't easy to get. I signed.

Taylor did something else that was to contribute largely
to the success of the album—he brought in a true triple-threat,
singer-actor-musician, Christopher Guest. Guest remains one
of the fine, somewhat unsung talents in *Lampoon* history. Why

73

he has never reached major success in the entertainment business has always been a mystery to me. Perhaps his most memorable role in more recent years was as the villain in *The Princess Bride*, and he was, of course, one of the not-all-together-with-it rock stars in *This is Spinal Tap*. He also directed a film called *The Big Picture* starring another *Lampoon* graduate, Kevin Bacon, and he's married to the actress Jamie Lee Curtis.

For "Radio Dinner," Guest sang, did impersonations of Bob Dylan and others, wrote music, and even brought in other players, including the backup singer for Hendra's "Deteriorata," a chubby young newcomer named Melissa Manchester. Over her singing, Norman Rose, whose voice has been compared favorably with God's, recited the extraordinary put-down of middle America's favorite contemporary poem. Guest also contributed a young sound engineer named Bob Tischler to the mix. We were all so impressed by his work that he was chosen to run the sound studio that we later built at the *Lampoon* offices. Later in his career, Tischler briefly replaced Lorne Michaels as producer of "Saturday Night Live."

O'Donoghue and Hendra did exactly what we all hoped would be done. They brought the *Lampoon* with all its comedy of shock from the eye to the ear. With Cerf and Kelly and, particularly, with Guest, they produced an album that was among the best-selling comedy recordings of the decade. It would be nominated for, but not win, a Grammy Award, but as importantly, it gave our advertising department even greater presence in the recording and sound industry.

Before all that happened, however, there was one small problem. RCA, which had guaranteed us total creative control, said one cut had to be excised before they would release the album. It was a rather dumb, mildly funny bit about the supposedly sterile married life of David Eisenhower and Julie

Nixon, taken from a piece that had appeared earlier in the magazine. RCA, a defense contractor, did not want to annoy the Nixon administration. They demanded that it be deleted. (Julie: David, I think we're supposed to use the hole in the front, not the one in the back. David: Gosh, you mean there are two of them?)

O'Donoghue, not used to anyone tinkering with his creations, was apoplectic. Hendra was ambivalent. Taylor wanted everybody to be friends. "Fuck 'em," I decided. "It stays or we go!" We went. RCA released us from the deal. We kept both the master recording and the advance. Within days, Taylor (Weintraub was somewhere in the Mediterranean balancing his checkbook) called Bob Krasnow at Blue Thumb Records, got a fast, no-holds-barred yes and a second twenty-five thousand dollars. This was getting better. We'd now grossed fifty thousand dollars on the album, and it had only cost us about ten thousand dollars to cut. We were to earn considerably more from royalties.

In *Rolling Stone*, almost a year later, Stephen Holden would say of "Radio Dinner" and *Lemmings*, our stage revue, "Sidesplitting laughs are hard to come by these days, but the *National Lampoon*, in its pages and now in assorted other enterprises, delivers them in spades."

And so, all seemed right with the world. In Chicago, a young Albanian hoodlum named John Belushi was in his second year at the Second City Comedy Club and was convulsing audiences and gaining wonderous admiration from his peers who were marveling at his energy and sheer presence on stage. In Toronto, an American-born actress named Gilda Radner was getting a similar reaction at the Second City Club there. In Greenwich Village, Cornelius Chase—Chevy to all who knew him—was looking for work. Also in Chicago, only a few blocks from where Belushi worked each night, an advertising man by the name of John Hughes was writing copy without great enthusiasm and filling in the hours by writing jokes and sending them through the mail to such comics as Rodney Dangerfield. In Orange County, California, a beautiful fifteen-year-old high school cheerleader, who shall remain nameless for now, but not for long, was dreaming about being a world-famous movie star, and, meanwhile, was considering a part-time job at her local supermarket. All of them would eventually come to the *Lampoon*.

By the spring of '72, the opponents for the forthcoming presidential election were just about set. Richard Nixon would definitely run for his second term in office. It appeared that a fuzzy egghead by the name of George McGovern would oppose him. The staff of the *Lampoon* knew on which side their bread was buttered. Nixon was a scoundrel, a liar, a crook—all character traits which made him better fodder for a humor magazine than McGovern who wasn't even as interesting as Teddy Kennedy—he wasn't a drunk or a philanderer, just a do-gooder who, if elected, was unlikely to get anything good done. It was decided, they'd vote for McGovern but root for Nixon.

John and Yoko posed for a "Foto Funnies"—a photo-comic strip that had gained instant popularity the year before. Yoko had insisted that she write the strip. Nobody understood what they were doing in it, but, what the hell, it was John and Yoko.

"Foto Funnies" had an additional surge of popularity that year after O'Donoghue came across a handbill advertising a massage parlor. On it was the photo of Danielle, a girl whose tits fell from her chest to her knees. Michael found her and invited her to be our official "Foto Funnies" model, a chore she handled until the late seventies. She became instantly recognizable for obvious reasons and would be hounded by auto-graph seekers in the street or in restaurants and especially at *Lampoon* parties or openings.

Michael found more than Danielle that year. He found love. The recipient of his affection was Amy Ephron, one of the three Ephron sisters, daughters of widely known Hollywood screenwriters and successful writers on their own. Michael was in heaven. He still lived in a dingy loft in Soho, but he was making money now. And, more importantly, he was being recognized everywhere as a master of black comedy. Kenney was undeniably a genius, and Beard was probably the most prolific of all and was the editor to whom all came with their ideas and their problems, but it was O'Donoghue, more than anybody who had set the fierce tone of the magazine and of comedy for years to come. It was O'Donoghue who figured out how to laugh at sickness and infirmity and poverty and death.

He had this growing image. He had the *Lampoon*. He had his girl friend, and he had his friends, closest of all now being Tony Hendra.

After working together on "Radio Dinner," the two had become inseparable. Tony had moved his wife and kids to farm country way out in western New Jersey and many nights, rather than taking the train back home, he'd flop on a couch in Michael's loft. Michael, who didn't like to collaborate with other writers, even created a couple of magazine pieces with Tony, who preferred to collaborate.

They were colleagues. They were friends. They were two of the wittiest and most outspoken members of the group that regularly gathered for the staff dinners.

Then it happened. Michael had one of his frequent migraines and was home, head swathed in ice. Tony showed up at Amy Ephron's apartment. They gabbed. They had a couple of drinks. They smoked a joint or two. They made love. He stayed the night and then went directly to the office. She called Michael and told him what happened.

In his book, Hendra excuses his actions by saying "in the hip-happening, going too far, nothing-is-sacred, dish-it-out world of the 1972 *Lampoon*, this sort of thing had happened once or twice before." Total bullshit. Certainly, guys had competed for girls and had, on occasion, slept with women who had slept with other Lampooners. But this was different. Amy was Michael's steady girl friend. Tony was married with two kids as well. And it was *Michael* who he made the cuckold in this scenario; Michael, with all his insecurities, with his feeling that everyone was out to steal his jokes or his girls; Michael who trusted almost no one but had trusted Tony. If it had happened to Doug, he would have probably figured out an appropriately funny punch line to the story, then driven out to New Jersey and fucked Tony's wife. But it happened to Michael and he didn't think it was funny.

He stopped talking to Amy and had one brief confrontation with Tony in the office the next day. Unable to fully convey to Hendra the depths of his animosity toward him, he marched into my office. By now the story had reached me. He demanded that I fire Tony at once. I tried to calm him down. I explained that I didn't feel it was my place to get involved in the personal lives of the people who worked at the *Lampoon*. We talked at length. He told me he would never again attend an editorial meeting at which Hendra was present. At the time their offices abutted each other's. He wanted Hendra's office moved. I agreed.

As we were having this conversation, Hendra was discussing the situation with Beard. This was not the kind of problem Henry was used to handling. He was an editor and a writer. He wasn't an executive and didn't want to be, although he had reluctantly accepted the title of vice-president of the company at my request. Beard was his usual, noncommittal self. In the face of adversity, he nodded or shrugged. As Tony tells the story, he nodded frequently.

Now, we had a problem. O'Donoghue was "A-Team." Hendra was good but not nearly as valuable. The easiest way out for me would have been to fire Tony. He was replaceable. O'Donoghue was not and never would be. I had honestly believed what I told Michael. This wasn't my business.

But I was the leader and this was serious. I decided to take Tony off the magazine for a while and assign him to put together another album. He aligned himself with Kelly who was the magazine's reigning poet and whose lyrics would be invaluable for any album. They came up with a great idea, a parody of Woodstock, the most celebrated rock concert of all times, the rock concert to which all other rock concerts would be compared, a historic blend of rock and drugs and sex replete with the most famous names of the time. It was the story of young people who were simply killing themselves with excess while running like hell to get nowhere. They were "Lemmings."

Soon after, the plan of doing an album was shelved. Instead we decided to do it as a musical comedy. We'd then have a play—and get an album to boot.

All that made O'Donoghue even angrier. "This is great!" he rationalized (not without good reason), "Hendra double-crosses me, and he's punished by being given a show to create." I assured him that I hadn't planned it this way. It had just evolved. We discussed Michael doing a special issue of the magazine over which he would have total control. He'd been talking for some time about an "Encyclopedia of Humor." This would be an A-to-Z book in which topics of every nature would be satirized. Special editions of the magazine with reprints had been quite profitable, but this would be the first original special edition. With the reprints, we created a royalty pool for contributors, and there were no other editorial costs. Overhead was minimal. On the encyclopedia project, O'Donoghue would need much of Gross's attention, a couple of full-time assistants, and a lot of editorial help. O'Rourke had been a contributing editor and was now on the payroll as my assistant. I gave O'Donoghue the green light on the project and assigned O'Rourke to work with him.

Michael wanted one more thing. He wanted a legend prominently displayed on the cover of the encyclopedia, "Edited By Michael O'Donoghue." We'd never done anything like that before but I agreed.

Amy Ephron passed out of Michael's life with the Hendra incident. She went on to become a Hollywood studio executive and a screenwriter. Now, Michael and Anne Beatts discovered each other. Michael seemed calmer than usual. While she was going with Michael, Amy had written one story for the *Lampoon*. It appeared in the May 1972 issue. Its title was "How To Make It With Men."

Late in 1972 we acquired *Ingenue* magazine from Dell Publishing. Before that we would copublish a *Harvard Lampoon* parody of *Cosmopolitan* which highlighted a pullout pinup of Henry Kissinger and outsold the highly successful *Time* parody. David Kaestle, a college classmate of Gross's joined the company as art director of special projects and would contribute importantly to the magazine's popularity. He would be the guiding artistic force behind the 1974 classic "High School Yearbook."

Brian McConnachie was put in charge of our book division and the first *Lampoon* paperbacks were published. Taking no chances, our initial release was *National Lampoon's Dirty Book*. It really wasn't very dirty, but it sold very well. We were now occupying two floors at 635 Madison, enough to get them to name the building after us. We passed on "The National Lampoon Building," figuring it would attract too many practical jokers. It was called "The Twenty First Century Communications Building."

CHAPTER SIX

BY 1973, circulation of the *Lampoon* topped 800,000. The magazine had passed *Time* and was now number one in sales on college campuses, but the piercing new humor that obviously had created this inertia had side effects that moderated its growth.

We were being hit by lawsuits, mostly for libel or copyright infringements, and supermarket and convenience store chains were regularly taking us off their magazine racks because management disapproved of some of the things we were doing.

Our first lawsuit, with Disney, had been resolved rather easily with our promise never to use a Disney character again. Shortly after, we had the same problem with a parody of the "Peanuts" strip. Cartoon characters are to be avoided, we learned. You can get away with murder with celebrities, but a copyright infringement is not going to be a winnable case. Once again, we backed off. The "Peanuts" lawyers were assured there would be no further use of Charlie Brown and company. With the Volkswagen suit, we'd again run into a trademark infringement. We would stick to celebrities. Was Mario Savio a celebrity? We thought so. The Berkeley campus radical had been front-page news in the sixties. Where'd he go? Doug Kenney "found him." He was now a "TV pitchman" or so Kenney's piece suggested. Suddenly, Savio did surface.

His lawyers hit us with a nine-million-dollar lawsuit. It dragged on for a year or so then was dropped. To win such a suit, the plaintiff has to prove damages. It was never clear what Savio's damages were.

Our next lawsuit was one for defamation. Although our lawyers insisted that you can't libel or defame a dead person, Liza Minnelli sued us for nine million dollars because of a feature the *Lampoon* did about her late mother, Judy Garland. Despite numerous suits over the years, I was never quite sure how the plaintiffs and their lawyers came up with the actual number they were suing for. Certainly, for example, Liza Minnelli in this case could not prove that her mother, who had been dead for several years, was deprived of nine-million-dollars-worth of income or that she, Liza, had had mental anguish on which a price could be affixed. But there it was, a nine-million-dollar lawsuit and more headlines.

A meeting with the lawyers was suggested, and Liza, looking thin and grey of face, showed up. This did not appear to be a happy woman. In all fairness, the satire was harsh. It suggested—hell no, it said—that Judy had OD'd on the john, which, sadly, was true. It was one of those *Lampoon* pieces that was vicious without being very funny. "Who says it isn't funny?" my staff would argue.

Most often I would go along with the majority vote, occasionally killing a feature or joke because it was so cruel or the humor so obscure that I simply said no. I probably should have done that with the Garland piece, but I tried not to make it a habit. One reason the *Lampoon* was working was because of this freedom. The editors felt that they could be nasty and preposterous and were.

Liza thought we had gone too far when we met that day in the lawyer's office. She sat sullenly, listening to the lawyers as they traded mild threats. After a half hour of this, I leaned across the large table that separated us and said to her, "Why don't we go somewhere and talk?" She nodded. When we were alone, I apologized. I told her I was a big fan of both her mother (I was) and her (w-e-l-l).

I agreed that the article was unkind but pointed out that a lawsuit would just mean a couple of years of name calling and finger pointing. "Why," I suggested, "don't you write an editorial in the next issue of the *Lampoon?* Say anything you want to say. Call us anything you want to call us. Get even and to the very readers who saw the offending feature in the first place." It made sense. She agreed. A couple of months later, her editorial appeared. It took us to task for being "ruthless and uncaring." It said flatly that we suffered from "a decided lack of good taste." "What a great idea," Brian McConnachie said when he read it. "Let's do another Bad Taste Issue!"

We didn't lose our first lawsuit until the late seventies. We'd run a picture of midget twins who had worked in a war plant during World War II. It showed them in front of two large pipes. The caption suggested that they were hired to crawl in and check out the hot and cold water faucets aboard aircraft carriers.

Of course, this was not exactly the case, and it apparently offended the twin who was still living. He sued us for six million dollars, and I was ordered to appear in a Columbia, South Carolina, court, Columbia being the hometown of the plaintiff. It is also the home of the University of South Carolina where, at the time, the *Lampoon* was the most popular magazine on campus. When I arrived, a line of youths were in front of the courthouse carrying placards which read "Free the Lampoon One," "S.O.S.—Save Our Satire," and "Let the Lampoon Satirize Short Subjects."

A hometown jury threw out the request for the six million and awarded the plaintiff fifteen thousand dollars for "misappropriation of his photographed image." This was the last damage suit the magazine suffered. Suits after that related to *Lampoon* films until I sued the magazine myself in 1992.

The lawsuits were never damaging. If anything, the publicity was beneficial.

But reaction from advertisers and retail outlets to humor that angered them stunted the rapid growth of the magazine and eventually almost destroyed it.

We knew right from the start that a lot of people were going to be unhappy with what we were putting on the pages of the *Lampoon*. Kenney's tweaking of Agnew and the ridicule of Nixon and his other henchmen were acceptable to most. They were politicians and "if you can't stand the heat, get out of the kitchen." Kenney's humor was more frequently self-deprecating. He made fun of his own youth and that of the reader's by writing about high school and college and "know-it-all" parents, about small-town America, and teenage sex, particularly about "first" experiences. ("My First Blowjob" was a very popular Kenney treatise.)

O'Donoghue was the master satirist, and for the most part his targets were famous people of legend (Howard Hughes, Winston Churchill, "The Diana Barrymore Drinking Songs"). Or he dealt in literature ("Pornocopia," "How To Write Good"). Or made fierce statements ("The Vietnamese Baby Book"). Or was just plain funny ("The Floor of the Sistine Chapel").

Beard's writings, other than in the "News" section, were beautifully crafted and rarely offensive ("My Gun Is Cute," "Truth In Advertising," "The Assassination Of Spiro Agnew" ... well, maybe a little offensive). It was usually material written by other editors and writers that brought us problems. We'd get rumblings; this would offend an advertiser here, a retailer there.

Gerry Taylor remembers losing Superscope, a subsidiary of Sony, as an advertiser, because of a feature on the late Dan Blocker of TV's "Bonanza" fame, with the account executive showing Taylor the door after letting him know he had been a close friend of Blocker's.

The vast Thrifty Drug Store chain in the western U.S. and Dart Drugs in the east refused to carry the magazine from the start because of the constant satire of conservative politicians and policies. In later years, Justin Dart became part of Ronald Reagan's kitchen cabinet. By coincidence, another of Reagan's close confidantes was Alfred Bloomingdale who had been my associate at the Diners' Club and in the late seventies served on the board of directors of the *Lampoon*. He resigned when Reagan became president. Before he did, he asked Thrifty and Dart (both run by close friends of his) to allow the *Lampoon* on their magazine racks. They refused, suggesting to him that the *Lampoon* was "a dirty magazine with left-wing leanings."

The complaints were occasional, the problems minimal, the losses minor, until we got into "religion." And we jumped feet first.

Beard was a WASP. Kenney, McConnachie, and O'Donoghue were Irish Catholics. None of them or any of the others seemed to pay much attention to religion in their writings in the first year or so of the magazine. It basically started with the January 1972 issue. The theme was "Is Nothing Sacred?" Nothing was.

The issue, guest edited by Hendra, featured O'Donoghue's "Vietnamese Baby Book," the Chris Miller story

"Remembering Mama," a remarkably unflattering history of the American Indian by Anne Beatts, and "Son-O-God" comics written by Kelly and Choquette and drawn by Neil Adams. Kelly and Choquette were disaffected Catholics. Hendra had briefly been a monk. The "Son-O-God" character was an Arnold Schwarzenegger look-alike rather on the dumb side. His heroics were basically at the expense of "anti-Christ," a bulbous caricature of the pope.

My complaint with the strip was and remains that it wasn't funny. Advertisers felt more strongly. The fallout was the first of any magnitude against the magazine. Until this, advertisers had merely refrained from going in. With "Son-O-God" comics and a piece called "The Joy Of Sects," a number of advertisers already running in the magazine got out, some immediately after the offending issue, others a little later. We talked this over. We'd already established that we pick on everybody. Could I say to the staff, "lay off the Catholic stuff. They're more sensitive than the WASPs and Jews and every other group we're savaging"? I suggested we just cool it for a while.

And then, the Catholic League For Religious and Civil Rights went to work. Something of a one-man operation working out of a small office near our own, the league wrote to all our advertisers, decrying our anti-Catholicism and demanding that they drop out of the magazine. An article followed in the Catholic newspaper, *Our Sunday Reader*, actually listing many of the advertisers.

Gerry Taylor remembers that one of our few vocal supporters was Bernie Mitchell, then president of Pioneer Electronics, the *Lampoon*'s biggest advertiser. "I'm not anti anything," Mitchell wrote to the league. "They, the *Lampoon*, merely see humor in everything. It seems to me they have a right to do that."

Within a few issues, most advertisers drifted back, lured by the magazine's skyrocketing circulation. Some did not return. What was happening was that our editorial was chipping away at both our advertising and retail base. The decision to give the writers what amounted to almost a free hand had created the consumer excitement, but over the years we found growth more and more difficult because of those we were alienating.

As a young public relations man in the 1950s, I had represented Heineken, the beer imported from Holland. The distributor in this country, Leo van Munching, whom we called the "Baron," became a good friend of mine. When we started the *Lampoon*, Heineken was one of our first national advertisers. The Baron was at my daughter's wedding and sat ringside when my son Michael opened his first major musical engagement, at the Rainbow Grill in Rockefeller Center.

In 1973, Beard and Cerf wrote a piece titled "Americans United to Beat the Dutch." As if the title wasn't enough, the text suggested that the Dutch were "warmongers, rowdies, and bullies" and that they were planning to invade America. Of course, the joke was that the Dutch hadn't invaded anyone for five hundred years, were hostile to no one, and even if they had been so inclined, were in no position to be hostile to America. Van Munching didn't think it was funny, and one of my oldest friends canceled his advertising.

In its first five years, the *Lampoon* would gain two advertisers for every one that dropped out, but that didn't account for the logical advertisers that never bought any space at all. Although more young men in college read the magazine than any other publication, no major jeans company (Lee's, Haggar, Levi Strauss) ever advertised in the magazine. Seagram's and Schenley stayed out as did the major manufacturers of boots

and socks and shirts. And, no car ads from Detroit. Our advertising people were invariably turned away with the same message, "*We* love you guys, but our clients think you're too...
dirty... nasty... cruel... liberal... wicked... insensitive."
Insensitive?! Us?!

To a degree, we'd overcome the Catholic league's boycott, and our advertising grew every year from 1970 through
1976, but that growth was never commensurate with the
impact the magazine made on the youth of America and
Canada.

One by one, as we offended different groups of people,
we started to lose not our reader base but many of the retail
outlets that sold the magazine. The *Lampoon* often could not
be found as readily as it had. A piece by Hendra in the 1975
199th Birthday Book Issue (we decided to celebrate a U.S.
birthday unencumbered by other ceremonies) called the
Mormons "the Morons." That slight omission of the letter "m"
lost us two thousand supermarkets owned by Mormons in the
West. On occasion we'd be lumped with *Playboy* and *Penthouse*
and even *Hustler* and labeled pornographic, which was totally
absurd. In only one issue in the history of the *Lampoon* was
male or female genitalia shown. A lot of breasts were flashed,
but at no time could such display have been called erotic or
pornographic. It was always part of a joke, sex and politics
being the primary targets for any satirist.

Again, it was Hendra, who (like Kelly) has spent recent
years complaining that I was an agent of smut, who did us in.
He came to me and asked if I would pose for some pictures for
a piece in the magazine. I hesitated. Mogel was usually the
model used for business executives but he wasn't available. I
agreed and I posed for the photographer, then for reasons I

cannot recall, probably because I was out of the city, never saw the other pictures my likeness would share a page with. In the words of the infamous Otter, once more, "I trusted" them. Some time later, I saw the printed piece. It was called "Blow Me!" My picture was inset in a series of photos of dwarfs in semipornographic poses, totally naked, dorks and all. My screams were heard throughout the office. Once again, Hendra—the Jekyll and Hyde of Lampooners, the man who gave us *Lemmings* but in the long run had lost us O'Donoghue —had kicked me in the gut.

Nineteen seventy-six was the first year in *Lampoon* history that revenues from sales of the magazine dropped. They bounced back the next year and took a sizeable jump in 1978 when *Animal House* came out and the name *Lampoon* was on the lips of nearly every young person in America, but we never got back the outlets and advertisers we lost because of the feature we started to speak of as "Dwarf Dork."

I was still reluctant to censure an editor for going too far. Going *too far* had gotten us *this far*, I again reasoned. The piece was ugly and unfunny. I ranted a lot and warned that this kind of thing must end. It was the most classless exhibition we'd ever had. Negative reaction to "Dwarf Dork" would be matched only once more by the "Baby in the Blender." When it was, Hendra would be long gone, and we'd be nearly put out of business.

In 1977, we went to court again. This time *we* sued someone. The producer George Schlatter, who had created "Laugh-In," came up with a new idea, a one-hour comedy show to be called "Lampoon." When his plans were announced, our lawyers immediately informed him by letter that the name, quite obviously, was ours and that we had not only used it on a national magazine but on syndicated radio, for national touring theater and that we'd already contracted to use it in motion pictures.

By return letter, we were notified that the lawyer for Mr. Schlatter disagreed with our claim to proprietorship and that his client had reached agreement with a major network and was proceeding with the taping of the show using the disputed title.

When the case came to court some months later, the judge quickly ruled for us and against Schlatter and anybody else who would use the *Lampoon* name.

We expected the decision. What we didn't anticipate was that Schlatter had taped more than half his show against a huge background that spelled out the name "Lampoon."

Now, the show was unusable. Had he not used the background, of course, he could have simply changed the name of the show. It was never heard of again.

This kind of irrationality amazed me at the time. In later years in Hollywood, I saw that being irrational, particularly when it came to spending money, was commonplace.

CHAPTER SEVEN

IT WAS QUITE a group Hendra assembled at the Village Gate. Chris Guest, who had been so impressive on "Radio Dinner," was once again involved. Paul Jacobs, a musician and composer who could also sing and act a little in the same manner that some of the other members of the troupe could play instruments a little, was the musical director.

Chris brought in another cast member, a tall, gangly clown by the name of Cornelius "Chevy" Chase, who had gone to Bard with Guest and had since bounced around from one job to another. He was a decent musician—could play piano and drums—and had good ideas, and could write comedy. But most of all he was a wonderful buffoon. His pratfalls and mugging would provide a physical comedy to be matched only by a third member of the cast, a husky, explosive barrel of talent, one John Belushi.

Hendra had gone to Chicago to see who in its Second City Revue might be right for our show. He'd called me after his first night there to excitedly tell me about this slightly insane young performer who literally tore the stage apart. He was, Hendra told me, "the actor everybody in Chicago is talking about."

Judy Belushi recalls the night that Hendra arrived.

"John wanted to go to New York badly," she said. "The idea of being in the first National Lampoon show just knocked him out. He'd heard that everybody in the show would have to play an instrument so he got fellow Second City actor Joe Flaherty's brother, Paul, to teach him how to play guitar. He only had time to learn one song, 'Louie, Louie.' The night Tony arrived, John made sure that he'd be noticed. He walked into ongoing scenes that he wasn't supposed to be a part of and ad-libbed characters and dialogue that never existed before. He did his Marlon Brando impression at least twice and on a couple of occasions, started hand-to-hand combat with astonished fellow actors or lapsed into a violent monologue about nothing in particular. The audience loved it. Hendra was delighted.

"After the show, Hendra went to our little apartment. We'd spent all afternoon trying to figure out what wine to serve to this 'big' [off] Broadway director. When Tony arrived, the place was jammed with other Second City people including the Murray brothers, Brian and Bill [who followed John to the *Lampoon* not too long afterward]. At the party, Hendra asked John if he'd play something on the guitar for him. John played 'Louie, Louie.' Hendra then asked if he could play another number. John played 'Louie, Louie' again."

Now the cast was almost complete. Hendra heard Gary Goodrow, an old friend and a former member of the Committee in San Francisco, was in town. Gary could act, was funny, and played a good saxophone. He was hired.

Melissa Manchester, at her husband's insistence, had turned down the lead female role. I had seen a young girl named Alice Playten on stage several times. We had no one who could really sing. Chris was a marvelous impersonator of singers, and Chevy had a pleasant, if small, voice, but I felt we needed at least one member of the cast who could really belt, and Alice Playten could belt. She was barely five feet tall, but her voice reached out resoundingly to the furthest corners of the Gate, and she moved with a small person's light, airy steps. Just before joining the show, Alice filmed a television commercial for Alka Seltzer. It made hers the only familiar face in a cast of unknowns. The final member chosen was Mary Jenifer Mitchell, right out of the nude musical *Oh Calcutta*, a sexy comedy actress with a terrible soprano voice which would be used to good effect.

This was the group. The show went into rehearsal with notes more than script. The first act would be a collection of blackouts and sketches including a high school parody written by Doug Kenney. Chevy would read the news which was newly written almost every day to stay topical. It was, of course, the very same performance he was to repeat some years later on "Saturday Night Live." A scene in an operating room in which all the doctors were working under the influence of drugs was, perhaps, the first-act highlight. Certainly, if *Lemmings* had a reoccurring theme, drugs was it.

The second act would be what had brought us to this point, the *Lampoon's* version of Woodstock, originally intended as a record album. Here, Kelly, Guest, Jacobs, and Hendra wrote parodies of the rock stars of the day. The lyrics, mostly by Kelly, for the music by Guest and Jacobs, remain biting, literate, and funny two decades later.

The rehearsals were frenetic. Hendra was not a take-charge director, and most of the cast had forceful personalities. At times, Guest, Chase, and Belushi would direct on their own, and they competed with and often ridiculed each other. It was chaotic but it was shaping up as opening night approached.

It was mid-January. The show was scheduled to open on January 25, 1973. What I had seen in rehearsal had excited me. I felt we not only had a cast album in the Woodstock parody, but it was starting to hit me that theater might be a new business for the *Lampoon*. I talked to the William Morris Agency about the possibility of touring the show if it was received well in New York. The magazine was flourishing although at the moment it was flourishing for the most part without the services of Hendra or Kelly or of O'Donoghue or O'Rourke who were at work on the "Encyclopedia." Michael's rumblings about Tony "being rewarded for being a scumbag" persisted. He talked about his own love for "show business."

Then, "show business" almost came to a halt. Peter Lavery was the company manager of *Lemmings*. He called me in a panic from a phone booth in the street outside the Gate. "We've been locked out!" he shrieked. "They've padlocked all the doors!"

He calmed down long enough to explain that a New York State tax collector had ordered everybody off the premises and had put locks on the doors. I asked Lavery to get him on the phone. The tax man told him he was leaving and wouldn't talk to anyone. Lavery dropped to his knees and pleaded. The tax man walked out into the street and took the phone which was now being held nervously by Tony's assistant, Dale Anglund. The bureaucrat explained to me that Art D'Lugoff, proprietor of the Village Gate, had been remiss in making tax payments to the state and now owed eighteen thousand dollars. Since D'Lugoff had ignored several warnings, he had followed the usual procedure and padlocked the premises.

I explained that I had a show opening there in less than ten days. Certainly D'Lugoff would be better able to pay his debt if the show opened and I paid him his rent and share of the ticket sales as well as his getting money from the sale of food and drink. "Sorry," I was told. "Once the padlocks are on, you can't take them off. It's the rule!"

I argued. I reasoned. Finally, I said, "Look, take the padlocks off, and I'll guarantee the eighteen thousand dollars." "Oh," the man said to me, "who are you?" I decided not to bother telling him. I had my bank immediately draw up a check for the eighteen thousand dollars, and a member of my staff rushed it down to the Gate. The tax man broke the rule and removed the padlocks.

A month after the show opened, D'Lugoff, a decent and honorable man, repaid the money and his club remained open.

A few days before the opening, disaster almost struck again. John Belushi walked into my office and told me that he was leaving New York and returning to Chicago. During the long pause that followed, an assessment of the situation ran through my head—I had invested a considerable amount of the company's money in this production. The burly, bearded ape standing before me was the star of the show. Was he replaceable? Unless Marlon Brando was immediately willing and available, I didn't believe anyone could replace Belushi for a long run, for the cast album, and certainly not for the opening night critics.

Stay calm, I advised myself. You love this guy, he can be irrational, but there must be an answer.

"Why are you leaving?" I asked. I was calm, very calm.

"Judy," he replied.

"Oh?" I responded.

"Judy hates it here," he told me. "She's got no friends, no job. She's goin' nuts. She wants to go back to Chicago and I can't let her go alone."

Another long pause. "What," I inquired, "does Judy do?"

"She's an artist."

I nodded. "She can't leave," I said. "Neither one of you can leave. Judy's got a job working in the *Lampoon* art department."

He grinned. This was exactly what he was angling for when he came in, but he wasn't going to tell me that. I picked up my phone, called Michael Gross, and told him I wanted Judy Jacklin (later Belushi) to be put to work in the art department.

"I don't need anyone else," he told me.

"Sure you do," I assured him. I hung up.

John looked at me, the grin still on his face. "Oh, by the way, Judy just got a new job and needs some clothes," he said. "Can I borrow a couple of hundred?"

There are events in your life that you remember with great clarity. The opening night of *Lemmings* was one of mine.

The Village Gate was jammed. All the critics were there, and as the show went along, we studied their faces to see if we could interpret their reactions. We couldn't. The first act was decidedly uneven. Gary Goodrow's rendition of "Deteriorata" got big laughs. Chevy's "News" was well received. Doug's high school sketch with six-foot, four-inch Chase in drag seemed to go on forever. Young people in the audience loved the "Doctors and Drugs" routine. Their elders seemed repulsed by it. Moderately successful was the best description of act one.

During the intermission, I walked by the table at which the *Lampoon* editors were sitting. Trow seemed to be mildly enjoying himself. McConnachie, as always, was pleasant but somewhat dazed. Beard was livid. He looked at me and mouthed, "I hate it!"

The second act started with Belushi ambling on stage and declaring, "All right, we all know why we came here—a million of us—we came here to off ourselves!"

The audience started laughing and didn't stop for more than an hour and a half. Guest was Dylan and James Taylor, Jacobs was Neil Young, Chase was John Denver, Mary Mitchell was an off-key Joan Baez, and Alice Playten was Jagger and Brenda Lee, thundering out a wonderfully funny song called "Pizza Man." And there was Belushi "falling asleep" as "James Taylor" sang, insulting Denver, slapping a stringless bass, and pouring his unlimited energy into every scene. And here was Chase as a biker, storming into the audience and threatening those at ringside with violence should he discover the culprit who had left fingerprints on his bike. And there were Belushi and Chevy together as two dopers testing a new way to get high, crashing into each other head on while wearing motorcycle helmets. "Nothing," Belushi tells his friend Chase, as he waits hopefully for some psychedelic effect. "I got nothing, man." The duel between the two classic comics to outdo each other had other members of the cast and crew glued to the stage each night. It was improvisational comedy at its best.

As the finale, in which the lemmings, the young people who flocked to Woodstock for sex, drugs, and rock and roll, all off themselves to Belushi's constant pleadings, screamed to an earsplitting finish, the audience leaped to their feet and screamed back in delight. The curtain calls came again and again. I reached for Hendra and pushed him onstage, and he took a deserved bow with Goodrow and Mitchell and Playten and Chase, who would later become a star, and Belushi, who became a star and like the lemmings, would "off himself" if unintentionally.

Later, we gathered at Minetta Tavern, a charming little Italian restaurant a few minutes from the Gate. My son Michael, now seventeen and working as ticket taker at the show, was posted at the entrance along with a half dozen friends from his school, Horace Mann. Only those with invitations were allowed in.

As the cast members arrived, the crowd in the restaurant broke into applause. When John came in, he hugged me nervously. Everybody was waiting for the reviews. In the New York theater, good reviews are essential and the review that means more than all the others is the one in the *New York Times*.

Shortly after midnight, the show's press agent came in with the *Times*. He had already turned it to the theater review. I glanced at it quickly, then, my heart racing, I jumped on a chair and read it to a hushed group. The review brushed off act one, suggesting it "suffers from a severe case of the puerilities." It then proceeded to rave about act two, about the music, the lyrics, and mostly about the performances. It was wildly enthusiastic about Belushi and hailed Chevy's performance as "the theater's best comedy turn of the year."

Once again, there was bedlam. I was so overwhelmed that moments later I greeted Chris Guest's father as "my old friend Ned," thinking he was Chevy's father who had edited my novel at Putnam. I looked for Beard but couldn't find him. The other members of the staff now started to find things they liked in the show. O'Donoghue, of course, was not there but Kenney was and didn't seem upset that his high school sketch had been a dud. Rather he was delighted that we had what appeared to be a hit show.

The reviews that came out over the following days displayed mostly the same enthusiasm. A week later, even the dowdy *New Yorker*, making sure at first to remind the world that the first act was lame, raved about the second. "It is, unlike the rotten first act, very, very good and very, very funny." Once again the performers were singled out as being "versatile and talented."

Of course, I agreed. There had been no doubt in my mind that Belushi and Chase would be stars. I always thought Guest would be, too. I also thought that the reviewers, and the audience, in their rush to anoint the cast, overlooked the brilliance of the parody and, in particular, of the music and lyrics.

A week or so later, Walter Kerr of the *Times* did a follow-up comment and was less enthusiastic. He claimed the show needed more comedy. It was "more nostalgia," he complained, "rather than the ribbing we've been promised." This was not a review and had no effect on the rush to the box office.

Hendra, who had risen from the muck of the O'Donoghue affair to bring this winner home, went back to the mire once more when he wrapped a fish in newspapers and sent it to Kerr with a note that read, "Swim with the fishes." Worse than being gauche, it wasn't clever or funny. The rest of us at the *Lampoon* wrote it off as being typically Tony.

Rock stars flocked to the Gate to see themselves being satirized. At one performance, James Taylor buried his head on the table while his wife Carly Simon soothed him, and the audience laughed hysterically at Chris Guest's devastating portrait of Taylor lamenting in song, "[I'm] shootin' up the highway on the road map of my wrists." Joe Cocker came to see Belushi's impeccable take on him and wound up on stage with him. The Gate, for 385 performances, housed not merely a show to see, but an event, a place to go and a place to be.

CHAPTER EIGHT

ASIDE FROM INGENUE, 1973 was a very good year.

Ingenue was a magazine, like *Seventeen*, for girls in their early teens and attracted a lot of advertising. This was the market that advertisers, particularly those selling makeup and clothing, wanted. When Dell Publishing owned it, the magazine had a decent circulation and a good advertising base.

We hired Joanna Brown, the beauty editor of *Glamour*, as editor-in-chief and Elliot Marion who had been *Glamour's* advertising director as publisher. With P. J. O'Rourke, then my assistant, and my teenage daughter Julie, I would supervise the editorial. Mogel would oversee Marion's work which was primarily advertising sales, with long-time assistant George Agoglia directing all production and distribution.

When we took over the magazine in February, Dell had one more issue, April, to publish before our inaugural issue. Marion and his staff were terrific. Advertising in our first issue would far outsell any previous issue published by Dell. Working with Joanna and the other editors, P. J., Julie, and I came up with new features. Julie was there primarily because she was a bright, ambitious teenager, and she gave us both a sounding board and fresh ideas for a teenage girl's magazine.

We brought in new features and new writers. It was a great start. We were confident that this would be a winner. Then Dell's April issue came out. In it, a widely known child psychologist recommended that girls indulge in heavy petting and under the right circumstances, not be wary of premarital sex. The reaction was akin to the dropping of a large bomb. Our first issue was locked up, but insertions after that were canceled by most national advertisers. Tens of thousands of subscribers also dropped out.

The irony of the situation escaped no one:

1. We were being destroyed by an editorial that we had nothing to do with.

2. We were victimized by a serious essay by a doctor who espoused a theory that favored a lessening of a young woman's tensions in regard to sex. Even if you didn't agree with it, it was just that, a theory. The company that published the *Lampoon*, which treated sex like a stop-off at McDonald's and featured pictures of naked women and four letter words, was actually being done in by a reasonable, intelligent opinion about sex. "I think," Mogel said to me with a shrug, "God's getting even with us."

We did what any red-blooded American company would do under the circumstances. We sued. Dell had agreed in the sale agreement that the last issue of the magazine published by them would deviate in no way from its normal editorial policies. This article sure as hell was different. Eventually we went to court and won nearly half a million dollars in damages, but *Ingenue* never recovered and in 1974, it died.

Otherwise, everything was great. *Lemmings* had received yet another great boost in the *New York Times*. Eric Lax wrote a piece titled "Why do young people love *Lemmings*?" In it he described the show as "theater turned into rock concert which completes the circle that began in the sixties when rock concerts became more and more theatrical." He wrote about the young people who were "flocking to and loving *Lemmings*." And he ended it with "The real message of the sixties wasn't love or peace, it was death—from needles or bullets, take your pick. Death is what *Lemmings* is about. It is also implicitly about laughter as a vital life sign."

There had been at least one crisis after the opening of *Lemmings*. The first act needed work, and Tony had inserted a new sketch called "Humor Lecture." It was quite funny and very dry and very, very British. Everyone assumed that Tony had written it. He never said otherwise. A week or so after it first appeared, we got a registered letter from the Monty Python group. The sketch, it seemed, was theirs. Hendra had simply borrowed it without permission.

I was livid. I wrote a letter of apology to Terry Jones and Michael Palin who had written the piece and assured them that "borrowing" in this manner was not something we would tolerate and that the sketch would be removed at once. It was. In his book, *Going Too Far*, Hendra describes Henry Beard's reaction as resulting in a few angry words and no more.

I recall a different scene.

For the second time in a year, a *Lampoon* editor, this time Beard, tore into my office and demanded that I fire Hendra. Now I was prone to do just that. I met with Tony and he unspooled a long story about how Jones and Palin had allowed him to use the piece when he had a comedy act with Nic Ullett and that he had simply taken for granted his right to use it once again in *Lemmings*.

The explanation, of course, was specious. "Loaning" material for a nightclub act was one thing; allowing it to be used without credit or remuneration in a musical comedy was another. I remember shaking my head in disbelief, thinking to myself, "Does he believe this shit, or does he think *I'm* stupid enough to believe it?" But, once again, I didn't fire him.

Hendra's habit of "borrowing" ideas and stories and sketches was now legendary.

A month or so after the opening, Blue Thumb sent two truckloads of sound engineers and equipment to the Gate, and the cast album was recorded live. It would be the first *Lampoon* album on the pop charts and was once again nominated for a Grammy, this time for "Best Musical Comedy Recording." Once again, it didn't win.

ITEM: DOUG SPEAKS

In 1973, Len Mogel was teaching at New York University and invited Doug Kenney to lecture his class. Doug walked in, looked at Mogel and the audience, then slid open the door to a closet and proceeded to give his lecture from inside the closed closet. About halfway through, he came out and continued while sitting cross-legged on Mogel's desk.

The NYU incident gave me an idea. We were already the best-selling magazine on college campuses. Why not a lecture tour of those campuses? We called a half dozen colleges and offered them Doug as a guest speaker. All accepted. With no closets to hide in and a prepared text to which he only occasionally referred, Doug was a smash hit.

Soon, other schools were calling from around the country. The colleges paid only his expenses. Everywhere he went, magazine sales went up. We were approached by a speaker's bureau. They suggested that we could have Doug speak at colleges and get paid for it at the rate of two or three thousand dollars a lecture.

I liked that. But Doug was not writing much for the magazine while he was on the road being received like a star at colleges and tasting frequently of their booze and drugs and co-eds. And Doug's writing was too important to do without.

I needed someone who was known on campus but, unlike Doug, wrote for us less frequently and who could do much of that writing in hotel rooms. The choice was Chris Miller. Chris wasn't on staff, so we agreed to split the lecture fee which was soon more than five thousand dollars an engagement. Doug's speeches were rambling discourses on *Lampoon* with the rest of the world thrown in as he saw fit. Chris would read his short stories which were—to say the least—ribald.

He remembers his college tours well. "My stories were dirty, but they were right on. The kids loved it. I was speaking their language. It was the seventies, a time when you could say anything and I sure did.

"One of my last engagements was at—I think it was Southwest Missouri State. When I got there and spoke to the people in charge, I said to myself, 'This is a Bible Belt school. I'm gonna get killed.' They set me up on a stand in the lunchroom. It was me and a microphone facing three or four hundred kids and a few teachers. I started reading one of my stories. I don't remember which one, but like most of my stuff, it had lots of scatological references and lots of sex, an awful lot of sex.

"I'm about ten minutes into the reading when out of the corner of my eye, I see the woman in charge of the lectures stomp out. Meanwhile, the student body was laughing, stamping their feet, and applauding every other line. A couple of minutes later, the woman comes back with a big, husky guy in tow. He walks over to me and in the middle of a sentence, switches off my mike. Then he looks at me like I'm dead meat and says, 'This is over!'

"Now, the kids are mad and so am I. I pick up my reading material and shout, 'Follow me!' There I am, Chris Miller, the

Pied Piper of Smut, walking through the school with hundreds of college kids following me. As we walk, more and more join us. We parade out to the quad and stop in front of a big tree. By now there are nearly a thousand kids settling down on the grass in front of me. And here come television cameras and reporters from the local radio stations and newspapers. This is now a freedom-of-speech story. When everyone quieted down, I picked up my short story and looked at them, 'Now,' I asked, 'where were we?'"

At the *Lampoon*, Doug and I had become good friends. His early fear of an older "business type" was gone. One Sunday night, my wife and I returned from a weekend holiday to discover two gold mints on our bed. They were the kind the maid leaves after she turns down the bed at night in a hotel. I asked my oldest son Michael, who had been home over the weekend, what the mints were all about. Michael is a rascal but a rascal incapable of telling a lie. He grinned. He blushed. He stammered. Finally he spoke. Doug and a girl friend had been by that Saturday, and Doug had conned Michael into letting them stay over, in our bed.

The next day I chided Kenney. He had this killer smile that made it very difficult to stay angry with him. "I just wanted to be like you," he said with a laugh. "Yeah," I said, "well, my bed is off limits." "That's OK," he shrugged. "I didn't enjoy it as much as John Belushi and Judy did Friday night."

Michael grew close to Doug and to John and Judy and later to Harold Ramis and Gilda Radner. It wasn't until years after the fact that I learned that on Michael's eighteenth birthday, Belushi gave my son a present. "Here's some coke," he intoned in rabbinical parody. "Today you are a man." I remember John fondly but not for everything.

ITEM: LIFTED FROM THE NEW YORK TIMES,
Thursday, November 1, 1973

"A tall lean, intense man showed up at the National Lampoon offices—and—said he'd like to buy 40 copies of the October issue which features a comic strip titled, 'G. Gordon Liddy, agent of C.R.E.E.P.' and portrays Daniel Ellsberg of Pentagon Papers fame, sympathetically. Writing out a check for thirty dollars for the copies, he signed it 'Daniel Ellsberg.' He is now negotiating for the original art work of the strip. "

As the year drew to a close, we could see that the company was probably going to earn close to two million dollars before taxes, most of that coming from the *Lampoon*. Nineteen seventy-three and 1974 were to be averaged out to determine the price we'd have to pay Beard, Kenney, and Hoffman for their minority interest. The way we were growing, 1974 was a sure bet to be even more profitable than '73. We were looking at a possible buyout price in the five million range. Our total cash assets were around two and a half million.

I revisited Graham Loving at his apartment. "This is great pot," he said, offering me a joint from a Wedgewood dish he held. I shook my head, no. "Coke?" he asked. Again, I demurred. We talked about the buyout due in 1975 and the company's present and anticipated earnings. Once again, he smiled comfortably. "It's a lock," he said. "It's better than ever. You've got the most talked-about magazine in America. Earnings are going up every year. Don't worry."

Changing the subject, he put a hand on my shoulder. "You have an eighteen-year-old son don't you?" I nodded.

"One of my daughters is coming into town. I was divorced years ago, and they live in Oklahoma and visit me a couple of times a year. She's sixteen and maybe your son could take her out and show her the town. My treat."

A couple of nights later, my son Michael, not thrilled with the idea of a blind date, left the house to do his dad "a favor." When he returned after midnight, I was reading. He walked into my room, a smile creasing his face from ear to ear. "Wow," he said. "I have been out with the most beautiful girl I have ever seen in my life."

He took Candy Loving out once more, then she went home to Oklahoma. A few years after that he walked into my office, once again grinning broadly. He tossed a copy of *Playboy* down in front of me. It was the twenty-fifth anniversary issue. The centerfold, who had been selected as "The Most Beautiful Playmate of the Twenty-Five Years of Playboy's History" was Candy Loving, lying there in all her naked glory.

A month or so before *Lemmings* closed, in November of '73, we formed a road company and sent it out on tour. Belushi and Chevy were in the group that left, while Chris Guest, Mary Mitchell, and Alice Playten stayed, with new members filling out both casts. I had offered the Belushi role with the group that remained at the Gate to Peter Boyle, hot off his film success in *Joe*. He toyed with the idea for weeks, then passed.

During the year at the Gate, I had ignored the rumors that drugs were being used regularly in the dressing rooms. I was assured it was mostly pot, and pot permeated the editorial offices of the *Lampoon* as it had those of *Cheetah*, so such use wasn't unusual. I learned much later that a petty cash fund I had given Hendra to buy dinners for the cast was being used primarily to buy drugs.

I was quite unsophisticated about drugs. My generation got off by getting drunk. It seemed to me there wasn't much difference, and the cast, like the editors, were always on the job and always seemed to look like they knew what they were doing. It was no secret that Belushi dropped "an occasional Quaalude" and that cocaine had become available midway through the run of the show but, I had been told, wasn't used to excess because the cast didn't have the money for it on a regular basis.

That summer my family rented a house in Westport, Connecticut, and the editors and the cast and crew of *Lemmings* were frequent Sunday visitors. The house was built around an indoor pool which occupied most of the vast living room, and we'd have great volleyball games, with a net being stretched midway across the pool. We set up a half-court basketball court in the garage area, and there'd be three-on-three games going all day long. Late in the day, I'd broil steaks for twenty or thirty on a back-porch grill. Of course, there'd be plenty of beer and liquor.

We had a wonderful black woman working for us as a maid that summer. She was round and short and had a wit that was as quick as any of the humorists there to party. One Sunday, Belushi, who drank and ate continuously, was on a Southern Comfort kick. He put a bottle in the refrigerator to cool. Later he opened the fridge and searched for it but it was gone. He turned and bellowed, "Where's my Southern Comfort!?" Our maid sidled up to him, smiled daintily, and said, "Here I is, honey."

The basketball games weren't limited to summers. All year long, in the city, I'd spend Sunday mornings in school yards playing pickup games with kids half my age and, for the most part, taller, faster, and stronger than I was. Often my son

Andy and I would drive up to Harlem and play pickup games in which we'd be the only white guys. I'd played in high school and college and could still shoot and pass with some skill. My "career" ended some years ago when I tried to block a pass thrown by a six-foot-four-inch twenty year old and broke my hand and two fingers. I proudly announced to my family when I got home that I'd finished the game, sinking the winning basket. It was my last basketball game, and at the age of fifty, I switched to tennis.

The editors rarely visited Westport when the *Lemmings* cast was there, except for Kenney who loved actors and show business and came whenever either group was invited. Of course, O'Donoghue and Hendra were never there on the same Sunday.

By now, O'Donoghue's "Encyclopedia of Humor" had reached bookstores and newsstands, appeared on the best-seller lists, and been well received by book critics, but the success of *Lemmings* and Hendra's involvement with it still irritated Michael.

We started to plan a weekly radio show. Bob Tischler was hired to set up a sound studio in newly rented space in our building, and Bob Michaelson, whose family was syndicating old radio shows like "The Shadow" and "The Green Hornet," was brought in to set up a *Lampoon* network. O'Donoghue became creative director of the "National Lampoon Radio Hour." Polly Bier, who would be the only one connected with the creative end of the show with any prior radio or television experience, was named producer. Judy Belushi moved from the art department to the radio show, and she and Janis Hirsch were to be Michael and Polly's assistants.

Lemmings toured colleges and concert halls until late winter of 1974. Company manager Trudy Brown and Dale

Anglund, who had been invaluable at the Gate, were on the road with the touring troupe. The cast flew from one engagement to another with the lights, sound, and props following in a truck. In February, the oil shortage of '74 struck and getting fuel became a serious problem. In April, Trudy called. The truck was stuck in Evanston, Illinois, and they couldn't get enough gas for it to continue. With no indication that the shortage would end soon, we canceled the tour and brought the group back to New York.

In 1974, the radio show would be heard on more than six hundred stations. In the same year, the circulation of the magazine would exceed one million, and advertising revenues would go over the two-million-dollar mark. The oil shortage would be cured and another production, *The National Lampoon Show*, would go on the road. A new recording contract would be signed with CBS, and a publishing deal for paperbacks was closed with New American Library. With all this going on, we resigned as the management group for *Weight Watchers Magazine*. Hendra and Kelly, flushed by the success of *Lemmings*, were now buddies. O'Donoghue now added Kelly to his list of "the dead."

Something else happened in 1974, the stock market went into one of its cyclical nose dives, a swoon which lasted well into 1975. There were virtually no underwritings on Wall Street. And Graham Loving, who had continually assured me that the buyout of the minority stockholders was "in the bag," closed his brokerage company, bought a hotel in Aspen, and left New York. I assume he took his "stash" with him. My worst nightmare was coming true—we were making a lot of money, but it was apparent that it might be impossible to come up with the kind of payment our deal with the "boys from Harvard" would command.

CHAPTER NINE

ROB HOFFMAN had returned to Dallas and his father's business after working for the *Lampoon* over the summer of 1970. He spoke to Doug and Henry frequently, and on several occasions when in New York visiting them, he stopped by my office to say hello.

In the summer of '74, he was back for the final negotiation. The original agreement had given the minority stockholders the right to cause the company to buy their 20 percent stock interest in the *Lampoon* no sooner than March 1975, five years after the publication of the first issue, and no later than the same month in 1977. They chose to exercise that option at the earliest date and the purchase figure came to more than six million dollars.

After Loving's company shut down, we had searched for a banker or an underwriter without success. Underwritings were just not available because of market conditions. There was no way we could come up with the six million dollars. We were advised that we could prolong any payout and perhaps sharply decrease the amount owed because the essence of the deal hadn't been lived up to by the minority stockholders. The intent of our agreement was that we would supply management and financing, and they would provide themselves. Hoffman, never a meaningful player on the creative side of the magazine, had worked on it only briefly, but Kenney, the star player, had disappeared for more than a year, at a time when the magazine had desperately needed his talents. It was pointed out that while there was no clear-cut wording that required all three men be there for the entire incubating period, it was certainly the intent of the agreement. Why would we have given them this lucrative deal if it wasn't to get "them" for the full five years? "There's a chance," we were told, "you might be able to beat them in court."

We weighed the consequences, years of litigation and hundreds of thousands of dollars in legal fees—and a breach that could rip the magazine apart, all on a chance we could win. We were not dealing with your everyday businessmen here—these were tough young people, and Beard and Hoffman were tough and rich young people, capable of hiring lawyers—Harvard lawyers, no doubt, who would flock to the side of a battling comrade.

I ruled out such a lawsuit and called a meeting with no lawyers—just Hoffman, Beard, Kenney, and Mogel and me. We talked for hours. We told them the obvious, we didn't have the six million, and we couldn't get a broker to underwrite it. Hoffman again did all the talking for them. "Sorry," he shrugged, "what do you suggest?" I told them we intended to pay them every cent of the six million, but we needed a moratorium on the debt until the stock market was more favorable, perhaps a year or two. That was quickly rejected. We offered part payment in common stock, part in cash, and part in some kind of long-term paper. He flatly rejected it. I then suggested a million to be paid on the anniversary date with the rest to be paid out over ten years or sooner if company earnings allowed it. Beard and Kenney said nothing as Hoffman again dismissed this offer. I increased the increments slightly. He suggested taking the entire amount in common stock which would have meant they'd have total control of the company. I countered with an offer of nonvoting stock which would mean I was still in charge. That was turned down. I had not put in seven years to become a passive stockholder. Finally, Hoffman looked at me and said, "If you can't pay, you'll be in default or you'll go into bankruptcy. Either way we'll take over the company."

I was furious. Their thinking of a takeover had never come up before. I turned to Kenney. "What ever happened to, 'we'll never hurt you!!?'" I snapped.

Now, Doug lost it and something happened that I'd never witnessed in a business meeting before. He jumped to his feet and started bouncing up and down like a two year old having a tantrum. "I want my money!" he screeched. "I want my money!"

Every head turned to him. Suddenly, he stopped. There was a long pause and total silence and then, for almost the first time, Mogel was heard from. He stood up and confronted Doug. The words came out of his throat like a growl, "I'm gonna punch you right in the mouth!"

Now we were all on our feet. I grabbed Len's arm and moved him away from Doug. Doug's tirade had come unexpectedly, but he was an unpredictable guy. Mogel, on the other hand, was normally a quiet, pleasant man. His reaction was so shocking that every one of us started to laugh. It broke the tension.

We continued to talk and came up with a formula: We pay them $100,000 on October 1, 1974, as sort of good intentions money. On the due date in March of '75, they would get $3 million. A year later they'd get $500,000 and the rest over four years. They left the room and caucused. When they returned, Doug apologized to us for losing his temper. In turn,

Len apologized to Doug for suggesting he was going to hit him.

Hoffman looked at some notes he'd made. "The deal sounds good," he said, "except for two things. The money has to be interest bearing. Let's say 8 percent." I nodded my assent. "And," he said, "we want a boost in the price because we're not getting paid everything up front. We want the price to be $7,500,000 instead of $6 million, and we want the additional 1.5 million to be paid on the due date."

His request struck me as being so oppressive that at first I couldn't answer him. Then we argued, but he wouldn't budge. I was now in a helluva position, I thought to myself. I can come up with about a million and a half from the company. I had offered to pay them three million on the due date without any idea where I would get the extra million and a half but where was I going to get three million dollars by March 1975? I wasn't concerned with the payout after that. I felt secure that company earnings would more than meet that.

I asked that we adjourn the meeting and resume discussions the next afternoon.

When they left, I had my secretary get Steve Ross on the phone.

Steve Ross had been a friend of mine since the early sixties when he and I had tried to merge the Diners' Club with his Kinney Corporation. My board of directors had fought me on the merger and killed the deal, deciding that the Diners' Club was too big for such a marriage. Ross instead merged with Independent News and then acquired Warner Bros. He was now chairman of the board of Warner Communications, later to become Time-Warner.

Steve was the best businessman I'd ever known, but more than that, he was the most decent man I'd ever done business with. We were important customers of Warner's magazine distribution company, but that had little to do with his reaction to my call. He was a friend. I needed his ear. He told me to come right over.

I doubt if I was in his office for more than half an hour. He listened to my story, heard what I needed, picked up a phone, and told his comptroller that on March 18, 1975, I would need three million dollars and that I was to get it at prime interest rate, the same rate they paid for their money, and could repay it with comfort.

Four years later, the first proceeds of *Animal House* repaid the Warner's loan. In 1987, another quick visit to his office resulted in a loan of $500 thousand which we needed badly and in a hurry. Four years after that, late in 1991, I flew to New York to discuss a project I had in mind with Steve. When I arrived at my hotel, his secretary called and, apologizing profusely, told me that Steve had a serious back problem and had to cancel the meeting. A week later the story broke about his having cancer. Only a few months earlier, I'd had pneumonia, and he'd sent me a stack of books to "read in bed." What do you send a billionaire? I wrote him a note wishing him well. From his sick bed, he sent back a letter thanking me for mine. When he died in 1992, I was stunned. He was a kind, gentle man. In the history of the *Lampoon*, he was the only person we ever asked for an important favor, and he always came through.

The next day we closed the deal. The following March we wrote checks totaling $4.5 million. Eventually Kenney and Beard would split close to $6 million with Hoffman getting more than $1.5 million.

Immediately afterwards, Hoffman took his check and caught a plane for Texas. Beard took his and resigned. He then went to his office and started packing. Hendra says that when he and Kelly went in to congratulate Beard, he let them

know in no uncertain terms that he had no intentions of cutting them in, even though they'd never asked for anything.
Hendra reports that Beard looked around the room to convey
a feeling of disgust and said, "I haven't felt this happy since
the day I got out of the army."

Michael Gross has told me that Henry loaned him
money to buy a house in Los Angeles some years later, eventually telling him to forget about paying him back.

Doug came back to my office after getting his check. He
was ashamed of the way he reacted during the negotiations
and told me that he would stay as long as I wanted him. We
shook hands. "Hey," I said, "that would be forever."

Doug did give Michael O'Donoghue $35,000, and the
word was that he gave Trow, his mentor, around twenty
grand.

Kenney stayed with the *Lampoon* until *Animal House*
opened, then he was off to Hollywood. Meanwhile, he wrote
frequently for the magazine and for the radio show and several stage shows and, of course, his "High School Yearbook"
became the best-selling special edition of a magazine ever
published.

The company was never to recover fully from the impact
of the buyout. In 1975 we put *Ingenue* out of business because
we couldn't risk the capital it needed to get rolling again.

We canceled plans we'd been formulating to publish a
movie magazine—years later came *Premiere*—and a magazine
of the future to be named after the company, Twenty First
Century. Years later came *Omni*.

To replace Beard as editor, we set up an editorial board
consisting of Hendra, Kelly, McConnachie, and Kenney who
wanted to participate but still didn't want to lead. Eventually,
we would realize that magazine by committee doesn't work.

CHAPTER TEN

HARPER'S MAGAZINE called "National Lampoon's High School Yearbook" "the finest example of group writing since the King James Bible." Other newspaper and magazine critics received it with almost equal enthusiasm. The least that can be said of it is that it ranks with *Animal House* as the best work of satire the *Lampoon* ever produced. Adapted from an early piece in the magazine by Kenney, it remained his creation but it involved the participation, before being printed, distributed, and sold, of 128 people, more than the cast and crew of many films. Kenney and P. J. O'Rourke conceived and directed it. Art director David Kaestle gave it form, and Chris Cerf, Ed Subitzky, Tim Mayer, George Trow, O'Donoghue, Gerry Sussman, Emily Prager, and Louise Gikow all wrote for it or contributed substantial ideas.

For months, the group, orchestrated by O'Rourke and Kenney, lived a scenario which seemed more like the making of a movie than a book or magazine The *Detroit Free Press* described it as "A masterpiece of parody." It was all of our high school yearbooks. From the bad poetry to the bad photographs of the faculty and graduating class, from the trite messages of farewell scribbled over the autographs of classmates under their photos, to the club pictures, it reminded us that much of the time we spent in high school was pretty ridiculous.

There was the corny tribute to the late John F. Kennedy (this was supposedly 1964) and the In Memorium lament about a dead classmate which appeared under Kenney's own high school graduation picture. And there was the principal of C. Estes Kefauver High School, Dr. Humphrey C. Cornholt, as played by Len Mogel, who wrote in his farewell letter in the yearbook, "The only true human waste is waste of time." Was this a subliminal admission that he—the principal—was "the mad crapper," the villain who left telltale excretions about the school?

Of course, there were the seniors themselves, Belinda Lynn Heinke known as "Metal Mouth," Madison Avenue "Zippy" Jones, the school's only black who is described thusly, "newcomer... stands out in a crowd." And there was Maria Tereza Spermatozoa, the class strumpet whose nickname was "Quickie" and for whom the yearbook editors inserted among her credits "Jayvee Tongue-wrestling Champ!" And, of course, there was Larry Kroeger, ostensibly the owner of this copy of the yearbook, of whom was written "nice guy... lives close to school," as if these were the highest words of praise available. Kenney was never one to discard a name. Larry Kroeger went on to become "Pinto" in *Animal House*.

Janis Hirsch, who came over from the radio show to buy props and help coordinate the action, wound up in the yearbook as "Ursula Jean Wattersky." Cast appropriately as the girl with the crutches, her Kefauver bio read: "'A' for effort ... always puts her best foot forward." Everyone loved Janis at the *Lampoon*. She'd contracted polio as a child only a few years before the Salk vaccine was developed. Affection notwithstanding, humor at the *Lampoon* was cruel, and she'd be the butt of jokes often. O'Donoghue, for example, called her

"Wobbles the Duck." None of this ever bothered her. She laughed at such humor, more than holding her own in this world of put-down.

After the yearbook was completed, I made her my assistant and then taught her how to handle publicity for the company. Within months she was offered an important job at a sizeable public relations company. We discussed it. The money was double what we paid her, and it promised a bright future. Nevertheless, she asked me what I thought she should do. I told her to grab it.

A few years later, she was writing comedy for television and is now producing television shows at Fox Broadcasting. She remembers the "High School Yearbook" well. "I did anything they told me to do. I was the hairdresser for the students. I called and woke them up if we had a morning call. I was low man on the totem pole. I was so happy to be at the *Lampoon*, I would have scrubbed the floor in the gym"

Getting the school and the kids who were to portray the students was a major problem. Kenney and O'Rourke visited a dozen schools, but they were turned down by every one of them. My youngest son Andy was attending Columbia Prep in Manhattan, so I spoke to Jim Stern, the headmaster. His mouth dropped. "The *National Lampoon* here? You want me to get killed?" He was just about echoing my mother's words, "that dirty magazine!"

I pleaded. "Jim, this will be a great education for your students—the making of a magazine—and they'll be a vital part of it. They'll be actors in a real production." He was weakening. "Talk to the students," I urged.

The next day, at a school assembly, he broached it to the students. They exploded in a burst of enthusiasm. He was off the hook. With the exception of "Wobbles" Hirsch and a couple of others, the students in the "High School Yearbook" were all from Columbia Prep.

We had wrapped the project and were near press time, and no one had come up with a cover. One night, after a day that included fruitless hours at a cover meeting, I woke up from a deep sleep. I started thinking about the cover, and suddenly I "saw" three high school cheerleaders twirling around in front of a crowd at a basketball game. Their skirts had flown to their waists. Two of the girls had the appropriate underpants under their dresses. The other had quite obviously forgotten hers. She was bare-assed! I knew that was it. The next morning I called Kaestle, Kenney, and O'Rourke into my office and described my vision. All three nodded at the same time.

Like the "dog" cover, the bare-assed cheerleader image has been "borrowed" more times than can be counted, only recently reappearing as part of an underwear advertisement in national magazines.

The best recent count I can get on the "High School Yearbook" is that it sold almost two million copies and is still selling. It first appeared in 1974 and was reprinted in '74, '76, and '79. If, as Kenney said, "we invented nostalgia," the yearbook was a major step in the process.

"Radio Dinner" had been the *Lampoon's* initial move into the entertainment business; *Lemmings* was the next. Thousands came to see *Lemmings* at the Gate and thousands more saw it when it toured concert halls and nightclubs around the country. With "Radio Dinner," we proved that we could entertain beyond the printed page and with *Lemmings* showed that we could attract exceptional entertainers and that we had ideas and talent that would usher in a whole new era in show

business. Stick-it-in-your-face comedy was here, and it flourished live. *Lemmings* was all about drugs and death, and people
had laughed. We would now give the world our kind of
comedy via a mass medium—radio—and we'd have it supervised by O'Donoghue, the master of the bizarre.

The "National Lampoon Radio Hour" first went on the
air in the late fall of 1973. Of the *Lemmings* group only Chris
Guest worked on the early shows, O'Donoghue refusing to
employ anyone tainted by association with Hendra. The
format of the show was basically the same as that used by
"Saturday Night Live" two years later. It usually opened with a
news broadcast, either a camp "Megaphone-News" written by
Bruce McCall or George Trow's Walter Winchell-like stream
of absurd gossip and innuendo. Sketches would follow to be
interspersed with recorded comedy songs

George Coe, now a noted character actor, and comic Sid
Davis were regulars as were comedienne Pat Bright. Soon
Guest convinced O'Donoghue that Chevy Chase should be
allowed out of purgatory and permitted to join the regular
performers. And soon after, Belushi and Brian Doyle-Murray
were writing and performing regularly.

Judy Belushi, who with Janis Hirsch worked for
O'Donoghue and Polly Bier on the show, recalls, "My first
introduction to Michael came when I was working downstairs
in the art department. I was doing some filing in the editorial
offices when I heard somebody shrieking. Just one voice was
yelling. I was so startled that I dropped everything I was
holding. Then, a strange, pale man with wispy red hair, a
beard, and granny glasses came running out of an office.

"He'd apparently been in there alone and was carrying a
walking stick. When he saw me, he came over to where I was
and raised the stick. I really thought he was going to hit me,

but instead he smashed it against the file cabinet I'd been working at. The cane shattered and he stood there looking at the handle in his hand. That seemed to calm him, and he looked down at me and asked very sweetly, 'You okay?' There's no question in my mind that Michael always wanted to be perceived as being crazy because he felt that other people would think of him as a genius and that a crazy genius is considered more of a genius than a sane genius.

"Anyway, after that we got to be friends, and when I heard he was going to do a radio show, I asked him if I could work with him on it. I remember he looked at me and said, 'You know, it's a little like going into the Pony Express business, starting a radio show in 1973.'

"Working with Michael and Polly and Janis and Bob Tischler and Bob Michaelson was great. Michael was really a very good director, and he surprised us because he was often sentimental and liked sweet things. Janis and I helped Michaelson ship the recorded show out to the radio stations, and we were always late. Station managers used to call and tell us they'd get the program an hour before it was supposed to go on the air or sometimes after it was supposed to go on the air, and they'd have to run a repeat show. [Matty] used to bitch about missing deadlines, but it was a one-hour show, and Michael was a perfectionist. He'd often sleep in the studio, and he and Tischler would work sometimes for eighteen hours without a break."

By early 1974 the show was being broadcast over six hundred stations, making it the number one program on radio and the first big variety show since the golden days of radio twenty-five years earlier. Many of the stations that carried it were located on college campuses. At the University of North Carolina, they'd play it on Saturday night and a thousand or more kids would gather around loudspeakers, drink beer, and listen to the show.

There were two problems. First, O'Donoghue was no longer writing for the magazine, and second, the show was losing money. The stations took the programs on a barter basis which meant you kept a number of the commercial spots, resold them, and kept the money. Early in the run, Taylor had sold a huge contract to Seven-Up. Their sponsorship paid the bills, but a program called "The Assassination of Richard Nixon," a parody of the Kennedy assassination, got a negative reaction from the Seven-Up bottler in Tulsa, Oklahoma, and steamrolled its way to the home office. The contract was canceled. After that there was very little national advertising.

Janis Hirsch recalls a fight between Trow and O'Donoghue that started over a disagreement about a sketch Trow had written. It began with some selective name-calling and reached its high point with objects of every description being hurled but rarely hitting anyone. The creative process was no less frenetic than that on the magazine.

Many of the regular bits were later to reemerge on "Saturday Night Live" including O'Donoghue's infamous portrayal of Ed Sullivan with needles in his eyes and somewhat later, Gilda Radner's Babwah Wahwah or Barbara Walters to the uninitiated.

Some of the most memorable routines involved Chris Guest as Mr. Rogers interviewing Bill Murray as anything from a jazz musician to a drunken bum.

As the show wended its way toward the spring of '74, I continued to urge O'Donoghue to return to the magazine. One night we had dinner at an East Side restaurant then walked the streets for two hours talking about how we would bring in other people to do much of the everyday work on the radio show—other people who would still be under his supervision.

The magazine, I reminded him, was still at the core of *Lampoon* operations, and we needed his input and, even more importantly, his output. He reminded me that he wouldn't work with Hendra. I assured him that he wouldn't have to, that he could deal with Kenney or McConnachie. He agreed.

The following Sunday was Easter.

I'd had a particularly hectic week, and I simply wanted to forget the *Lampoon* and the company for the weekend. O'Donoghue called. Someone, he thundered, had moved Anne Beatts's desk from an office in the recording studio. I didn't even know such a desk existed. "Anne Beatts has to have a desk at the radio show!" he screamed. "And she's got to have an office. She must have it or else!" I tried to stay calm, "Michael. I'm home. It's Sunday—Easter Sunday. We'll talk about it in the office."

"No," he shouted. "We discuss it now or I quit!"

I'd had it. "OK," I said, "if that's how you feel about it, you can quit!" We didn't speak again for nineteen years.

A few days after the Easter Sunday incident, Hendra burst into my office, eluding the grasp of my secretary, Barbara Sabatino, who for nearly twenty years made going into my office unannounced a capital offense. I had an important meeting in progress, and I remember glaring at Tony for interrupting us. "I found him," he announced gleefully, "O'Donoghue's replacement." With that, Zippy the chimpanzee roller-skated into my office.

At the time, I didn't consider it very funny.

I put Bob Tischler in charge of the "Radio Hour" and asked Sean Kelly to supervise the creative end of the show. By

Staff meeting, the early years. Left to right: Michael O'Donoghue, Barbara Sabatino (my assistant), Brian McConnachie, Len Mogel, Henry Beard (back to camera), Michael Gross, me, and David Kaestle—1972. PHOTO COURTESY OF MICHAEL GROSS

Michael O'Donoghue, with hat—not cap— and army jacket. His 1973 summerwear.
PHOTO COURTESY OF
MICHAEL GROSS

Henry Beard wearing his familiar tweed jacket and turtleneck and chomping on his trademark unlit pipe—1973. PHOTO COURTESY OF MICHAEL GROSS

Doug Kenney—1975. PHOTO COURTESY OF MICHAEL GROSS

Michael O'Donoghue and Tony Hendra, before the war—1972. PHOTO COURTESY OF
MICHAEL O'DONOGHUE

Michael Gross and the Trojan Panda cover—1974. PHOTO COURTESY OF MICHAEL GROSS

now, the road show had closed, and John Belushi was putting together a new revue. While that was being prepared, the cast—Belushi, Brian Doyle-Murray, Joe Flaherty, Harold Ramis, and Gilda Radner—appeared regularly on the "Radio Hour." Before Michael had left, Brian and John wrote a show called "Welcome Back, Death Penalty." It was a sardonic call to end the practice. More than four hundred of the six hundred radio stations carrying the show had refused to air it. Every week anywhere from one to two dozen stations kept us off the air because something offended them, but this was, by far, the record. John and Brian beamed with pride. *Lampoon* editors and writers congratulated them.

In his book, Tony Hendra says that during *Lemmings* I suggested he fire Belushi. Of the many inaccuracies in the book, many strangely where I was involved, this bothered me the most. Belushi and I were very close during *Lemmings* and for several years afterward. When I decided to do a second show, I thought so highly of him that I put him in charge of it. I would later name Belushi to replace Kelly as the radio show's creative director. I had dinner with John and occasionally his family, including his kid brother Jim, on numerous occasions, usually at the Minetta Tavern which had become a hangout for me. And, certainly, there would have been no intelligent reason for my wanting John fired from *Lemmings* where he delighted audiences every night. Aside from that, I really liked him.

"John was the sweetest guy you could ever work with," Janis Hirsch said to me once. "He'd be late if his kitten fell asleep on him."

Belushi and his friends now became the resident company for the radio show. Brian Doyle-Murray was hired as staff writer. The others were paid both as actors and writers.

This group was even more creative than the *Lemmings* troupe. Every one of them could write as well as act. By now, I had cut the one-hour format in half to reduce the continuing losses. We changed the name to "Half the National Lampoon Radio Hour." One show they wrote was called "The Immigrants," a hilarious potpourri of misinformation about various groups that immigrated to this country earlier in the century. It crackled with sly jokes and an uncanny display of foreign accents by the cast. It was to me, the finest radio comedy in my memory matched perhaps only by Jack Benny or Fred Allen at their peaks.

In 1974, we broke in the new musical comedy, *The National Lampoon Show*, at a nightclub in Mineola, Long Island, called My Father's Place. A few nights later, the troupe left on an extended tour which started in Philadelphia. I drove there for the opening. As I pulled into the city, a local station was broadcasting "The Immigrants."

Back in New York, Brian Doyle-Murray had convinced me that I should hire his younger brother Bill to replace him on the radio show.

After four years of O'Donoghue, Bill Murray's volatility should have been no more than a minor annoyance to me. Michael had been "A Team" and at this point, Bill was a staff writer but, like Michael, he was "nuts," and you always knew when he was around. Once, he tore into my office and declared that the bookkeeping department was trying to steal from him. I looked at him blankly. "There's $1.86 missing from my paycheck," he hissed. "And I wanna know where it is!" I suggested that he trot down the hall and check it out with the comptroller. He refused. He wanted me to get to the bottom of this larceny personally. Once again, I'd had enough. I told him not only to leave my office but to leave the recording studio, leave the building, and leave the *Lampoon* forever. He stomped out. For the next three days, Tischler called me regularly and asked me to reconsider and allow a now-repentant Bill to "come home." Finally, I relented.

The $1.86, it turned out, was an accurate deduction for some minor tax item.

A few weeks later, Brian called me from Philadelphia and told me he had to leave the show. It seems he was madly in love with Gilda and after reciprocating for a while she, in turn, was now enamored of another member of the cast. Under the circumstances, he explained, he couldn't remain with the show. He suggested that Bill replace him. I was delighted to get Bill out of our building. Brian returned to the radio show for its closing months.

When it ended, we had a well-equipped recording studio and a staff but nothing to record or produce other than the two comedy albums a year we'd been turning out in addition to the radio show. Anxious to expand beyond the *Lampoon*, we conceived "The Mary Travers Show."

The format was simple—Mary would interview rock stars. Her name would attract them to our studios. It did just that. For starters, Bob Dylan, who almost never did interviews and never appeared on talk shows, would be one of the first guests. Rock stations eagerly subscribed to the show. Finally, Michaelson and I agreed, we had a show that was easy to produce, would ship on time, and wouldn't alienate sponsors. What we didn't figure on was that Mary was dull on the air and difficult off.

The much-hyped show with Dylan was slow and uneventful. Subsequent shows with other rock giants were equally tedious. Away from the microphone, Travers would rail at Janis and Judy. Marty Charnin, the director who later wrote and directed *Annie*, was constantly at her side. It was obvious that he had "replaced" Taylor to whom she was still married. Once again, that wasn't any of my business, but her treatment of her staff and the quality of the show was.

I closed down "The Mary Travers Show" after eight programs. We wound up in a bitter screaming match in the hall outside the studio, and I literally threw her and her belongings out of the building.

The October 1974 issue of the *Lampoon* sold an all-time number of issues, 1,083,425. Not much by *Playboy* standards but a lot for a humor magazine that wasn't sold at a third of the retail outlets in the country because it ridiculed people and ideas that some considered above such nonsense. Surveys indicated that there were twelve readers for every copy of the *Lampoon* sold, which meant twelve million people a month, mostly young men, were reading the magazine. The average reader was twenty-three years old.

In 1975, circulation hovered just under the million mark. Advertising revenues were at an all-time high. We closed the radio show, and a special edition of the magazine called "The National Lampoon Bathroom Reader" was a big success.

The National Lampoon Show rolled into 1975, picked up an additional producer, had a second and third company, and somehow evolved into "Saturday Night Live."

CHAPTER ELEVEN

ITEM: GILDA SOARS

Gilda Radner was deathly afraid of flying. On the road with The National Lampoon Show, she always arranged to go from one engagement to another by car or bus or by train for longer distances. On one occasion, the distance was too great and the time too short. The company manager announced that everyone had to fly. Gilda refused. Harold Ramis said that he'd convince her she should do it. They spent the entire night together, Ramis plying her with assorted drugs and stories, the basic theme of which was, "the show must go on." The next morning the cast gathered in the hotel lobby to board the bus taking them to the airport. Everyone kept glancing at their watches as departure time approached, but there was no Gilda. Finally, the elevator door opened, and Gilda, eyes glazed and body moving only barely, emerged. Around her neck was hung a handwritten sign that read: "Hi! I'm Gilda and I'm not afraid to fly!" She wore it until the plane landed, and they got her to the next hotel.

JOHN BELUSHI felt great having the show on the road. He'd relished the excitement of *Lemmings*, playing to New York audiences, and the way the critics had received him and, he loved becoming an overnight celebrity in New York. He and Judy would walk into a bar or restaurant, and people would applaud him and ask for autographs. That was "great," but he was never close to the rest of the cast. Chris and Chevy had gone to college together and were very tight. The others were basically out on their own after the show.

It was important to John to be close to the people he worked with, and that's how it was with *The National Lampoon Show.* He'd always gotten along well with the Murray brothers; Ramis was like a rock, talented, dependable, always ready with the answer to a problem. Joe Flaherty, too, was a steadying presence and everybody loved Gilda—so vulnerable, so genuinely nice, and so funny. This was the cast's show, almost all of it. They had created it with only a little help from the editors. Doug had written a Patty Hearst spoof, and Sean had written some of the songs, but it had been assembled mostly by the cast.

When he joined the show, Bill Murray inserted some bits he was later to use on "Saturday Night Live," "the Honker" and the small-time bar singer. John romped from scene to scene, changing characters like socks. But this was a real ensemble and the cast really liked and helped each other. Offstage, they smoked a lot of pot and traveled and ate and clowned together.

At a longer-than-usual stopover in Toronto, the show settled in at the El Mocombo nightclub for a two-week engagement. There were two shows a night. The first one was always packed and the second, often deserted.

There was also a problem we hadn't anticipated. The agent who booked the tour neglected to tell us that customers could stay for two shows in an Ontario nightclub in any one evening and not be asked to pay an additional cover charge.

They frequently stayed. We had prepared only one show. Rather than repeat the same show to many of the same customers, the cast, having been trained at Second City, which was, to a degree, improvisational theater, winged it.

One night, Belushi, Ramis, and Bill Murray were struggling through some improv to a small, rather indifferent group who had already sat through an entire first show and was well into their cups. It was not going well. Suddenly, someone at the rear of the club began laughing hysterically. Every time one of the actors said something, the same shrill roar of pleasure resounded throughout the room. As laughter will be, it was infectious, and soon everybody in the place was laughing. Now, the hysteria from the back of the room grew even more raucous. Michael Simmons, filling in for an ailing company manager, was standing in the wings. He walked along the side of the club determined to see who had started this avalanche of laughter. There, in the back of the room, sitting alone at a table and laughing so hard that the tears were flowing freely down her cheeks, was Gilda.

Dan Aykroyd and other members of the Second City Club in Toronto were regular visitors to the El Mocombo, and after the evening performances, the cast would hang out at a little after-hours bar owned by Dan and his brother Peter. Another regular visitor to the El Mocombo was a thin, ingratiating young producer named Ivan Reitman. Ivan's family had migrated from Czechoslovakia when he was an infant and had settled in Toronto. He studied music as a boy but early on had decided he wanted to be a producer. His early film efforts were financed by wealthy Jewish families in Toronto and had done moderately well.

In later years, I would suggest to interviewers that Ivan's early films were all called *The Beast From Under Your Armpits*, and indeed, in one, the heroine grew a third arm. Most recently, he'd produced a musical called *The Magic Show* starring the magician, Doug Henning. The show had done so well in Toronto that other producers had moved it to Broadway where it was again enjoying a successful run. Ivan still owned part of the show and was listed as one of the producers.

Ivan had (and has) a very astute mind. As he watched the show at the El Mocombo, he envisioned these actors, and more importantly, the *National Lampoon*, as his ticket to Hollywood. Somehow, he had to get "in." He got friendly with Michael Simmons and told him how anxious he was to do business with me. Michael suggested he call me. He did, the next day. It was a pleasant conversation, and we agreed to talk again. His experience with *The Magic Show* interested me. Meanwhile, without my knowing it, he started talking to Ramis about possibly working together.

Weeks later with the show still on the road, I decided I wanted to bring it into New York for a limited engagement to get the benefit of the flurry of publicity that would surely result. I hesitated because I didn't want to have to mother another musical in New York. On the road, the show played at other people's theaters or clubs. The cast performed and you got paid. It was that simple. In New York you had to rent a theater, sell tickets, promote, advertise, publicize, and worry about the day-to-day problems of a theater project. I'd had my hands full with *Lemmings*, and I worried about doing it again. It was during that period of indecision that Ivan called, and we spoke three or four times. I finally told him to come to New York so we could meet. When he did, I didn't waste any time. "How would you like to bring the show to New York for a limited engagement?" I asked. "You could be the producer." Titles have never meant a lot to me unless accompanied by money. I recall his words clearly. "I'd give my right arm to produce a *Lampoon* show," he said breathlessly.

ITEM: IVAN PRODUCES

Ramis remembers the first rehearsal in New York. "It was a cold day. Everybody came in wearing winter clothing. We'd started rehearsing, when Ivan walked in. It was his first day as the show's producer. He had on a woolen stocking hat, a big scarf, and a heavy jacket. He was grinning from ear to ear as he greeted everybody. As he did, he took off the hat and scarf and jacket. When he was finished, Bill Murray put an arm around his shoulder and picking up the clothing he'd discarded, put them back on him, one by one. Then—and Ivan was still grinning—he walked him to the door, opened it, eased him out, and slammed the door shut. Ivan didn't come back for two days, and when he did, he never mentioned what had happened."

The show opened at the now-defunct Palladium Club in Rockefeller Center in March of 1975. The reviews were good if not as spectacular as those for *Lemmings*.

Once again, the *Lampoon* had a successful show in New York. Once again, it became the hot ticket in town. The six-week limited run that we had agreed on was sold out at nearly every performance. I had approved the artwork that Michael Gross created for the show's poster which included the credit "Ivan Reitman Presents." The show with some minor changes was the same one that I had produced that had been on the road for months. Ivan had brought in a director who made some minor changes. His name, Martin Charnin.

Murray was, as expected, the most volatile of all *Lampoon* performers. He worried a lot about the show and particularly about his performances. He couldn't cope with distractions. One night, the actor Martin Mull came in drunk and proceeded to get even drunker. This, of course, was a nightclub and the waiter, as requested, kept bringing the drinks.

Toward the end of the show, Murray was onstage, doing his beloved "Honker" routine. Now, Mull started an incoherent conversation with Bill. Murray gave him a stare that would have immobilized Mull or any other normal man when sober, but it didn't stop this harangue. Bill exploded and leaping off the stage into the audience, grabbed Mull by the throat and shook him. The audience recoiled in horror. Suddenly Belushi was in the audience, too. He pulled Bill off what seemed to be a now-sober Mull and dragged him back to the dressing room.

Ivan asked me if he could put the show on the road again. I said yes, but the cast demurred. Belushi, in particular, had been on the road with *Lemmings* and the *National Lampoon Show* for the greater part of a year and he missed Judy. He wanted to stay put in New York. Ramis had an offer to do some writing in California, and there was talk of doing a Second City TV show in Toronto. Everybody else was too tired to continue traveling, especially Gilda with her fear of flying. Reitman cast a new show, and, most notably, replaced Gilda with Mimi Kennedy and Ellen Foley and Belushi with Meat Loaf who wasn't as funny as John but sure as hell could sing better. The show toured for several months then closed quietly.

At the *Lampoon*, O'Donoghue and Beard were gone. Trow, whose contributions had diminished after the second year, asked that his name be removed from the list of contributing editors, suggesting to one of the editors that I should have paid him off as I did Beard, Kenney, and Hoffman. John Weidman, already a Harvard graduate, had left to study law at Yale and now returned to the magazine. Gerry Sussman became a major contributor.

With Beard gone and Hendra, Kelly, and McConnachie running things, deadlines were being missed. Beard had always been available to plug a hole if editorial copy was needed. Except for Kenney, the staff was not capable of "instant" humor. Perhaps, as importantly, Gross was missed badly; he and Kaestle having left to form their own art studio. The new art director, Peter Kleinman was a young man with talent, a drug problem, and a desire to be an editor. The most cohesive force at the magazine was O'Rourke. Hendra and Kelly hated him and resisted my giving him more and more responsibility. Nevertheless, I soon made him executive editor, then in 1975, managing editor. He was tough and dedicated and talented; the first two attributes being qualities some of the other members of the staff resented.

There were good issues and memorable pieces: "American Bride Magazine" by Emily Prager, Ed Bluestone's totally insane "Iceless Icecapades," "Beep the Little Bus," by Hendra and Kelly, McConnachie's "Our Wonderful Bodies," Sussman's hilarious "Mel Brooks Is God" interview, and a flood of material from Chris Miller, O'Rourke, and newcomers Ted Mann and Todd Carroll. Nineteen seventy-five was the year Vaughn Bode, reaching for a new high or possibly a new orgasm, experimented with dangling from a noose hanging from the rafters in his home and accidentally hung himself.

Nineteen seventy-six was the year Mitch Markowitz, who was later to write *Good Morning Vietnam*, and Jeff Greenfield, who would become a key reporter on ABC's "Nightline," became contributors, and it was the year Sussman first introduced the adventures of the New York cabby "Bernie X."

Nineteen seventy-six was also the first year that the *Lampoon*'s circulation temporarily stopped growing. Publishing revenues were down nearly two million dollars, primarily because we had no important special editions; no "Yearbook" or "Encyclopedia." Advertising sales were up, but there was no *Lampoon* show, no radio program—nothing that was new and challenging and fun. So, we decided to make a movie.

CHAPTER TWELVE

WITHOUT MY knowing it, Reitman and Ramis had started discussing a *Lampoon* movie, Reitman figuring that they'd develop something and then bring it to me. Ramis had a film about his college days in mind and started putting some ideas together. Early in 1976, Kenney had come to me and told me that he was tired of meeting deadlines. He obviously didn't need the salary but assured me he'd stay until the end of the year if I wanted him to, but no longer.

I didn't want to lose Kenney any more than I had wanted to lose O'Donoghue or Gross or Beard. I thought about it for a week or so then came up with an idea. Kenney, above all, wanted to be in show business. His happiest times at the *Lampoon* had been while hanging out at *Lemmings* or at the radio show. He loved performers. He often suggested that he might want to become an actor and had a small role in *Between the Lines*, a film directed by Joan Macklin Silver.

"You can't leave," I said to him, "we're going to do a movie."

He smiled immediately.

"I want to do a film based on 'The High School Yearbook,'" I said, "and I want you to write it."

We had not yet put Doug and Harold together. They had met during *The National Lampoon Show* rehearsals. Despite

141

Harold having told Doug that he hated his Patty Hearst sketch, they liked and respected each other.

Ramis remembers Doug coming to his tiny Manhattan apartment shortly after they met to work on the Hearst sketch. "Doug walked straight to my bookcase and pulled a book out. He looked at the first couple of pages, then started reading it aloud. I couldn't imagine what he was doing until maybe five minutes later I realized that after the first couple of pages, he was making up his own story, using the same characters and setting. I was astonished and he'd glance up and tell from my face that I was, and grin. He was ad-libbing a better story than the author had written. Finally, he closed the book and put it back in the case. Then, he turned to me and shrugged, 'I can do that with any book.'"

Ivan called me only a week or so after my discussion with Doug and told me that Harold had written a rough draft on a proposed film titled *Freshman Year.* I read the draft and shook my head. It put down the fraternity system. It wasn't much fun. You weren't rooting for anyone. It simply didn't work. This, it should be noted, was the first screenplay from the man who would eventually write or cowrite *Animal House, Caddyshack, Ghostbusters, Stripes, Meatballs, Groundhog Day,* and other films and would become the most sought-after comedy script doctor in the motion picture business.

Ivan agreed the script was wrong, but we both wanted to pursue the idea of making a movie. I told him of my discussion with Doug. Then I suggested we team the writers and have Doug and Harold write a treatment for "The High School Yearbook" movie which, then, Ivan and I would produce. On the spot we cut a deal, 75 percent of the producer's earnings to the *Lampoon,* 25 percent to Ivan. We set up a corporation with that split in the stock and called it the Yearbook Movie Company.

I made the deal with Ivan for one reason—certainly, Doug and Harold or Doug and someone else would have written the film without Ivan's involvement, but here was a bright, aggressive young man and at the *Lampoon's* management level, I, as always, had a desperate need for bright, aggressive young men. I envisioned the *Lampoon* going into the film business for more than one film and that Ivan would work with us—all the way. That vision and the quick deal we agreed on that day resulted in a four-million-dollar windfall for Reitman. My plan backfired. Ivan became so successful, he didn't need the *Lampoon*.

After *Animal House*, and at least partly because of it, he became one of the richest and most powerful men in Hollywood and, more precisely, one of the two most important people in film comedy; the other being John Hughes who arrived at the *Lampoon* the following year when we were shooting *Animal House* and when everybody—especially Hughes—started dreaming about California gold.

Ramis and Kenney's work on the *Yearbook* screenplay was going nowhere; we all felt there was too much sex and drugs in their screenplay for a movie about high school. We told them to move it to college where Ramis had wanted it in the first place. Doug suggested using Chris Miller's short stories about his fraternity days at Dartmouth as a base. Miller happily joined the group. The time of the movie was established as 1962 when Chris was in school, and the writers came up with a name, *Animal House*.

We decided that instead of a script, they'd write a treatment which I would then try to sell to a major film studio. Ivan talked about getting Canadian financing for it, but we agreed that we'd first attempt to make a deal in Hollywood. No one connected with the project had ever been involved with a major motion picture, but even before the treatment was written, we were deciding how we'd sell it.

I gave the three writers an office, and they started writing. Once or twice a week, they dropped by and we reviewed what they were doing. They chatted with Ivan on the phone about as often. Meanwhile, Kenney and Miller were still writing for the *Lampoon*, and Ramis was into various other projects.

A few months later, they finished the treatment. A normal treatment covers about twenty pages. Studio executives have notoriously short attention spans. Anything too long is given to a reader who then writes a synopsis that might cover six or eight pages and include his own recommendations. Thus, the original input on which the decision to make a movie often lies, rests, in good part, with a man or woman making perhaps forty thousand dollars a year and is then passed on to an executive making at least ten times that much. There are studio executives—men who make the final decisions—who never read a full script but will commit millions of dollars to a project based on a reader's synopsis, comments, and recommendations, the reactions of other members of the decision-making team, and, most importantly, the key ingredients—the stars and director.

The treatment the writers completed in 1976 was 114 pages long, longer than most scripts. It didn't bother me—I had no idea how long a treatment should be—nor did it bother Ivan when he got his copy. It wasn't only too long, it was too busy. A script adapted from this treatment would have resulted in a four-hour picture. But we loved it.

Once again, I called Steve Ross. After all, Warner Bros. was part of his Warner Communications empire. He got on it at once. A few hours later, Jay Emmett, the president of Warner Communications, called me. As with Steve, I'd known Jay for many years. I told him about the treatment. He was enthusiastic.

"Look Matty," he said, "I'm going to Los Angeles in a couple of days. Send the treatment over to my office. I'll give it to Ted Ashley personally and ask him to read it himself at once."

Ashley was the chairman of Warner Bros. We'd go right to the top, but I hesitated. "Jay," I said, "why don't you just set up a meeting with Ted for me? I'd like to explain this to him before he reads it."

Jay laughed. "Matty, I'm his boss. He'll give this top priority. Let *me* walk in with the treatment."

I did. Three days later Jay called me. "I'm sorry," he told me, sounding genuinely sad, "but Ashley says to forget it. It'll never make a movie."

"Success in Hollywood," someone once said, "is half talent, half coincidence, and half knowing how to add." I know a producer who got a film made because he was hit by a golf ball. The guy whose ball hit him was a studio executive who invited him for a drink after his ball and the producer's head met somewhere around the sixteenth hole. They chatted. The conversation got around to movies. The producer mentioned a project he'd been trying to sell and that became that.

A week or so after the Warner Bros. rejection, a Jerry Miller called me from Los Angeles. "Mr. Simmons," he said, "I'm the assistant to Ned Tanen, president of Universal Pictures. I'm just calling to tell you that I'm a big *Lampoon* fan. I want you to know that if you ever get an idea for a movie, we'd be very receptive."

There was a slight pause as I digested this. "Mmm," I said (as though I had to check my brain for the multitude of film projects we were working on). "I may have something for you" (very slowly so as not to exhibit excitement). "Yeah. We do. Actually we have a treatment."

"Great!" He was excited. "Can I get it? I'll have our office in New York pick it up in an hour."

"No," I said. I wasn't going to let this happen twice. "The only way I'd be interested in pursuing this is if I can see Mr. Tanen and discuss this story with him. Then all of you can read it."

"Terrific!" he enthused. "I'll call you back!"

Ivan and I flew to Los Angeles the following week and checked into the Beverly Hills Hotel. We met with Tanen the next day and pitched our proposed film as succinctly as we could. "These stories may be hard to believe," I remember telling him, "but they're true. Much of this really happened on college campuses in the sixties, and young people everywhere will relate to them."

He took the treatment and, noting its heft, stared at it for what seemed like a very long time. "How many pages in this treatment?" he asked. I smiled, "One hundred and fourteen." He nodded in amazement. "A 114-page treatment?"

Two days passed, then Jerry Miller called and asked if we'd drop by to see Ned again. When we walked into his office, Tanen got right to it. "I hate this!" he said. "The story is all over the place. There are too many characters, too many things happening, and I don't like anybody in it." Tanen leaned over and looked me in the eye. "Can you make this for two and a half million?" he asked.

At that point I didn't have the slightest idea whether the picture could be made for a million, ten million, or two and a half million. My background was in publishing and theater. I couldn't even take a wild guess about the budget of a movie. I looked at Ivan. He shrugged. Why not. "Absolutely," I told Tanen. "I guarantee it!"

Tanen still seemed uncomfortable. He fidgeted. "I hate this," he repeated as we shuddered, "but the *Lampoon* is so hot, it's worth a shot. Let's make a deal."

I returned to New York and Ivan to Toronto. Kenney and Ramis and Miller were ecstatic. There were mixed reactions from the rest of the staff, some of whom resented the fact that Kenney who had already been rewarded for his efforts and Miller who was a contributor but not a member of the inner circle and Ramis who had never even written for the magazine had been given this plum.

I flew back to L.A. a week later, this time accompanied by the *Lampoon's* entertainment attorney Bob Levine. Bob had never negotiated a movie contract before. I, of course, had never even read one. I was warned by all before I left, "Don't trust these people! They'll steal you blind! And don't take net points!" Net points are percentages of the profit of a movie. In more recent years, after stars and major directors would only make a movie in which they received a share of the gross, net points have become even less valuable. Eddie Murphy, a few years ago, characterized them as "monkey points" because before reaching net, the studios included their overhead and various other expenses even including a percentage tacked on top of a movie's paid advertising. Rarely is there anything left for the net participants.

When we sat down in the office of Universal's head of business affairs, Mel Sattler, the first thing I said was, "No net points!" This time, I decided, I would not be the hungry person in the deal. Sattler complained for a while, explaining that almost nobody except for a few major stars were getting gross points. In 1977 that was true, but I shook my head and held my ground. "OK," he relented. "I'll give you 5 percent of the gross from break-even." I shook my head, "Five percent from the first dollar." Again, he complained, then, after a while, agreed. I jumped right in, "And 10 percent after you break even." He looked at me like I was crazy. Again we heard a lecture on current profit-sharing policy, and again he finally agreed. When, he did, I snapped, "And I want 15 percent of everything up to $10 million dollars and 20 percent after that."

Two hours later we'd hammered out a deal: 5 percent to break-even, 10 percent after break to $15 million in gross revenues. Fifteen percent on grosses from $15 million to $20 million and 17.5 percent after that.

To my knowledge, this was the best profit participation deal anyone at that time had gotten from a major studio. I believe that Universal thought this movie (the actual budget was $2.7 million) might gross $8 million or $10 million at the box office. And that the contract they agreed to was an exercise in deal making.

The picture eventually would gross $170 million at theaters in the United States and Canada. Receipts from domestic cable and television alone have exceeded $25 million dollars. It became the most popular film comedy of all time. Using today's ticket prices, its domestic box office gross would have exceeded $300 million. It was released before the foreign market became the major factor it is today so worldwide grosses are not comparable. Interestingly, it was an R-rated film and few R movies reach these heights.

For the year 1993 alone, fifteen years after the picture was released, the gross points we negotiated that day earned more than $114,000. Through 1993, the *Lampoon* earned more than $12 million from *Animal House*, while Reitman earned the aforementioned $4 million.

An agent representing the writers wrapped up their deal a few days later, and they started to write the screenplay.

CHAPTER THIRTEEN

IN 1975, I WAS approached by an executive at NBC who asked if I'd be interested in bringing the *National Lampoon* to television. He told me they were thinking of a weekly ninety-minute variety format not unlike the shows we were producing.

I thought this over carefully. The one-hour radio show had been a backbreaking business—the staff worked through the night and still we were unable to put the shows together with the consistency of quality we were used to without taking a great deal of time from the magazine. That was the principal reason we'd changed it to a half hour. Furthermore, we lived through constant rejection from many national advertisers with both the magazine and the radio show. Would this problem follow us to television?

Most of all, there was the manpower problem. If this offer had come a few years earlier, I probably would have jumped at it, but Beard had left that year as had O'Donoghue. I knew Kenney, particularly now that he was rich, couldn't be counted on to be around much longer. I simply didn't have the talent at hand to spare and starting a search for new writers for television would only cause problems. The key people on the magazine would rebel if they weren't given the more lucrative television work.

I worried most about spreading the *Lampoon* too thin. Radio had devoured a lot of material, but it would be nothing compared to television, and would the reader, being able to see the *Lampoon* free every week for ninety minutes, desert the magazine?

I decided not to enter into any further discussions with the network. A short time later, the comedian Alan King and his producing partner Rupert Hitzig came to me with what seemed like a more palatable idea. They were going to produce a one-hour television show every week—a variety show with Howard Cosell as host, "Prime Time Live." Would I be interested in putting together a *National Lampoon* troupe which would perform, let's say, two sketches on each show? It was to be, as the name indicated, prime-time while the NBC offer was for a late-hour show.

We discussed money, and they offered more for two sketches than NBC had for ninety minutes. I accepted their offer and our lawyers started negotiating a deal. Meanwhile, I put together a troupe, Bill and Brian Murray, Chris Guest, Rhonda Coullet, who had been in the road company of *Lemmings,* and Belushi. But Belushi kept changing his mind. NBC had gone ahead with the project and had named a comedy writer by the name of Lorne Michaels to put it together. He'd already hired Chevy Chase and Anne Beatts as writers and— the head writer was Michael O'Donoghue. Gilda Radner became the first member of the cast. Now, all of these ex-Lampooners urged Michaels to hire John Belushi. He seemed to be unsure. In turn, Belushi wavered on my offer. He'd met Michaels and greeted him by telling him, "You know I hate television! I go home every night and spit on my TV set." Michaels wondered if such a maniac should be part of his cast. Finally, Chevy and the others persuaded him that Belushi was a great talent, worth the antics and temperment. John came to my office and sheepishly told me that he was accepting Lorne's offer. I was not happy. I complained, mentioned loyalty thirty or forty times, and finally wished him luck.

In later years, Michaels would deny that in any way "Saturday Night Live" had its roots in the *Lampoon*. Once, on a TV talk show, I chided him for having been quoted as saying, "No, I'd say we were more influenced by the *New Yorker*" (the *New Yorker*!!!) in a *Playboy* interview. His attorneys threatened to sue me for libel or disparagement or telling the truth or something.

Belushi, of course, was right. I was wrong to reject the NBC offer and wrong to suggest he turn down the "Saturday Night Live" show for the Cosell gig.

The next week, our negotiations with King-Hitzig-Cosell hit a snag. They insisted on total creative control. I had never surrendered control on a *Lampoon* project. I said that I would allow them only final word on matters involving network standards. They refused. I called off the negotiations and told the troupe they could stay with the show but without the *Lampoon* name. And they did. They were great. The show was awful. It folded in its sixth week. Cosell never again ventured outside the sports scene.

By 1976 "Saturday Night Live" was a huge success. O'Donoghue, once again, had set the tone. Chevy, John, and Gilda became stars.

Ramis, Miller, and Kenney were crafting the first rough draft of the *Animal House* script. In it was a gregarious hoodlum by the name of John Blutarsky, Bluto to his friends. From the start we all knew that John Belushi had to be that character.

It was now early 1977, and we still had no director. Universal had set up Ivan and me in a couple of small offices in a motel directly across from the lot. There was little doubt that our picture had low priority. There was even less enthusiasm among the Hollywood creative community.

A rough draft of the script was given to about a dozen directors who we thought would be right for the job. All passed. It's interesting to note that at the time, the two men who would become the most successful comedy directors in perhaps fifty years were associated with the *Lampoon;* Reitman on the *Animal House* project as coproducer and commuting between Chicago and New York for the magazine was *Lampoon* editor John Hughes. Box office receipts of pictures directed, written, or produced by these two men would, in 1993, be in the neighborhood of four billion dollars and going up. Reitman had let it be known that he wanted to direct *Animal House* but, at the time, he hadn't even directed one of his own Canadian potboilers. Hughes casually mentioned directing around 1980. The discussion never got further than that.

I was in Los Angeles. In Canada, Ivan had started preproduction on one of his own films. At the studio, the enthusiasm level went up as the power base went down. Universal's chairman, Lew Wasserman, never heard of us. Its president, Sid Sheinberg, thought of us and our movie as a minor venture. Tanen, who was president of film operations, still didn't relate to the project but thought there was hope. His assistant, Thom Mount, a sixties revolutionary turned "suit," liked the antiestablishment thrust of the story. *His* assistant, Sean Daniel, loved the whole thing. By now, Jerry Miller who had brought us to Universal, was gone. No one ever explained to me the reason for his departure or told me where he went.

I was getting antsy. Until we had a director, the studio wouldn't green-light the movie. Then one day Daniel called me. His girl friend was working on an independent film, a rough cut of which was being screened that night. She had told him that the director seemed to know what he was doing.

The picture was *Kentucky Fried Movie*, the first film written and produced by the now-estimable team of Jim Abrahams and Jerry and David Zucker whose next effort was *Airplane!*, which all three also directed. The director of *Kentucky Fried* was John Landis who previously had produced, directed, and written a picture in which he also starred—as a gorilla. *Kentucky Fried* had a budget of $500,000. It had no plot, just wandered from sketch to sketch to blackout, most of which was hilarious.

When the lights went up after the screening, I turned to Sean Daniel. "I like this guy's work," I said. "He's got *Lampoon* sensibilities." This meant, of course, that his film was very funny, a little sick, moved rapidly, and looked good. When we walked out of the screening room, Daniel said to me, "Call Tanen tomorrow and tell him you like him." I agreed, not quite sure why Sean couldn't have told Ned the same thing. But the difficulty in communication between studio executives whose offices are within a hundred feet of each other has always puzzled me.

The next day, I called Tanen. "You like this guy?" he asked rhetorically. I assured him I did. "Then, it's okay with me." A few days later Landis was hired, and he flew to New York to meet the writers. We met at my office.

He remembers that Doug was hostile, Harold wary, and Chris totally affable.

"We talked about the script and what I thought was wrong with it," he recalled recently. "I told them it was the funniest thing I ever read, but it was truly offensive. It had a major problem. You hated the Deltas as much as you hated the Omegas. You have to have heroes and villains, good guys and bad guys. And the script was too long, and there were scenes in it that had to go. They had this long, long scene where the Deltas got roaring drunk, and as an initiation into the fraternity, the pledges had to walk around a mountainside and throw up on seven campfires they'd started. Gotta go, I emphasized, *no one* will watch ten minutes of vomiting."

As John spoke, I smiled. I had always hated humor based on bodily excretions and had criticized this particular scene, but we'd agreed to wait before deciding on it. But now, Landis was firm. "Another thing," he said. "This road trip would be great if you cut it by two thirds. Christ, you've got these guys driving for days, going to Canada. Too long. Not necessary."

Of course, he was right. The sequence as originally written was much too long, but in the eventual trimming of it, one of my favorite scenes had to be deleted. Remember that this all takes place in 1962. The Deltas are cruising along in Flounder's brother's car. Suddenly, they see a bedraggled looking guy hitchhiking along the highway. He's carrying a worn suitcase, and a guitar is strapped to his back. The car screeches to a halt, and the hitchhiker piles in the back. Noting the guitar, Boone asks him if he sings. He says he does. "What's your name?" Flounder asks. "Robert Zimmerman," he tells them. "Hey," says Boone, "sing us a song." Zimmerman (Dylan) starts singing in that unmistakable growly, off-key voice. Go to a long shot. Again, the car screeches to a halt. A door swings open, and Zimmerman/ Dylan is tossed out of the car followed by guitar and suitcase.

As he went on, I knew that selecting John as director had been the right choice. He'd immediately understood what Doug and the rest of us had learned at the outset of the *Lampoon* and what Michael Gross had insisted on as soon as he became art director of the magazine; the best comedy comes from reality and the closer you stay to reality, the funnier you get. He implored the writers not to get hokey, not to try too hard for the jokes.

As John worked with the writers over the months, any hostility disappeared. Doug's early reaction had been that John was "Hollywood," all gloss and no substance. He wasn't. He was brash and outspoken, but he was smart and his ideas were terrific. With John working out of Universal in Los Angeles and Ivan producing a film in Canada, the three writers would meet me once or twice a week in the *Lampoon* boardroom in New York to go over notes from John and Ivan or just discuss new variations they'd come up with. Soon, Harold went to Toronto to become the head writer and one of the stars of "SCTV." Several times after he got there, the other writers flew up to work on the script with him and Ivan.

To their credit, the studio never interfered with the writing of the script. The usual, uninformed sources have reported Mount as saying he was part of the writing process, but when he was quoted in print as saying that, he quickly denied it. At any rate, the statement was a mystery to the writers who vaguely remember meeting Mount once—at a social occasion—before the movie opened.

Two or three times, as the writing neared completion, Landis flew into New York and Ramis and Reitman from Canada. We sat around the *Lampoon* boardroom table discussing the script. Ramis recently recalled my responding to Landis asking for a funny line or two to add to the scene near the end of the picture when all the Deltas have been kicked out of school. "How about Bluto saying," I offered, "seven years of college down the drain!" I remembered feeling very good when everybody in the room liked the line. I felt even better when it got laughs in theaters.

Except for the excitement being generated by the preparation and shooting of *Animal House*, 1977 was not a good year for the *Lampoon*. Circulation and advertising revenues dipped slightly and income from the usually profitable book division started to fall off. The company for the first time showed a loss. It was only $25,227, but it was our only loss since the first year of Twenty First Century Communications' eleven-year history. In addition to the drop in revenues, the loss occurred for three reasons. First, for the second year in a row we'd made interest payments on the minority stock purchase of nearly $400,000. In 1975 we'd started having to take a paper loss on the monies paid for that buyout. We introduced a new magazine and had the resultant start-up costs.

Len Mogel had gone to Europe to attend an international publishing trade show. He came back with a French adult comic book called *Metal Hurlant*, which literally translated means "screaming metal." This was unlike any comic book we'd ever seen in the United States. The art was breathtaking. The men were heroic or evil with bulging muscles and little desire to do anything but fight or make love. The women were equally heroic and even more beautiful. They all had heaving breasts and curving buttocks and thighs. And all *they* wanted to do was fight or make love.

"It's great," I agreed. "Let's do it." Len contacted *Metal Hurlant* and made a deal with them and with other French and Spanish publishers of similar materials. They sent us the film of the artwork, saving us thousands of dollars an issue. And since this was material that had already been published in Europe, we paid a reprint fee and didn't incur the high cost for original material. All we had to do was select the material we wanted to use, translate it, and publish. We decided to call it

Heavy Metal because the heavy metal music seemed to convey some sense of recklessness, violence, and sex.

Still struggling to figure out where to best use him, we moved Sean Kelly from the *Lampoon* and made him editor of the new magazine. By the end of 1977, I would take Hendra off the *Lampoon* as well and put him in charge of special entertainment projects. Earlier in the year, Kelly and Hendra had put together materials from past stage shows, the radio show, and the magazine and once again we had a musical comedy, *That's Not Funny, That's Sick!*, touring America's clubs and college campuses.

By now, Gerry Taylor had left to become the publisher of *Harper's Bazaar*, Brian McConnachie to join "Saturday Night Live."

P. J. O'Rourke was made editor-in-chief. New editors and writers would now come to the *Lampoon*. It seemed like 1970 all over again. We felt good about the future. The magazine had stopped growing, but we were confident that P. J and bright, funny people like Ted Mann, Jeff Greenfield, Peter Kaminsky, and John Hughes would bring us back into orbit.

CHAPTER FOURTEEN

LANDIS AND casting director Michael Chinich must be given most of the credit for the superb casting in *Animal House*, particularly since only Belushi and Donald Sutherland were known quantities before the movie was shot. Belushi's reputation on "Saturday Night Live" was growing every week, but certainly he was not a star when he signed for the role of Bluto. He was paid forty thousand dollars for the film and contractually had no points or participation in the picture.

Sutherland, of course, was a star. He'd been a hot property since *M*A*S*H* and took the cameo role of Jennings, the Faber English professor, only as a favor to Landis who he'd known for several years. He'd done a cameo in *Kentucky Fried Movie* for John and was paid union scale, something like five hundred dollars, but that took a few hours of his time. His cameo in *Animal House* involved two days of shooting. Moreover, it was not, like *Kentucky Fried*, an independent picture. Although the budget was certainly small enough, it was, nevertheless, a Universal film, and Sutherland said he'd do it but wanted some real money—suggesting fifty thousand for the two days. The studio, anxious to keep costs down and potential losses to a minimum, countered with ten thousand dollars and 10 percent of the net profits of the movie. Sutherland dismissed that at once. He wanted to do a friend a favor, he said, he didn't want to be a partner. Finally, a deal was struck at thirty-five thousand and no points in the film. To this day, Sutherland tells the story of the "prodigious" deal he negotiated for himself and the one he turned down. The ten points he passed on would have netted him close to $10 million.

The rest of the casting was going well except that Tanen had sent down a memo with suggestions for the key roles, "Dom DeLuise for Mayor DaPasto, Jack Webb as Dean Wormer and Kim Novak as Mrs. Wormer." The memo was filed and forgotten. Now, came a request that was more of a demand than a suggestion, "Chevy Chase as Eric Stratton."

Landis, who subsequently made a number of pictures with Chevy, thought he was wrong for the role and at a luncheon with Chevy, Ivan, and Sean Daniel, held ostensibly to convince Chase that he should take the part, Landis wondered out loud why Chevy would even consider an ensemble movie where he'd have to share both screen time and screen credit with a dozen other actors when he'd been offered a costarring role with Goldie Hawn in the film, *Foul Play*.

I agreed with John for two reasons. First, I thought that Chevy was too old for the role. He was past thirty and in no way looked like a college student. Secondly, a pairing of Belushi and Chase would have inevitably caused people to suggest this was not a *Lampoon* movie, but a "Saturday Night Live" movie, even though both actors had been with the *Lampoon* before going to television. I told both Chevy and his manager only that he was no longer twenty-one and sure as hell didn't look it. Only five years later, he would play the father of two teenagers in *Vacation*. Actually, neither Landis nor I affected Chevy's decision very much. He's a very bright guy and, after thinking about it for not too long, he took the *Foul Play* role.

Tim Matheson, best known as a kid actor on television, was cast as Otter. It was a perfect fit. Matheson *was* Otter just as Belushi was Bluto. A wonderfully ingratiating actor named Peter Riegert was Boone; tall, lanky, nervous WASP Jamie Widdoes was Hoover; tough, taciturn Bruce McGill was the motorcycle bum D-Day; a nerdy, nervous Tom Hulce was Pinto; and a sweet, overwhelmed-by-it-all cherub named Stephen Furst was Flounder.

The role of Clorette DaPasto, the Mayor's fourteen-year-old sexpot daughter, was passed on by Roseanne Arquette and finally given to Sarah Holcomb, an exquisite girl still in her teens.

Verna Bloom was cast as the hard-drinking, sexy wife of the dean. Landis recalls the day Thom Mount heard that John Vernon and Cesare Danova had been chosen as the villains. The studio hadn't wanted "real" actors in the roles. They wanted broader performances. Landis, just as he had done with the writers and the script, had opted for reality and not burlesque. Of course, I agreed with him, reminding all, again and again, that reality was what had made the magazine funny.

"Mount lost it," Landis remembers. "For the first time since I was a child, an adult was screaming at me. [We later learned that Ned had screamed at Thom about the same casting.] 'This studio,' he wailed, 'is not going to make a comedy with John Vernon and Cesare Danova!' Chinich and I just looked at him, astonished at the ferocity of his reproach. Finally, he cooled down just a little, got up, started to leave, then turned to us, 'You guys go ahead and make your fucking movie,' he said. 'It's on your head!' When he left, Chinich turned to me and smiled. 'We win,' he said."

The writers were still rewriting the script. I would remind them almost daily that the Deltas had to be more likable and the Omegas more detestable. "Black hat-white hat," I repeated again and again, recalling the standard thrust of the western movies we'd all loved as kids. Finally, a rewrite of the script was approved and with Belushi and Sutherland and the rest of the cast set, the picture was green-lighted.

Five colleges had turned down the idea of shooting a *National Lampoon* movie on their campus. The sixth, the University of Oregon, thought it was a great idea, thanks mostly to the school's dean, William Boyd, who figured that it would be a good educational experience for his students, the same line of reasoning I'd used to get Columbia Prep's Jim Stern to let us use his school for "The High School Yearbook."

In the fall of 1977, Landis, cameraman Charlie Correll, production manager Peter McGregor Scott, first assistant director Cliff Coleman, and the rest of the crew and cast arrived in Eugene, Oregon, for what was to be a thirty-day shoot (plus two at Universal). I remember discussing that with a director friend some years later. "Thirty days," he mused. "That's just about as long as it takes to get Bruce Willis out of his trailer."

Reitman, whose wife was having their first child, arrived two weeks after the shoot began. I traveled back and forth from New York, stopping several times in Los Angeles to work with Universal's advertising and marketing chiefs Charlie Powell and Buddy Young.

Landis remembers that as soon as they got there, the actors playing the Deltas fell into their roles. "The Deltas got to Eugene first," John recalls. "We'd rehearse, then we'd all have dinner together at the hotel we were staying at. One night I looked across the dining room, and there were Mark Metcalf, James Daughton, Kevin Bacon, and some of the other actors who were going to play Omegas.

"'Hey,' I said to the group at my table. 'It's the Omegas.' I was, of course, thinking we'd invite them over, buy them some drinks, chat for a while. Instead, Belushi leaps up and shouts,

'Food fight!' and every actor at the table started throwing food at these poor guys. That's how it was for the entire shoot. The Deltas hung out together, drank together, smoked pot together, and didn't associate with any of the Omegas until the movie wrapped."

Stephen Furst recalls the days in Eugene very well. "I'd been working as a pizza delivery boy when they hired me for the role of Flounder. It took months for them to make a final decision. I'd sit down in a waiting room with a bunch of other fat guys and I'd read, and Chinich would make a point of telling me how much they liked me. When I finally got the part, I couldn't think or speak all day. It was my first professional acting job, and I was in a *Lampoon* movie with John Belushi and Donald Sutherland. When we got to Eugene, I was a nervous wreck. All I wanted to do was please people and be good as Flounder. I loved being on the set, and I'd hang around all day even when I wasn't on call. I hated weekends because I missed the filming so much. The other Deltas thought I was nuts, but I had never known anything this exciting. Riegert was going with Bette Midler at the time, and I remember lending them a car I had rented so they could drive somewhere for dinner. I kept saying to myself, 'Bette Midler is driving in my rented car.' I was in a total daze.

"Guys like Matheson and McGill thought I was naive and I was. I felt like I was getting on people's nerves, and that was probably true, too.

"I'd never smoked pot or done any kind of drugs. I was high all the time just because I was where I was and was doing what I was doing."

Doug Kenney and Chris Miller had paid their own way to Eugene, and Landis made them Deltas, Doug as the nerd Stork and Miller as Hardbar. The studio had refused to pay their way out so they were there as actors, not writers. Nevertheless, when a classroom scene was needed for Sutherland's character, Kenney wrote the remarkable Milton speech for him. This is the scene in which Sutherland's character finally tells an inattentive class, "All right. I find Milton as boring as you find Milton. Mrs. Milton thought so, too."

When the shooting of a picture starts, it becomes the director's film. All a producer can and should do at that point is make suggestions and help keep everything on time, on budget, and in harmony.

Landis's theory is that *Animal House*, like all movies, went through a series of proprietorships. He puts it this way:

"First it was a Matty Simmons movie.

"Then it was a Matty Simmons-Ivan Reitman movie.

"Then a John Landis movie.

"And then a John Belushi movie."

To his credit, Landis, only twenty-six in 1977, was in total command. He knew what he was doing and acted like it. To their credit, the studio executives stayed away from the set, Daniel paying a brief visit to see his girl friend who was, once again, Landis's script supervisor. Always fully prepared, John could also be spontaneous. Furst recalls the scene in the supermarket when Matheson is supposedly throwing cans and packages of food at him. "What actually happened," Stephen relates, "is that Landis, off camera, told me to walk down the grocery aisle then turn to the camera. As I did, he started tossing all this stuff at me. It wasn't in the script or anything. I just kept catching it. I was, like, in shock."

Karen Allen played Boone's girl friend, the female lead in the film. As in the case of Furst, Tom Hulce, Kevin Bacon, Sarah Holcomb, and most others in the cast, it was her first movie. She brought her own home movie to her audition, and I remember all of us being fascinated by her look on screen. Her eyes were sparkling green and intriguingly intense. The amateur film got her the job.

Belushi spent only three days a week on the set, commuting between Eugene and New York where he was still doing "Saturday Night Live." He was tired but ready and on time.

"Belushi had an incredible rapport with an audience," Landis says. "I remember when we were filming the scene where John is on the ladder watching these half naked co-eds frolicking in their bedroom. Well, let's face it, he was playing a Peeping Tom, and that's not normally a very admirable role, but when John turned around and smiled at the camera, he made everybody a coconspirator with Bluto.

"On screen he was a cross between Harpo Marx and the Cookie Monster. Harpo had that sweetness and yet was completely destructive. I made him watch the Cookie Monster on 'Sesame Street' for the cafeteria scene when he jams all that food down his mouth. The Cookie Monster, like Bluto, is gruff with a prodigious appetite. Of course, John was all of those things in real life—destructive, gruff with a huge appetite for everything, and very sweet."

When you're shooting a movie for a major studio, copies of the prints are made and shipped overnight back to the home base. The next day, the studio executives gather to view the "dailies," the previous day's filming of all the pictures then being shot for the studio. An interesting thing was happening back at Universal. The brass watching the dailies began to realize they had more than a little movie that might make a few bucks because of the *Lampoon* name. People in the screening room were laughing—often and loudly. At first, Sean Daniel would call us and tell us what was happening.

After a while, Mount started to call, and toward the end of the shoot, Tanen called. "You know," he said to me, "I think we've got something here." The enthusiasm was moving up the power base.

Looking back to 1977 and the making of *Animal House*, Tanen now says, "Sure, I may have been apprehensive. Remember that I was seeing dailies, bits and pieces of guys killing horses, spitting food in other people's faces, trying to seduce every woman in sight, swilling liquor, and destroying property. Let's not forget though, the guys who used to work for me may have been taking bows for years, but I'm the one who went on the line and said, 'Let's make it!'"

Tanen is right. He had the guts that the head guy at Warner Bros didn't have and the intuitiveness to figure out that somehow this script, which he didn't fully understand or particularly like, would make a movie that his company might possibly make a couple of bucks on.

Tanen was a gruff, outspoken studio head in the mode of the old Hollywood moguls who liked to yell a lot but had the right instincts for making good movies. Under his aegis, Universal made *American Graffiti*, *The Sting*, *Animal House*, *Jaws*, and *E.T.*, among other, perhaps not as awesome, successes.

Actually, with *Animal House*, he was like me at the outset of the *Lampoon* magazine, not quite understanding what was so goddamn funny about death and lying politicians, about being broke and being sick.

After a while, I think we both got it—if you can laugh, you won't cry. Death and avarice and hunger are stupid. And stupid is funny.

Despite my eventual problems with him, I liked Ned and still do. He's smart and he was accessible. Some studio people you have to work with are neither.

CHAPTER FIFTEEN

CIRCULATION OF the magazine was down, but revenues from books and special editions had increased *Lampoon* revenues by more than a million dollars in 1977, and in 1978 total revenues would increase by another $5 million, much of it from early *Animal House* profits. Before *Animal House* was released, O'Rourke, Hughes, and Kaestle had put together a classic parody of a small-town newspaper, appropriately called "The Sunday Newspaper Parody." There would be four printings of it for a total sale of 350,000, at the previously unheard of price for a magazine of $4.95. *Animal House* opened on the last Friday of July in 1978. It would dominate our conversation and our planning and change the lives of all of us at the *Lampoon*.

Even before it opened, the sweet smell of success had pervaded the spacious halls of Universal Studios and had wended its way eastward to the less austere confines of the *National Lampoon* where its editors and writers were now thinking of writing movies or, at least, television. Success in the mass media had first struck with O'Donoghue, Beatts, McConnachie, and others at "Saturday Night Live," but that was not yet big money or big time. *Animal House* would, as the weeks and months went by, be talked of more and more as a blockbuster, and blockbusters meant lots and lots of money and prestige.

O'Rourke was one of the few who wanted no part of Hollywood. Like Beard, O'Rourke always felt the movies were not for *real* writers, *real* writers wrote for magazines and wrote books.

At Universal we had a new champion. Bob Wilkinson, who was head of distribution, walked out of the screening room after seeing a rough cut of *Animal House* and turning to Tanen, uttered the magic words that had been heard until now only at the *Lampoon*. "What we've got here," he said, "is a blockbuster." His enthusiasm for the project soon had theater owners around the country eagerly awaiting it.

Tanen still wasn't sure. Watching a rough cut one day with Landis, Mount, and Daniel, he ordered the projectionist to stop the picture. It froze on a shot of Otter being kicked in the groin and beaten severely by a group of Omegas. He pointed to the screen. "He's just been kicked in the groin," he said. "Was that funny?" Landis was puzzled. Where was he going? "It wasn't meant to be funny," he replied meekly. Tanen leapt to his feet. "Oh!" he screamed, "so—you're making a comedy that isn't supposed to be funny!" At that, he turned and stormed out of the room with Mount right behind him.

The first test screening settled the matter of insecurity once and for all. A test screening is held under controlled cir-cumstances. A group simulating the actual audience that a movie is expected to attract is invited to a screening room or theater. After the screening, they are given cards on which they indicate their level of enthusiasm or lack of it for the movie and are asked various other questions as well as making any comments they choose to make. Often, the comments can lead to editing changes in the film.

At the *Animal House* test screening, 92 percent of the par-ticipants rated the picture as excellent. It was the highest such rating a picture had ever gotten in the studio's history of such tests. The comments weren't merely encouraging. They were, to say the least, laudatory; to say the most, ecstatic.

The next move was to screen the movie at a preview at which everybody paid to get in. There would be no cards. No questions would be asked. If the audience liked it, they'd laugh a lot.

A theater in Denver was selected for the first preview. We flew there with Tanen, his boss Sid Sheinberg, Mount, Daniel, Wilkinson, and several other Universal executives. We—were Landis, Reitman, and me.

The opening night of *Lemmings* had been, I had promised myself, a night I would never forget. The swell of enthusiasm from the audience had left me proud and, without realizing it, grinning broadly. The reaction that night in Denver was so incredible that I couldn't even smile. I just stared blankly as the audience stood, many on their chairs, and screamed their approval when the picture ended.

"They didn't like it! They didn't even love it! They devoured it!" Charlie Powell said to me later that night.

None of the producing group said anything as we trooped out of the theater. Even Sid Sheinberg seemed stunned. We left the theater, still without a word. Now, Tanen came over and put an arm around my shoulder. It was a "my buddy" arm around the shoulder. "What," he asked quietly, "if I asked you to cut the black bar scene?"

The black bar scene is the one in which the Deltas and their dates visit an all-black bar and are invited to leave by some large, dangerous-looking blacks who then proceed to dance with their dates. The Deltas leave—hurriedly. I had, during the shoot, asked Landis to temper the scene by adding a sort of postscript which showed the girls returning to their sorority house talking only about the Deltas. Clearly, it indicated that nothing untoward had happened other than the Deltas leaving them.

When Tanen asked me the question, I stopped and looked at him. It had been quite obvious from the audience reaction that we had a winner. "No," I said. "Absolutely not. Everybody will love the scene, and blacks will love it most of all. One liberal writer in Greenwich Village will complain about it." Tanen dropped the subject.

When the picture came out, Andrew Sarris in the *Village Voice* was the only critic who complained about the black bar scene. At every showing I attended after the picture opened, blacks laughed louder than anyone else.

In 1977, the third *Lampoon* show, *That's Not Funny, That's Sick!*, had gone on the road. I wanted a touring show because I felt it was the best kind of marketing for the magazine. It made some money, nothing meaningful. The material for this particular show was excellent since it was comprised only of earlier "good stuff."

The cast was quite good if not in the same league as the stars of *Lemmings* and *The National Lampoon Show*. A pert young redhead named Wendy Goldman sang and mugged her way through it with success. An energetic performer named Eleanor Reissa, out of the Yiddish theater, no less, made sure that no moments were quiet and the *Lampoon* prerequisite, an actor who could portray a dozen characters including the traditional Dylan, was found in Andrew Moses. Broadway director Jerry Adler staged the show. And for the first time, a *Lampoon* revue was backed by a band.

My son, Michael Simmons, and his group had played clubs and concert halls around the country. He and his band were the first brief act of the show and then backed the performers, giving it the drive and support that a good musical comedy needs. But the star of the show was a frail, kind of sweet-looking guy named Rodger Bumpass, and his was a story that Damon Runyon might have written fifty years before Rodger lived it.

He had come to New York from Little Rock, Arkansas, to be an actor. He went to audition after audition without success. Nearly six months went by, and he was running out of money. He took what was almost his last hundred bucks and went to bartender's school but continued to go to auditions. The last one he went to was ours for *That's Not Funny, That's Sick!* We liked him at once. He could act. He was funny as hell. He sang very well, and he moved like an acrobat. He was hired as an understudy but was quickly promoted to the regular group when Lee Wilkof, who'd already been cast, asked us to let him out so he could join the off-Broadway cast of *Little Shop Of Horrors*, a show destined to be a huge hit and then a film.

In rehearsal, it was soon obvious that Bumpass was going to be the star of the show. Aside from his many talents, he had a perfect temperament. He was always on time, always knew his lines and everybody else's, and everybody liked him. The show went on an extensive tour. Wherever it went, business was good and the reviews were excellent. Always, they singled out Bumpass's performance.

Here the story must detour slightly before we meet Bumpass again. The word on *Animal House* was now all over Hollywood. It was late spring and the picture hadn't opened yet, but it had previewed all over the country and the reaction was always the same. I signed a three-year, exclusive movie and television deal with Universal giving us $500,000 a year for expenses and development. We moved into one of the biggest producer's office suites on the lot with three secretaries and an assistant, all paid by the studio. Our first film hadn't even come out yet, and we were "moguls." Down the hall from our new lodgings were the offices of Dick Zanuck and David Brown.

Zanuck, the son of the legendary Darryl Zanuck, and Brown had coproduced *The Sting* and many other successful pictures including what was then the number one film of all time, *Jaws*. I'd known David Brown for many years. Like me, he'd been in the publishing business before films. He still wrote the cover lines for *Cosmopolitan*. The editor was his wife, Helen Gurley Brown.

One day, David and I bumped into each other in the hallway. We discovered we would both be in New York the following week and arranged to have lunch there at the Friar's Club, the show business club I'd belonged to for many years.

At lunch, the subject naturally got around to making movies. "God, I'd love to make a movie with you fellows," David said. "I got it," I said, *"National Lampoon's Jaws 3—People 0."* He laughed so I continued, just making things up as I went along, never thinking he would take me seriously.

"It opens at night at Peter Benchley's home. [Benchley wrote *Jaws*.] He goes to his pool for a midnight swim, dives in and—disappears. Suddenly, a shark fin circles the surface of the pool and slowly we fade." I went on, telling the story of a vengeful shark desperately trying to prevent the filming of *Jaws 3*. The villains were the studio heads and the director who'd made the first two *Jaws* films. The heroes were an assortment of actors, writers, and a "vulnerable, young guy from Dimter, Idaho." A good friend of mine, a lawyer at Universal by the name of Gerry Barton was, at the time, married to an actress named Jeannie Dimter, and the name had always intrigued me. I simply usurped Dimter and added Idaho.

David, who hadn't said a word during this entire rendition, now got excited. "I love it!" he enthused. He excused himself, raced to the phone, and called his partner who was also in New York. He was glowing when he came back. He was so excited he couldn't sit down. "Dick loves it, too! We're seeing Tanen tonight. We'll talk to him and call you in the morning. We'll make this picture! You produce it and we'll exec produce."

I nodded, still not believing what had just happened. We shook hands and left. My office was four blocks away. I ran all the way. I wanted to dictate the story I'd just concocted while I still remembered it.

David called me the next day and told me that Tanen liked it as much as they did. "We're in business," he assured me. I called two of my editors into my office and described what had happened. "I want you to write it," I told them. For both of them, it was their first film. One was Tod Carroll who would later write *O. C. & Stiggs* and *Clean and Sober*. The other was John Hughes.

That day, I decided as well that Rodger Bumpass would play the young man from Dimter, Idaho.

That's Not Funny, That's Sick! was wending its way westward.

The reviews continued to be uniformly good and continued to single out Bumpass. *The New York Times* had said in its review of the show: "It is most consistently funny whenever a dour-faced man with the unlikely name of Rodger Bumpass is doing anything at all. Mr. Bumpass has a malleable face, a malleable voice, and, apparently, a malleable mind. Like all great comedians, he is basically an actor. Whatever surface effects he may use with that remarkable face and his collection of voices, they are logical extensions of the basic character that he is projecting."

In May of 1978, the show opened in Los Angeles to a packed audience at the Roxy, the rock-and-roll mecca on Sunset Boulevard. When it closed, management estimated that during the three-night engagement, they had turned away more than four thousand people. The opening night crowd included much of the cast of *Animal House*, a lot of movie stars, and Thom Mount, Sean Daniel, and other Universal executives who had primarily come to "audition" Bumpass, to see if they agreed that he could star in *Jaws 3—People 0*, which Hughes and Carroll were writing, using the ad-lib story I had told to David Brown as its base.

The show was well received. The entire cast got long and well-deserved ovations, but Bumpass brought them to their feet. It was quite simply, a star-turn. It was suggested by many that he ranked with such previous *Lampoon* stars as Belushi, Chase, Radner, and Bill Murray.

Mount grabbed me at the door of the club. "You were right!" he gushed excitedly. "This guy's sensational! Let's sign him!"

Rodger Bumpass, eight months out of Little Rock and six months out of bartender's school, was signed a few days later to a Universal contract. He was to get fifty thousand for the film, more, I reminded him, than Belushi had been paid for *Animal House*. The show was scheduled to end its run by August. Bumpass would stay with it until the closing, then return to Los Angeles, be put on salary and expense account by the studio, and prepare for the film. When it did close, he detoured to Little Rock where the locals greeted him with front-page stories and TV and radio interviews. The friends he grew up with and his family threw parties for him and assured him that they'd known all along that he'd be a star.

In the fall of 1978, the writers handed in the first draft of the *Jaws 3* script, and everyone liked it. Notes were given and changes were suggested. Now, they were working on a second draft. Tanen told me to hire a director, and I had selected a little-known Roger Corman discovery named Joe Dante.

Stephen Furst (Flounder) was recruited to play the role of an ex-matinee idol who, as the writers noted, "had let himself go." Mariette Hartley would play a tough studio executive, and we were trying to get Richard Dreyfuss for the role of a shifty, wheeler-dealer moviemaker.

We needed a leading lady. Blake Edwards had just completed a film called *10* and invited me to a screening. In our script, our leading lady had to be remarkably beautiful, sexy as hell, not necessarily a great actress, and willing to appear nude frequently. There on Blake's screen was the unknown Bo Derek. She agreed two days later to do the picture. Dante and I picked our principal location, the Salton Sea in the California desert. At Universal, they started making sharks.

When two weeks later *10* opened and Bo Derek became an instant star, Bumpass was numb with excitement. He was going to star in a major motion picture, and his leading lady was going to be the world's new sex symbol.

Dick Zanuck, David Brown, and I congratulated each other as well. We had a surefire winner: the third *Jaws* film, the first *National Lampoon* movie after *Animal House*, and Bo Derek's first picture after *10*. We also had a funny script and, all agreed, a capable director. "What do you think?" I asked David one day. "The sky," he said. "At least $100 million at the domestic box office."

I was, like Bumpass, riding high. Another hit, coupled with the profits we'd receive from *Animal House*, would repay all of the debts incurred by the buyout of "the boys" and leave plenty over for expansion. Another hit could drive our stock from twenty-two, where it had risen after *Animal House*, to fifty.

Then, one day, in late fall, Tanen called and said he had to see me. When I walked into his office, I could swear he looked as if he was going to cry. He greeted me warmly. "Matty," he said after I sat down, "I'm going to have to close down the picture."

What was discussed after that was clouded in my mind within minutes after I left his office. I do know that he told me he couldn't give me a reason for the cancellation. I remembered thinking that I'd spent a year on this project—a year wasted when the *Lampoon* was the hottest name in the film business. Tanen had said he would talk to David and Dick. I knew I had to tell Dante and Hughes and Carroll. And what the hell was I going to say to Rodger Bumpass?

A few days later, my confusion and disappointment turned to anger. Both the *Lampoon* and I had two years to go on our contracts with Universal. I wrote Tanen a letter, telling him I was moving off the lot and that I wanted the contract canceled or I'd go back to New York and he could just send the checks to my New York office.

The press got wind of this, and it was given major coverage. In the *Los Angeles Times*, Tanen suggested, "Matty Simmons thinks he's David Lean." I retorted with an equally stupid riposte, "Yeah, well maybe, but Ned Tanen is not Louis B. Mayer. Louis B. Mayer would have had the sense to make the picture."

I was so angry, so frustrated, so hurt that this surefire project that I had counted on for so much, had not only been canceled, but canceled without my ever being given a reason, that I had shelved a terrific deal and opened new offices and started developing at our own expense. Zanuck and Brown left Universal soon afterward. Years later, a former Universal executive told me that the picture had been canceled at the insistence of Steven Spielberg, the director of *Jaws*. I don't know if that's true, but I do know that the order to kill the picture came from Tanen's bosses.

Rodger Bumpass didn't go back to show business for a year or two, working around Hollywood as a messenger and delivery boy. Later he appeared in two of our shows and toured for a while in the Low Moan production, *El Grande de Coca Cola*. He also appeared briefly in an early and forgettable *Lampoon* film, *National Lampoon Goes to the Movies*, and starred in the *Lampoon's* off-Broadway and Showtime musical, *Class of '86*. The *New York Times* once again addressed Bumpass's talents. "The man," the reviewer suggested, "can do anything. He could do Iago if he wanted to."

Today, Rodger is a successful voice-over actor for commercials and animated films. He's as hopeful as ever. "You never know," he told me recently. "It's kind of a crazy business."

CHAPTER SIXTEEN

ON THE EVENING of July 26, 1978, *National Lampoon's Animal House* had its world premiere in New York City. Three thousand invited guests filled the Astor Theater on Broadway. Another thousand, last-minute invitees who had enough clout to get what had to be "the invite" of the summer, were shuttled by bus to the Lincoln Center Theater where a second print would be shown. Universal had turned the running of the premiere and the party that would follow over to me. My aides at the *Lampoon*, primarily my assistant Barbara Sabatino and my longtime right-hand man George Agoglia, worked for weeks on setting up both the screening and the party, which would be held at the Village Gate as an homage to *Lemmings*.

We told all guests that the film would start at precisely 8:00 P.M. At that hour, the Astor Theater was packed. Celebrities, key press, *Lampoon* staff, Universal brass, cast members, and scores of other VIPs were seated and ready. Some couldn't find seats and scrambled for places on the balcony steps. I turned to tell Agoglia to let the projection booth know that we were ready to begin when a white-faced Sean Daniel dashed up to me.

"We can't start!" he whispered nervously. "Landis isn't here yet."

I told George to wait.

179

As in the case of Belushi and the other stars of the movie, we had sent a limousine to pick up John and his wife, the film's costume designer Deborah Nadoolman, at their hotel. I knew he had to be a nervous wreck because I was, and everybody in the theater connected with the movie was tense.

"We'll wait another five or ten minutes," I said.

By 8:15, Landis still hadn't shown. Daniel implored me to wait a little longer, but I felt it could dampen the crowd's enthusiasm. I told George to start the picture. When the theater lights went down, I walked into the lobby, too nervous to sit through the movie. A few minutes later Barbara, who had been stationed at the entrance to the theater, came tearing in with John and Deborah in tow.

He was livid. He'd arrived late, had forgotten his tickets, and the cordon of guards we'd put around the theater to keep out gate-crashers had also managed to keep out our director. He'd then lost his temper with a theater doorman, and the guy actually punched him in the stomach. Barbara had rescued him. As soon as he saw that the film had started, he got even angrier, blaming me for what had happened and asking how I could start a world premiere screening without the film's director. We exchanged snarls for a few minutes, even threatening to do violence to each other until Daniel and Thom Mount pulled us apart, Daniel taking him and Mount trying to cool me down. So, at the world premiere, the director and his wife watched the movie from their seats on the balcony stairs.

The scene in the theater lobby after the audience had given the film a thunderous ovation was one of wild enthusiasm. Belushi was hugging everybody, and everybody else was kissing, embracing or, at the very least, shaking hands and slapping backs. At one point Landis and I saw each other in the crowd. We held out our hands to each other, and he leaned over, and despite the din in the lobby, said very clearly, "I'm sorry. I should have been on time."

Chartered buses took more than three thousand people from the two theaters to the Gate. There, as I had done for the much smaller *Lemmings* opening night party with my son Michael's friends, my younger son Andy and some twenty of his classmates from Columbia Prep (many of them veterans of the "High School Yearbook") guarded all entrances except one. Guests were funneled through the main gate where uniformed guards checked their invitations. Several thousand gawkers blocked off Bleecker Street to get a glimpse of celebrities and share in the festivities.

ITEM: THE KID WHO HAD HIS NOSE PRESSED AGAINST THE BAKERY WINDOW

Like most of the cast, Animal House was Kevin Bacon's first film. Unlike Belushi or Matheson who'd had successful careers on television or Tom Hulce who had starred on Broadway, Kevin had been a struggling young actor before Animal House and now, on the eve of the opening of his first film, was once again a struggling young actor.

He'd returned to New York after the shoot and auditioned without any luck. He was supporting himself by waiting on tables. That July day, at lunch, someone had asked him if he was going to the world premiere of his picture that very night. Shocked because he not only hadn't been invited but hadn't even known about the premiere, he'd mumbled something like, "Oh, yeah—sure I'm going," told his boss he'd have to have the night off to go to the premiere of his movie, and departed.

Somehow, somebody had either goofed or didn't know where to contact him. Too shy to call my office and ask to be invited, he showed up that night at the Astor Theater. He ran into the same ring of impenetrable steel that Landis encountered, so he just stood outside the theater. When it was over he tried to spot Tim Matheson or Peter Riegert or Landis or any of the other people he'd worked with but, once out of the theater, those people were rushed into limousines, and he couldn't get close to them. He heard someone call out that there was a big party at the Village Gate, so as his fellow cast members were being whisked downtown in limousines, he took the subway. By the time he got there, most of the people he knew had already passed through the closely guarded entrance. He did see McGill and called out his name, but Bruce didn't hear him over the noise from the crowd.

Kevin stood outside of the Gate all night as the music from the sixties rock bands echoed through Bleecker Street.

In the club, there were barrels of wine and beer and endless supplies of food, and nobody minded the crush of the joyous crowd. It ran well into the early hours of the morning when the entire cast of Animal House was brought on stage to sing the film's title song. A couple of them jumped into the audience and pulled Landis up with them while others found me and hoisted me up as well. It was a raucous final note to an evening few of us there will ever forget. When we all finished singing, mostly off-key, I jumped back into the crowd. Doug grabbed me. "I'm glad I stayed!" he shouted in my ear. He meant, he was glad he stayed back in 1975 when Beard took the money and left and he had remained.

As the crowds poured out of the Gate, Kevin Bacon stood across the street and continued to watch. Years later when he was a star, we met and, of course, reminisced about Animal House. He never mentioned that he wasn't invited to the party. Landis told me about it only recently.

ITEM: MY SCREEN DEBUT

John Landis had an idea. The studio wanted a teaser—a one-minute film—to promote the picture before the longer trailer was available. John's idea was to open it with me sitting at a desk. I would look up at the camera as a voice says, "Ladies and gentlemen, Matty Simmons, chairman of the board of the National Lampoon." I then would say, "It's with great pleasure that I announce that our first motion picture will be opening soon." As I finish, a huge klieg light drops from the ceiling, crashes into the desk in front of me, and destroys it, segueing into a collection of brief moments from the movie. John assured me that the fall of the klieg light would be calculated carefully and that I was in no danger of death or brain concussion. I agreed to do it.

Several days before it was to be filmed, I came down with a terrible head cold. The day of the filming every aperture in my head was clogged. I was swallowing antihistamine pills by the hour. When I walked onto the sound stage at Universal, I was totally stoned. I vaguely heard Landis tell me not to be nervous, not to anticipate the klieg light, and above all, "Don't worry about a thing. We can do this in fifty takes if we have to."

After makeup, they led me to the desk and the camera rolled. Landis yelled action and, almost oblivious of what was going on around me, I recited my line. As I uttered the last word, the klieg light dropped and shattered the desk. I didn't move. I didn't blink. I was as calm as though nothing had happened. Landis was delighted. He ran up to me. "My God!" he shouted. "That was great! You did it in one take. And, I can't believe it, but you didn't even blink when the goddamn light came down!" I turned to him slowly and asked, "What'd you say?"

The success of *Animal House* was, in 1978, unparalleled in the history of movie comedies. At the box office, ticket sales exceeded the film that had previously been the most popular comedy, *Blazing Saddles*. Its box office gross was not topped until six years later when a group of former *Lampoon* people, Reitman, Ramis, and Bill Murray, scored with *Ghostbusters*.

Their mark was to be passed in 1990 by *Home Alone*, written and produced by still another former *Lampoon* graduate, John Hughes. It is estimated that, when comparing ticket prices in 1990, $6 average, to those in 1978, *Animal House* would still be number one. To this day, cuts from the movie sound track are played over the radio, and Bluto's pep talk to the Deltas is used to energize crowds at sporting events. Hardly a week goes by when the film isn't shown on a television or cable station somewhere in America and in the rest of the world.

The name Animal House has become a term readily identifiable with a rowdy or unseemly group. Most recently, the Philadelphia Phillies, a rough collection of retreads who cause havoc both on and off the baseball field, have gotten to calling their clubhouse the Animal House.

In the fall of 1978, for eight straight weeks, the film was the number one movie in the country. It dropped to second place for one week, then retook the lead for an additional three weeks.

At this point, the *Lampoon* was locked into Universal, and we were developing *Jaws 3–People 0*. Sid Sheinberg, the president of Universal's parent company, asked me if I'd bring a version of *Animal House* to television. I agreed to do it but asked that it be given a different name, and "Delta House" was hatched.

The popularity of the movie was boosting magazine sales. We finished the year with monthly sales of more than 600,000 for the first time since 1975.

Socially, I was a hot new man in Hollywood. I was being invited to parties at the homes of Sheinberg and other luminaries. A hotshot young studio executive at Paramount by the name of Jeff Katzenberg started calling me regularly, figuring that maybe "something would fall from the tree."

I lunched almost daily at the studio commissary and almost daily, Lew Wasserman, considered then the most important person in the film business, the top of "the power structure" at Universal, would stop by my table on the way to his, pat me on the shoulder benevolently, and ask, "How's my partner today?"

While we were preparing *Jaws 3*, I invited Bo Derek, who had already signed as Bumpass's leading lady, to lunch with me at the Universal commissary. As the hostess escorted us to our table, the room, which was normally alive with the clamor of actors and agents and other moviemakers and television people exchanging midday gossip or talking deals, suddenly hushed. I remember thinking that I'd never heard it that quiet before. I looked around to see if there was a reason—there was—and the reason was slipping into the booth beside me. Everyone in the room was staring at the exquisite young woman with me. Even at a movie studio which abounds with attractive young people, her beauty had brought the entire commissary to a stop.

We talked about the script, and we talked about the feedback I'd gotten from Blake Edwards's people who had told me that her husband, John Derek, had been a "pain in the ass" on the set of *10* with his ideas on how Bo's part should be portrayed. I was concerned. If, indeed, this was so and he'd pulled that on Blake Edwards, a powerhouse director, what would he do with Joe Dante, new to the world of big-time moviemaking? Bo assured me that John would not interfere.

Meanwhile, more than a dozen men from various tables around the room dropped by the table to greet me—most of them men I didn't recall meeting before and whose names I didn't know. I was suddenly enormously popular. Notes started arriving—"Who is she?" "I owe you my life if you introduce us!" "Matty, who is this amazing creature? I am madly in love." I showed her the notes and we laughed. "That's the main thing John does on the set," she said, smiling. "He reads the notes."

"There's no such thing as an original idea for a movie," the late Mark Rosenberg, a former president of Warner Bros., once said to me. "Somewhere, someplace, some guy thought of the same idea you did for your movie and got nowhere with it. Now, he wants to collect."

A month or so after *Animal House* opened, Universal, the writers, and the *Lampoon* were all served with a lawsuit which stated that the plaintiff had written a screenplay based on fraternity life and delivered it to Universal some years earlier. We pointed out immediately, of course, that *Animal House* had been culled from articles that appeared in the *National Lampoon* as early as 1972, that the treatment on which the movie was based was written and presented to another company, Warner Bros., before Universal had seen it, and that the executives of Universal had little or nothing to do with the writing of the final script.

Nevertheless, the suit dragged on for two or three years. It was finally resolved by Universal's insurance company without our involvement. Whether the plaintiff got anything for an obvious baseless complaint, we were never told.

When *Vacation* opened, the comic David Brenner sued Warners, claiming he'd submitted a script a few years earlier that was about a family taking a vacation trip and having to put a dead relative on the roof of their car; the same scenario that John Hughes had written in *Vacation*.

Hughes, however, had also written the same scene in the short story on which *Vacation* was based, and that story had appeared in the *Lampoon* several years before Brenner had given his script to Warners or had written the material.

The suit was dropped.

No one ever sued us on our failures.

At this point my wife and I were renting a house in Beverly Hills, but still had our principal residence in New York. Harold Ramis decided to buy a house in L.A. but was having trouble getting a mortgage. He went to the bank with his *Animal House* contract and showed them he owned 1.6 percent of the profits of the movie. He got the mortgage.

Late in '78, ABC approved the "Delta House" series without our having to do a pilot. I decided we would move to L.A. permanently which meant I needed stronger leadership in New York. Len Mogel was now devoting most of his time to *Heavy Metal* and to teaching and writing textbooks on publishing. I asked our longtime attorney Julian Weber if he'd replace him as president of the company after the first of the year. He agreed.

The move to L.A. had been inevitable. I had become completely captivated by the allure of Hollywood's entertainment business. I'd always been a gambler. I'd opted to become a publicity agent instead of returning to newspaper work after my stint in the army because I thought the fields were greener. I'd left a successful publicity business to join the Diners' Club, and I'd walked out of a high-paying job at the Diners' Club to start a publishing business from scratch. I loved playing poker and gin for high stakes and had owned racehorses on which I'd bet prodigiously.

Now, my gambling instincts had reached nirvana. Movies and television involved huge payoffs. You invested time and energy and talent, and if you won, as we had with *Animal House*, it paid off, not in making-a-living-money but in millions. I envisioned successes in film and television that would send the *Lampoon* stock skyrocketing and in turn, of course, make me very, very rich.

Living in Los Angeles, however, didn't please my wife. I was busy making films and television, mixing that life with tennis and swimming. She had no career and no interest in one or in hobbies or sports. She missed New York badly. In 1980, riding high in films and with the company stock soaring, we bought a two-million-dollar home on Canon Drive in Beverly Hills, a block or so south of the Beverly Hills Hotel. We were to live there for five years. When we sold it and returned to New York in 1985, taking a loss on the house of more than a half a million dollars, our marriage had virtually ended.

Stephen Furst, Bruce McGill, and Jamie Widdoes, three of the six most prominent Deltas, agreed to do the TV version, as did John Vernon who had been so good as Dean Wormer. Belushi, Hulce, Matheson, and Peter Riegert passed. We needed an Otter and a Bluto for sure. They represented sex and free-for-all fun. Raucous behavior from a character like Bluto gave the picture, and would give the TV show, much of its energy, and Otter represented the lech in all of us.

In an August issue of *Time* magazine, a writer covering the *Animal House* success, wrote, "Before *National Lampoon's Animal House*, no one ever had the guff to make an honest movie about college life, the *Lampoon* people understand the darkest secret of an American college education: one of the noblest reasons to go is to spend four years studying sex."

CHAPTER SEVENTEEN

ONE OF THE many people who called me after *Animal House* was Michael Fuchs, president of the burgeoning Home Box Office cable system. He wanted a *Lampoon* show, "One like *Lemmings*." "Why not?" was my reaction.

Hendra was now running our New York entertainment division, and certainly he had been the prime mover of *Lemmings*. We made an HBO deal, and a few months later, he delivered "Disco Beaver From Outer Space." Starring Lynn Redgrave, Jamie Widdoes, Rodger Bumpass, Lee Wilkof, and Alice Playten, it was quite funny but when we viewed the first rough cut, very confusing and haphazard. It had no fluidity, jumping or staggering from one sketch, song, or blackout to another.

"It needs work," Fuchs moaned.

I was in L.A. working on "Delta House." The story editors of that show were Michael and Stephen Tolkin. The three of us and Fuchs locked ourselves in an editing room loaned to me by Universal, and recut the show, adding a running commentary on arts and politics and societal mores by a couple in bed watching the show as though it was many TV shows rather than just one.

There were some wonderful moments: Playten as a junkie addicted to Perrier water; Michael Simmons as a gay cowboy singing a red-neck's lament for a lost lover as written with his usual skillfulness by Kelly; a frantic parody of TV quiz shows called "The Breast Game." The show suffered from homo-bashing, a literary sport favored by Hendra and Kelly, but many critics applauded it. In New York's *Newsday*, Marvin Kitman wrote, "If you want to see one of the advantages of being rich [having cable in 1979 marked you as wealthy] then watch 'Disco Beavers From Outer Space.'"

The next production became the only *Lampoon* theater project to flop. By this time, according to several of the editors who worked with them in 1979, Hendra and Kelly were both looking into other situations. Without Julian Weber's knowledge (and certainly without mine), Hendra was trying to raise money for a humor magazine which would compete with the *Lampoon*; this while he was still on staff. Kelly had nibbles from "Saturday Night Live" and would soon depart for that pasture.

I asked them to put together another touring show. All I contributed was a title, *If We're Late, Start Without Us!* Then, I returned to Los Angeles.

I desperately wanted other people in the company to run with projects from start to finish. Hendra, obviously preoccupied, had immediately turned the show over to Peter Elbling, a close friend of his. There is nothing from the production worth mentioning here. It was simply bad. It opened at the New Locust Theater in Philadelphia on March 12, 1979, and I flew in for the night to see it for the first time. In the *Philadelphia Bulletin* the next day a critic wrote, "A catatonic audience sat in stunned silence, wondering if it had been ripped off." He actually had some nice words about the cast but devastated the material. I had the company manager post a closing notice that night.

Kelly and Hendra left the *Lampoon* soon thereafter.

"Delta House" was now taking almost all my time. I remember thinking about my passing on the NBC offer to do a ninety minute weekly show because I'd thought it would be too time consuming.

We added Richard Seer and Wendy Goldman. He was the ever-present Larry Kroeger (Pinto), and she played Muffy, his girl friend. We needed a Bluto. We went through fat, surly guys, chunky, nasty guys—dozens of guys who reminded us even slightly of Bluto. We weren't going to recreate Bluto, we were going to introduce his brother, Blotto.

At one audition, a 250-pound madman invaded our studio. He roared. He mugged. He was Josh Mostel, the son of Zero, one of the most adept and energetic and outrageous comedy actors of our time. Primarily a stage actor, Zero had soared to stardom in *Fiddler on the Roof* and other Broadway productions and had given one of the great performances in film comedy in Mel Brooks's first movie, *The Producers*. His son was *not* his father, but he had the same madness and the energy we were looking for. We hired him on the spot. A number of years later, John Goodman, now a major star whose fame reaches far beyond his role on "Roseanne," told me that he had auditioned and been turned down for the role of Blotto.

Finding Otter was more difficult. We needed someone who had looks and charm but conveyed an underlying impression of mistrust. We picked Peter Fox, a good actor who was handsome and affable but never did quite project the slyness and lack of altruism that Tim Matheson had conveyed so well.

We planned on adding one more character, a devastatingly beautiful co-ed whose name would be the Bombshell. We started daily auditions. For weeks we couldn't find the right actress, then we had what is known in the trade as a "cattle call." In these, an endless stream of actors or actresses are paraded through the room until you see someone with just the right look. You then have these people read, check their credits, talk to them.

A cattle call is widely promoted in the acting community and almost always gets a big turnout. This one drew more than a thousand young women and the parade began. Around number eight hundred, a girl walked in who looked great. The ABC casting vice-president who was working with us told us that the actress had starred in a movie-of-the-week only a few months before. We were now even more hopeful. She read for us and sounded like Minnie Mouse on helium.

When she left the room, I turned to the man from ABC. "How could she have possibly had the lead role in a TV movie?" I asked.

"Oh," he shrugged, "someone else looped all her lines. She was sleeping with the director." We moved on.

At approximately 980, the most beautiful young woman I had ever seen walked into the room. Heads snapped to her immediately. She had perfect features, pale blue eyes, blonde hair that poured over her shoulders, and a slim, elegant body. She looked to be around twenty. Without trying to be, she was incredibly sexy. She had on little makeup and needed even less. Her sex appeal lay in her natural beauty.

We talked and she was intelligent and had a good, controlled actress's voice. She had, she told us, briefly appeared on the TV show "Fantasy Island" but had not acted, was just part of the scenery. Other than that, she had no professional experience. We had her read and she was fine. She needed training, but in a world where you can stop filming and then redo a shot to get it right, she was ready.

Marcy Carsey, more recently the producer of the "Cosby" and "Roseanne" shows, was head of sitcom productions at ABC. Permanent cast members had to be cleared through her.

"No experience," she repeated, "then you have to screen-test her."

"It's a waste of time," I argued. "The camera will love this girl."

She persisted.

The next week I directed her screen test myself. She did a scene from "Delta House" with Richard Seer. When it was over she came running to me, raising her hand like she was in school and wanted permission to leave the room. "Mr. Simmons! Mr. Simmons!" she called. "What about my job?"

"What job?" I asked.

"My job. I work the check-out counter at a Von's supermarket in Orange County."

I patted her shoulder. "Forget about it," I said. "You're out of the grocery business forever."

When they saw the test, the network agreed. As the weeks went by, we enlarged her part and her acting got better and better. Her unusual beauty was used as a story line for a number of episodes including one called "Hoover and the Bombshell," in which Jamie Widdoes falls madly in love with her while tutoring her for midterm exams.

A number of the people in the show did fall in love with her, but she remained friendly and seemingly unobtainable. When the show ended, she went into films. There's a great satisfaction in finding people early in their careers and in knowing you called one right, but of course, many of the people connected with "Delta House" thought that someday Michelle Pfeiffer would be a star.

Wendy Goldman was Michelle's confidante during the series. She remembers that Michelle was uncomfortable with her role. She felt she was not a femme fatale and that the role was gratuitously sexy in that she was usually asked to parade around in sweaters, shorts, bathing suits, or other rather obvious apparel. She also resented the fact that she was known only by the Bombshell and a real name was never used.

"She wasn't a *person*," Wendy says now. "And she was unhappy about it. I agreed with her and still do. It was male chauvinism."

I pointed out to Wendy that Blotto, Otter, Flounder, D-Day, and others in the group had real names that weren't used either, that Michelle's character, like Michelle, was intelligent, soft-spoken, and did not overtly use her sex appeal. It was just there! She simply was so damn good-looking that the male animal reacted. Wendy still doesn't agree with my reasoning. Michelle never voiced those objections to me or any of the other producers or writers. But she has suggested in magazine interviews that her role on the show was merely that of a sex object. Of course, we weren't exactly doing Hamlet.

Stephen Furst remembers that she was very nervous. "She smoked all the time, and she was always asking if she was doing OK. Of course, she was and we told her so—all the time."

He also remembers that his son Nathan, then three months old, did a scene with Michelle. Now fourteen, he still reminds people that he costarred on a TV show with Michelle Pfeiffer.

The show ran for only thirteen episodes on ABC, had decent ratings, and got very good reviews including a full-page rave from the critic for *TV Guide* in which he thanked us for bringing physical comedy back to television after a long hiatus since the days of Lucille Ball, Phil Silvers, and others.

The same week it first aired, both CBS and NBC premiered college fraternity shows. Neither lasted more than a few weeks. The press suggested that we, like them, were ripping off *Animal House*, actually accusing us of stealing from our own movie. Both of those shows had offered roles to the original Deltas before we signed them and were turned down.

In those days, the hour from eight to nine p.m., was called the "family hour" and physical interaction between sexes or drinking—any kind of suggestive or untoward behavior—was out. We were, over my loud protests, assigned to that time period. "How," I screamed at Carsey, "can you put *Animal House* in the goddamn family hour?" She shrugged. "Don't ask me. New York makes those decisions."

Finally, New York made the decision not to pick up our show for the '79-'80 season. No explanation. No apology. The show had a strong cast, the *Animal House* and *Lampoon* names behind it, and writing talent that was, to say the least, extraordinary for a sitcom, including Kenney, Ramis and Miller, John Hughes, Tod Carroll, Ted Mann, Michael and Stephen Tolkin and David Pollack and Elias Davis who worked with me as writer-producers and later went on to produce the last years of "M*A*S*H."

The *Lampoon* never did a series on network television after that.

ITEM: THE GOURMAND

John Belushi's excesses were becoming legendary in the film community. At a party, he stayed longer and played harder than anyone else. His heavy drug use was talked about even in a community where, in the seventies particularly, cocaine had become as much an everyday leisure as beer at a football game. And he ate prodigiously.

Before filming Blues Brothers, he'd gained enough weight so that his belly hung well over his belt. Landis, who was to direct the movie, talked him into going to La Costa, the obscenely priced health resort where you pay four hundred dollars a day to dine on carrots and lemon-water.

After a few days there, Landis was congratulating himself on Belushi's adherence to the resort's discipline. At dinner, he'd wolf down the celery and wafer-thin entrees and remark on their tastiness. On the third night, Landis knocked on Belushi's door around midnight to tell him about an idea he'd come up with for the film. There was no answer. Concerned, he turned the door handle and discovering that the room was unlocked, entered it. It was empty. He turned to leave. As he did, he heard a noise at the open window. Landis saw it was Belushi and snapped on the lights. Under John's burly arms were a foot-long salami, a loaf of Italian bread, and a bagful of condiments and other goodies. When he saw Landis, he smiled his charming, sheepish grin. "Just dropped down to the general store in town," he said. "A man needs nourishment." When they left La Costa, Landis, who wasn't overweight when they got there, had lost four pounds. Belushi had gained one.

In 1979, Stephen Spielberg's own "sequel" to *Animal House*, *1941*, reached the screen. It had Belushi and Matheson plus Dan Aykroyd and perhaps two dozen other well-known faces. Doug Kenney and I bumped into each other at a screening in New York. The film had ended only moments before, and we were both rushing out, hoping not to run into anybody we knew who was connected to the picture. Doug put an arm on my shoulder. "We gotta talk about this turkey," he said to me. "Hey," I shrugged, "thank God it's not our turkey."

In October of 1979, Doug, who had left the *Lampoon* and moved to Los Angeles right after *Animal House*, produced *Caddyshack*. He had written it with Harold Ramis and Brian Doyle-Murray, and Ramis directed it. It was shot on a golf course in the tiny town of Davie, Florida. "This," he announced to all, "will be bigger than *Animal House*."

Members of the cast and crew still wonder how this movie—any movie—could have been completed under the conditions that this one was filmed. The late Ted Knight, the delightful actor featured for so many years on the "Mary Tyler Moore Show," was unique in this group. Word was that he was the only prominent member of the company who wasn't doing drugs, including the producers, writers, and director. Chevy Chase, who makes no secret about his problems with drugs in those years, arrived with a satchel full of assorted goodies. Rodney Dangerfield came with a suitcase. Doug was doing cocaine by the ounce. Ramis, who has long since sworn off anything stronger than some occasional pot, often admits that he frequently looked into the camera and saw twice as many actors as were supposed to be there.

Remarkably, the movie was quite funny. Chevy and Bill Murray and Dangerfield were at their best, and there was a lot of splendid comedy. People in the industry, however, coyly suggested at the time that there was a certain disjointedness about the film that made it look like all involved were not exactly aware of what was going on. It was a moderate hit, did well on cable and television, and quite a few years later spawned a sequel, which, like *1941*, is better not discussed.

The tragedy of *Caddyshack* was the leading lady, Sarah Holcomb. After her debut in *Animal House*, Sarah went on to star in several films, then came to Florida to do *Caddyshack* and got hooked on drugs. Her career ended with that picture. In 1982, while we were shooting *Vacation*, Sarah visited us on location somewhere in Colorado. She was now living with Brian Doyle-Murray who was doing a cameo in the film. She was still very pretty but looked as if she might have had a real rough couple of years. We reminisced about *Animal House*, Brian did his cameo, and they left.

Sarah's most memorable scene in *Animal House* is the one in which she seduces Pinto, then passes out before anything happens. As she lies there, looking incredibly delicious, Pinto (Tom Hulce) tries to decide whether he should take advantage of her condition or be a gentleman. A devil appears over one of his shoulders and orders him to "Fuck 'er!" (It was John Landis's voice.) He's about to obey when an angel pops up on the other shoulder and convinces him that it would be wrong. I'm not sure why, but I thought of that scene as they drove off.

Before *Caddyshack*, Doug had met Kathryn Walker at a party in New York. He was so taken with her that he got her attention by calmly eating a crystal glass. Kathryn was a successful actress and quite attractive and smart. He, of course, was attractive and smart, too, and successful and funny, if erratic. They fell in love and moved to Los Angeles where they rented a home in pricey Coldwater Canyon. Doug, at Kathryn's insistence, made an effort to cure his drug addiction, but during *Caddyshack*, he was a wild man. In the *Esquire* article on Doug published in 1981, friends are quoted on the subject of his cocaine habit. "What he dropped on the floor," said one, "would keep most people high for a lifetime." Another described his lust for the drug thusly: "He went after it like an animal in heat—stuffing it into his nose with his thumb—great gobs of it."

After *Caddyshack*, Kathryn begged him to get help. He went to see a psychiatrist but returned only a few times. The reaction to *Caddyshack* gnawed at him. It simply wasn't *Animal House*. And he was, perhaps, too used to success. He'd gone from college to being one of the principals who created the most popular humor magazine of all time. He'd conceived and orchestrated the "High School Yearbook," which critics still called a "masterpiece." And he'd cowritten the most popular movie comedy of all time.

At one point, we met and talked for an hour or so in my office in Los Angeles. He was feeling lousy about *Caddyshack*, blaming himself as though there were no other coconspirators. "Hey," I told him, "Billy Wilder made an occasional bad movie, too."

He looked at me and nodded, then he repeated what he had said to Michael Gross. "Yeah—but we invented nostalgia."

In late August 1980, Doug was on the Hawaiian island of Kauai. Kathryn, Chevy Chase, and other friends who had gone there with him had returned to the mainland. He stood alone on a cliff overlooking the Pacific. He then either walked out on a precipice which crumbled under his feet, or he jumped. His body was flown to Connecticut for the funeral. Kathryn and Chevy, who were the last of the people close to him to see and talk to him, insist that he did not commit suicide and that it was an accident.

At the *Lampoon*, one wag said what Doug would have said under similar circumstances. "He was looking for a place to jump off when he slipped."

In his hotel room, he had written a note, supposedly to himself. "These are the happiest days I've ever ignored."

When the funeral services ended and Doug was buried, Peter Ivers stood alone at his grave and played a song on his harmonica. It was "Beautiful Dreamer."

Kenney's ex-wife Alex would in later years describe him well. "He was like an onion. You would get down to what you thought was the core, and there'd be another layer."

He was thirty-three and not the last of the lemmings who would run headlong to their death.

Two years later, Belushi was dead.

CHAPTER EIGHTEEN

IN 1979, mostly because of the company's share of *Animal House* profits and the impact the film had on magazine sales, the pretax earnings were substantially more than $3 million. Two million dollars were borrowed from the Chemical Bank in New York and all other outstanding debts for the purchase of the minority shares in the *Lampoon* were repaid. In 1980, we lost $744,000. This was primarily because of a series of write-offs when a book company we'd contracted with went into bankruptcy crippling our book and special edition sales. In 1981 we earned almost the same amount. In 1982, the company again lost money, $55,000. In 1983, we finished repaying the Chemical Bank loan. The purchase of the minority stock was now finally completed. We were out of debt but cash-starved during what should have been the most important growth period in the company's history.

Since 1975, we had paid nearly $3 million in interest on money borrowed for the buyout. In addition we'd written off $1.6 million for amortization on the purchase. For the rest of the century, *Lampoon* earnings would be affected by the near $200,000-a-year amortization. It was merely bookkeeping and didn't cost us a dime in real dollars, but in years when losses or profits were thin, that added $200,000 could have given our statements a different look and might have avoided the nagging complaints from the press and analysts even in years when losses were paper deductions.

There is no doubt in my mind that if in 1975 an underwriting had been available or if "the three kids from Harvard" had been willing to accept a reasonable deal in preferred stock or in stock and cash for their shares, or had waited until an underwriting could be made, National Lampoon, Inc., would have grown, diversified, and become a major publishing and entertainment company. If they had chosen stock, I believe they would have eventually earned more than they did. Here's why.

Cost of buyout	$7,500,000
Interest on loans	$3,000,000
Amortization	$1,600,000
	$12,100,000

Not included is the interest that could have been earned by money that was paid out in loan interest had it stayed in the company. Nor have I included the interest on the $7.5 million, had the purchase been paid for in preferred stock or if an underwriting had been effected.

In nine years, the cost of the buyout could have added as much as twenty million dollars to *Lampoon* earnings which, with the film successes, could have seen a stock price as high as forty or fifty dollars a share.

In the late seventies, the stock at times traded in the more than twenty-dollar-a-share range.

"What always amazed me," Julian Weber, himself a graduate of Harvard Law School, said to me recently, "was the constant stream of intelligence that flocked to the magazine." He was not referring only to the early years of Kenney, Beard, O'Donoghue, and the others already chronicled here. Julian became president of the *Lampoon* in 1979. P. J. O'Rourke was already editor-in-chief. Hendra and Kelly finished the chores they had been assigned that year and left. Bill Lippe, who had replaced Gerry Taylor as advertising director of the magazine, left and was replaced by Seena Harris, the first woman to hold a top post at the company.

Ted Mann, Danny Abelson, Tod Carroll, John Hughes, and Gerry Sussman were the editors, and Peter Klienman and Skip Johnson were art directors. To come from the *Harvard Lampoon* were Kevin Curran, Michael Reiss, Al Jean, and Brian McCormick. And over the next few years they would be joined or be replaced by Jeff Greenfield, Ellis Weiner, Peter Kaminsky, and Fred Graver. By 1984, all of them would be gone, Hughes and Carroll to the movies, Reiss, Jean, Curran, Graver, Kaminsky, and Greenfield to television.

"P. J. wanted longer prose pieces," Weber remembers. "Something you were always against." I remember thinking that when P. J. and I argued about lengthier prose that it was funny that O'Rourke, with his disdain of almost anything human, believed that the average reader had a longer atten-tion span than I thought they had.

P. J. left the *Lampoon* in 1981, saying at the time that since Doug's death, he had begun to realize that meeting a deadline every month wasn't how he wanted to spend the rest of his life. It was reminiscent of Doug's words when he left. The fact that P. J. and I no longer agreed about either the format of the magazine or the political direction it was taking did have, I'm sure, some bearing on his departure.

Now, none of the editors who had been on staff in the magazine's early years remained. Making movies was taking nearly all my time, so there would be no one around who had originally shaped the *Lampoon*. For the early eighties, it would be Julian's magazine and it would be all new.

Ted Mann, another Canadian expatriate, had written for the magazine as a free-lancer for several years before joining the staff in 1979. Tall, blond, kind of pudgy, usually cynical and frequently drunk, he was, nevertheless, one of the magazine's most consistently funny writers. He often arrived at midday, totally fried. Gerry Taylor remembers him rushing into his office one day and demanding that he "Buy gold at once!" Since the two had never discussed gold or any other financial matters before and since Mann was swaying discernibly as he barked out the instructions, Taylor immediately agreed and ushered him out.

Mann and I had at least one testy encounter during my regular visits to New York. At a party one night, he cornered me and berated me for twenty minutes on matters such as his salary, bonus, and the size of his office. Following that, he disappeared for the rest of the evening, to be discovered at the party's end, sleeping in the host's bed. Once, he hired a bagpiper and marched him into a meeting I was having in our boardroom. It was a scene out of hell, the bagpipe screeching, a drunk Mann cackling, and me pushing them both out of the room.

ITEM: OUT OF AFRICA

It was my habit when I came to the New York office every month or so to walk around and say hello to members of the staff. On one such occasion, I knocked on Ted's door. A voice said, "Come in." I opened the door and entered. For a full minute I stood at the entrance to the room in shock. I had entered a "jungle." The room was filled with palms and various jungle plants. On the floor was a tiger skin and on the walls were spears and shields painted in tribal colors. The ceiling was completely covered by what appeared to be the roof of a tent. Ted's desk and chairs were gone. Instead, a hammock hung from one wall to another. Stretched out in it, sipping languidly on a tall tropical drink and wearing a pith helmet, was Sahib Mann himself. He looked up at me and grinned, "Mr. Simmons, I presume."

ITEM: MORE MANN

I'm in the New York office when an emergency call comes through from Ted Mann in a midtown phone booth. It seems he has locked himself in the booth after being pursued through the city streets by three large black men who have given him two choices regarding the future. Either pay for the windshield on their car that he just demolished or face extreme violence. Ted has selected the first option, but he has no cash on him and apparently these fellows will not accept a credit card. I immediately dispatch the mail-room clerk to the scene with the required funds.

Meanwhile, O'Rourke, also having received a distress call from Mann, quickly assembles the editorial staff in his office and calls for an immediate march to the phone booth, only blocks away, to engage the enemy and free their trapped comrade. His idea is rejected by an eight to one vote; his, of course, being the only one in favor of warfare.

Unscathed, Mann finally arrives at the office carrying a mangled bicycle. He explains what happened:

It seems he was cycling to work up Fifth Avenue, his head heavy from a bout the night before with Jack Daniels, when a car clipped his bicycle and sent him reeling into the gutter. This only further aggravated his already distressed condition, so he jumped back on the bike, sprinted after the car, whipped out his bike chain, and smashed the windshield. Then, without looking back, raced off and turned up a one-way street, against traffic. This did not deter the occupants of the glass-shredded car. They followed him, the wrong way up the one-way street, this at midday, in midtown Manhattan. Finally, the congested traffic halted the chase, and Ted ran into the aforementioned phone booth which was encased in steel and heavy glass.

"Why," I asked him, "why would you do a thing like smashing someone's windshield?" He mulled that over then shrugged. "I never thought they'd be crazy enough to follow me." I stared at him.

"Do you think I can say I was on company business," he finally asked, "and get the insurance company to pay for my bike?"

Now, years later, Ted is perhaps thirty pounds lighter. He looks fit and rugged. He tells me that he runs five miles a day and hasn't had a drink in five years. When I met him to discuss this book, he was producing the television show, "NYPD Blue." I asked him what he thought of P. J. and Sean, and Tony, with whom he had worked.

"I liked P. J. A lot of people didn't. Some because he was tough and opinionated and others, like Tony and Sean, because he worked harder than they did. A lot of us weren't crazy about his right-wing theories, but I don't believe they hurt the magazine.

"Tony was always working on something else when he was supposed to be working for the *Lampoon,* like a screenplay about someone trapped in a snowstorm or another humor magazine that would compete with the one that was paying his salary.

"Sean didn't do much, but he seemed so awfully smart, nobody really cared. A lot of people made the mistake of confessing their sins to Sean, and he'd go right out and tell everyone else. He was wise and dangerous to be around." He thinks for a moment. "He was like Socrates. You know, the people of Athens killed Socrates for a reason.

"One day P. J. and I heard that a big storm was going to hit the town of Islip, way out on Long Island. We got hold of a truck and piled it with ladders and all sorts of rescue equipment as well as a goodly supply of beer and liquor in case anyone had frostbite. We drove out there, but the storm was so bad we checked into a motel, found a diner, and eventually rescued a couple of waitresses from a dull evening."

Ted left the *Lampoon* in 1983. Before he did, he cowrote the series of stories about two wayward teenagers, O. C. and Stiggs, with fellow editor Tod Carroll.

Kevin Curran, one of the bright lights at the *Harvard Lampoon* after the Beard-Kenney years, joined the *National Lampoon* staff in 1981. When I met him recently, he had taken brief leave from television's "Married With Children," where he's a producer and head writer, to develop a show of his own. It was to be called "The Bowmans" and was about a locksmith whose shop kept getting broken into and a fat Jesus freak who kept getting nailed to a cross but was so heavy he kept falling off. It was later retitled "The Good Life."

"The one thing I remember most clearly," Kevin insisted, "was that Tod Carroll ate the same thing for lunch every day—a grilled cheese sandwich." He also remembered, however, that in his years at the magazine, there was no sense of direction. "What had happened," he believes, "is the sensibilities of our readers had changed, and the magazine wasn't growing older and more mature with its base readership."

In 1982, Michael Grossman, who would later become art director of *Sports Illustrated*, was brought in and totally redesigned the magazine, even the logo which had been so widely exploited in the *Animal House* marketing. I disagreed with these decisions. I felt that there was nothing wrong with either the makeup of the magazine or the logo. But I had given Weber a mandate to change and improve the magazine, and my interference would have robbed him of any initiative to try to do just that.

What was wrong, from 1982 through 1984, I felt, was the magazine simply wasn't *funny* enough. O'Rourke's desire to create what he would call "A *New Yorker* for our own generation" simply hadn't worked. The *New Yorker* itself was dying slowly and would eventually undergo a dastic overhaul. Sussman, who replaced him, was a marvelous satirist but just too pleasant a guy to be a tough editor on a tough magazine. He had not been the answer. He was primarily my choice and my mistake. When he left, Julian brought Sean Kelly back.

After his departure from the *Lampoon*, Kelly, the defender of pristine humor at the *Lampoon* according to subsequent magazine interviews, wrote a book called *Fart* and then joined the writing staff of "Saturday Night Live" where he'd stayed not too long before being fired. A fellow staffer there told me that, while at the show Kelly had, as usual, "taken the hand that fed him firmly between his teeth and bit."

I was not happy about Kelly returning to the *Lampoon*, but Weber reasoned that having one of the old group back would help settle everybody down. Sean, he felt, would provide leadership and knowledge and a sense of security and maybe some funny writing.

Over the next two years, none of the above was forthcoming. Unwilling to assume leadership, Kelly came up with the idea of having a fictitious editor-in-chief, L. Dennis Plunkett. He and Carroll and Mann would serve as senior editors, presumably under "Plunkett," and Curran and Fred Graver were editors. Both Mann and Curran portrayed Kelly's leadership as being nebulous. "He was smart as hell," another editor told me, "but mostly he sat around cracking wonderful one-liners and putting down anyone not in sight."

The period, however, was not without its gems. A Warren Leight "survey" comparing 1984 and 1969 college graduates "revealed," among other things, that 97 percent of the '84 alumni would "fire my own mother if the bottom line demanded it" while among the '69 group only 45 percent would. Similarly, only 27 percent of the '69 graduates said that they were "willing to kill" if it would look good on their resumes while 83 percent of the '84s said they would.

Michael Reiss and Al Jean did a lengthy dissection of the boxing business including a computer analysis of the intellectual powers of former heavyweight champs in which Primo Carnera was declared smarter than Joe Frazier and a blender won a narrow decision over Leon Spinks. Cartoonist Ron Barrett introduced Politenessman, adding another firmament in the *Lampoon* universe.

Kelly and Graver grew very close. Fred was sort of Sean's protege. He wanted to work hard. He wanted to learn and he was bright as hell. A pleasant-looking young man, he'd been an editor at a book publishing company where Gerry Sussman had met him and invited him to join the *Lampoon* staff. While he was working at the *Lampoon*, Graver started having trouble at home. He and his wife discussed a trial separation. Kelly, Fred's mentor, said he'd talk to the lady and try to patch things up for them.

Hey! Nineteen seventy-three redux! We're reliving the O'Donoghue-Ephron-Hendra episode. Kelly is best friend.

Kelly comforts best friend's wife. Kelly gets cozy with best friend's wife! When Graver found out what happened, he, like O'Donoghue, refused to talk or work with the best friend who had turned on him.

Within weeks, five different editors and executives repeated the story to me. In researching this book, it was again brought up to me as a point at which things started falling apart. The man who had been brought in to "settle everybody down" had punched still another hole in the side of the ship.

A *Rolling Stone* article in late September 1983 reviewed the state of affairs at the *Lampoon*. Of course, it didn't mention the Kelly-Graver affair. It emphasized, after careful discussions with various people in the know, that whatever problems the *Lampoon* was having were my doing. "Simmons is preoccupied with sex in the magazine," the article decreed, stating that the Pubescence Issue, which supposedly started a trend toward sex in the *Lampoon* because it was so successful, came after Beard's departure instead of a year before it—as was actually the case—the suggestion being that Beard would have never agreed to the issue.

"If I didn't work for the *National Lampoon*, I'm not sure I would read it every month," senior editor Sean Kelly was quoted as saying; a statement comparable to a vice-president of the Ford Motor Company saying, "Hell, if I didn't work for this goddamn company, I wouldn't drive their shitty cars."

Throughout the article were other statements of discontent. Michael Grossman said, "There's nobody shaping the magazine. It sort of happens every month." As though an art director brought in to redesign the magazine was an outsider looking in.

The story, published in the magazine with the greatest crossover readership with the *Lampoon*, caused even more reader desertion. I had been on location, filming *Lampoon* movies, for almost the entire prior two years. That very summer, the *Lampoon* had its second huge hit. *National Lampoon's Vacation* had been the number one picture in America for more than a month and would eventually net more than six million dollars for the company.

But the *Rolling Stone* article, despite its twisting of facts and outright errors, revealed a serious problem at the magazine, one of which I had not been fully aware. I'd been unhappy with the quality of the humor. The look of the magazine didn't have the punch it used to have. But the article showed that these editors and art director, unlike those before and those to follow, just didn't care.

I knew then I'd have to make changes—a lot of them.

CHAPTER NINETEEN

IN THE YEARS between *Animal House* and the release of *National Lampoon's European Vacation* in 1985, I produced four *Lampoon* motion pictures and one television show. I also developed numerous other comedy scripts for the screen and created a pilot for NBC television and another for syndication. At the same time, Len Mogel had produced the animated science fiction film *Heavy Metal* with Ivan Reitman, and Hendra and Kelly put together *That's Not Funny, That's Sick!*, the cable review, "Disco Beaver From Outer Space," and the aborted stage show, *If We're Late, Start Without Us*. We had become a formidable entertainment company. And I was working like hell.

Meanwhile, my personal life was falling apart. My wife and I had been married for many years. Very soon after we moved to the West Coast in 1979, we realized that our marriage was no longer working. Our kids were all adults and could certainly handle a divorce, but Lee and I agreed to try and make it work. It was a bad decision, and both of us were soon depending heavily on prescription drugs to quiet our nerves. One particularly harried day with a picture in preproduction at one location, another in development, and the magazine back in New York having serious financial problems, I dashed out of my office to rush to a meeting about still-another film. I flung open my car door and jumped in. As I did, my jaw dropped in disbelief. The steering wheel was missing! Someone had stolen my steering wheel!!! I was stunned, then slowly I looked around and realized that I had, in my rush, jumped into the backseat of the car.

The company's first movie after *Animal House* was *National Lampoon Goes to the Movies*. It had been written by a group of *Lampoon* editors and had a format that had been tried before without success—four completely unrelated stories with only a slight thread tying them together. The script was intentionally very, very broad. The jokes flew by every minute or so.

This kind of buckshot comedy can be hugely successful (*Airplane*, *Police Academy*) or a failure, as we demonstrated. From the start, it was conceived as a little movie and had a budget of less than three million dollars. My original plan was to have a different director for each segment, but it was finally decided to go with two, directing two episodes each.

The studio was United Artists, which was about to release one of the most expensive movies of all time, *Heaven's Gate*. The studio's policy was to turn the money over to the film maker and get out of the way. After a lot of digging, I hired Bob Giraldi, one of the top commercial directors of that, or this time, and Henry Jaglom who had previously made only his own movies, presumably with his own money. Wiser heads than mine told me to pass on Jaglom, but I had seen a picture he'd made called *Sitting Ducks* and had liked it a lot. I thought he could do it. Among the people we cast were Robby Benson, Richard Widmark, Olympia Dukakis, Diane Lane, and Peter Riegert, who has always been one of my favorite actors.

Our schedule called for us to shoot the picture in three weeks in Los Angeles. With two separate crews and, of course, different casts, it meant a total of six weeks. I was the sole producer. When shooting began, I raced between the production office and the two sets, trying to solve problems, soothe nerves, keep costs down and comedy values up, frequently missing dailies, and never being able to stay on a set long enough to offer any meaningful advice or repair all hemorrhaging. The Giraldi shoot was going well. He was in total command of his segment. The cast liked and respected him, and he was using much of the same crew he used for his commercials so they were at ease.

The Jaglom set, on the other hand, was in total chaos. Everybody hated the director who would scream at people and embarrass them in front of the cast and crew. His favorite target was his own brother, an actor named Michael Emil, who was actually quite funny and has since worked for other directors. Halfway through the shoot, I walked onto the set to come upon Henry ranting at Emil who was literally cowering in a corner. Everyone else stood, transfixed, just glaring at the ugly scene. I took Henry aside and asked him not to do that again. He agreed meekly. It was two weeks into filming, and I realized I had a problem. On Jaglom's set nobody was happy and what was appearing on film was totally wrong.

Back at United Artists, they had a bigger problem. *Heaven's Gate* had been released and was being called the greatest financial disaster in film history. The studio would lose fifty million dollars and heads would roll.

ITEM: TAKE MY ACTOR, PLEASE!

I'd known Henny Youngman since my days as a New York press agent, before the Diners' Club. I'd run into him in New York, and he asked me for a cameo role in one of my films. We had such a role in one of the Jaglom sequences, "The Sentinels." Henny arrived in L.A. with his close friend, the owner of New York's Carnegie Deli, who brought along a large box of corned beef and pastrami sandwiches. Henny had a simple scene. Christopher Lloyd, playing a gangster, is holed up in his house. The police have him totally surrounded. Now, Henny, who has apparently been in the house, breaks a window with his briefcase and yells to the cops, "I'm a lawyer and I've just taken this man's case!" (I told you it was broad) Easy right? Well, Jaglom keeps yelling, "Ready Henny? OK roll 'em!" Henny keeps breaking the window and blurting out, "Don't take this man. Take my wife, please!" Jaglom pleads with him to just try to say the right line, but Henny can't get it out. Finally, I said to Jaglom, "You know, I think I like his line better than ours." It stayed.

When I got to the editing room we discovered that Giraldi's stuff looked good and was funny, but Jaglom's was almost unusable.

In his contract, the director is given a certain length of time to make what is appropriately called "the director's cut." When Jaglom's time ran out and we saw what a mess his two sequences were in, I notified him that his relationship with the film had ended.

Immediately, his agent, Harry Ufland, demanded and got a meeting with the United Artists brass. There, I explained that we had a deadline for delivery of the film and that Jaglom's continued presence, in my opinion, would do nothing but delay any chance of saving the movie and of meeting that deadline. Ufland, for reasons I cannot understand to this day, went wild. He started calling me obscene names and threatened to punch me out.

Finally Stephen Bach, the president of UA, and several other executives jumped between us. Jaglom's editing was not extended. I lived in the cutting room for the next month. Eventually, "The Sentinels" was usable but the fourth sequence, one which had in a mysterious burst of intuitiveness, been dubbed 'The Bomb,' was a total disaster. It simply could not be used. What we had was a three-segment, seventy-eight minute movie, one that was obviously too short to release.

While we were editing, Bach, one of the most intelligent and nicest people I've known in the film business, was fired because of *Heaven's Gate*. Later, he would write a book, *Final Cut*, about that legendary disaster. In it, he also discussed my near-battle with Ufland.

Paula Weinstein, a widely known producer, was made temporary president of the studio. I went to her and explained that I had about three-quarters of a movie. "I need to reshoot," I told her. "Giraldi has said that he'll come in and work on 'The Bomb.' But I'll need about $300,000 for the new filming." Paula shook her head. "I have no money," she said. I looked at her plaintively, "Then I have no movie."

The picture, in its shortened version, was released on cable and in video. I have not seen Jaglom or Ufland since. Henry has continued to produce and direct his own films, has his own following, and his movies often get good reviews but, to the best of my knowledge, no one has offered him a studio picture since *National Lampoon Goes to the Movies*.

In 1982, Mogel's *Heavy Metal* movie was released by Columbia and with about thirty million dollars at the box office became the highest grossing non-Disney animated film. The sound track album of the film sold almost a million copies and spawned three number-one hit singles. As had happened with *Animal House*, the film boosted magazine sales, and *Heavy Metal* circulation soared over the 200,000 mark.

Brandon Tartikoff was head of NBC television. He and I sat in his office one day and conceived a sitcom called "Two Reelers." It would star two not-too-bright young men who decide they're going to travel around the world with a very limited bankroll, work when they could and, run into high adventure, they hoped, wherever they went. As the stars I selected Stephen Furst and, fresh out of his depression from *Jaws 3–People 0*, Rodger Bumpass. Former Lampooner John Hughes and I were working closely on a number of entertainment projects. We cowrote the pilot script, and Tartikoff was delighted with it. Film director Jim Frawley directed the episode, and we all felt good about it. The network considered it then passed without comment. When I asked Tartikoff what happened, he shrugged, "What can I tell you?"

Once again, Rodger Bumpass's bubble burst and disappeared.

Toward the end of 1981, Hughes showed me a script he'd just completed. It was called *Class Reunion*. He asked if I wanted to produce it and allow the *Lampoon* name to be used over it. At the time we were working on two other films together. I read the script and thought it was too broad and after *Goes to the Movies*, I wanted to go back to reality comedy. I passed.

Hughes gave it to another producer whose agent promptly sent it to ABC. Films, the ABC subsidiary newly arrived in the theatrical film business. This, they decided, would be their first film if—they could get the *Lampoon* name on it, but I turned them down. The *Lampoon* was now being represented by John Ptak at the William Morris Agency. He asked me to reconsider. Hughes again urged me to do it.

Reluctantly, I agreed and we made a deal for use of the *Lampoon* name, the only time I'd ever allow the name to be used on a property we didn't, at least, share control on.

Two months later, after a director and much of the cast had been selected, Brandon Stoddard, the ABC Films executive who supervised the project, fired the producer. He called Ptak, this time asking if I'd replace him.

"I hate the script," I told Ptak. "It's not a movie I want to make. I probably never should have agreed to let them use the *Lampoon* name." "But you did agree," he reasoned, "and now they're in trouble, and they're willing to pay you a lot of money to come in and straighten things out. You have to do it to protect the name."

It made sense. It should be pointed out that my producer's fees and profit participation went to the *Lampoon* from which I, in turn, received a salary and bonuses. My decision, therefore, was not influenced by my getting a sizeable fee. He was right. If they were in trouble and I could protect the name, I had to do it.

The shoot on *Class Reunion* was easily the most boring I would ever work on. It didn't have the problems that *Goes to the Movies* had, but it just seemed to crawl along, and I never had a sense that it was going to be a good movie.

Hughes had set the entire film in a darkened, abandoned high school. Everything was black or grey and looked cold and dull. It was a horror spoof, and the look was not unintentional, but it was claustrophobic. Finally, I got him to write a couple of scenes that would bring the action outside of the school and would give the audience a chance to breathe a little.

It didn't help the movie much. At the last minute, I brought in a burly comic named Barry Diamond who'd been in a couple of *Lampoon* stage shows. He was funny and gave it some life as did an actress named Miriam Flynn who I later used as Cousin Catherine in *Vacation* and the always-dependable Stephen Furst but, as I feared, the humor was too broad. It was trying too hard.

My wife uttered the funniest line involved with the film the night it was previewed in Westwood. Our car was being repaired, and the garage loaned us one of those Japanese cars that talked to you. If you forgot to fully close a door, it would tell you "your door is ajar," or it would let you know if you didn't put on your seat belt.

We picked up the director, Michael Miller, and his wife and drove to the preview. When it ended, the four of us trudged back to the car. The audience had greeted the movie with a mixture of unhappiness and indifference. After we glumly got into the car, I switched on the ignition. "Hey," I announced, "I don't have my seat belt on, and the car didn't say anything. It's not talking!" "Maybe," my wife intoned, "it saw the movie."

Surprisingly, the movie opened well, grossing more than seven million dollars its first weekend. It also had a handful of decent reviews to go with a majority of negatives. The budget on the film was just over four million dollars. Eventually, ABC would recoup its investment from domestic theatrical rental, free and pay TV and video. The injured party was the *Lampoon*. For years, the film would be described, with gross exaggeration, as a "disaster," "a bomb," "*Lampoon's Heaven's Gate*."

ITEM: LIVING IN MAKE-BELIEVE LAND

One of the scripts we developed in the early eighties was called Georgia Baby. It was about two veteran cops trying to solve the murder of a young college professor when one falls in love with their prime suspect, a seductive night-club hostess. It was comedy with a startling dramatic twist, and we were quite enthusiastic about the screenplay.

Jack Klugman and Tony Randall, most famous for their roles as Oscar and Felix in "The Odd Couple," were anxious to star in the film. At the time, Klugman was in television in a show called "Quincy," about a coroner who often investigated the murders of the victims he examined. One afternoon, Randall and I were having lunch at the Bistro Gardens, a pleasant if overpriced eatery in Beverly Hills that caters primarily to the overpaid. As we finished lunch, a woman at the next table waved furiously at Randall. He looked up and winced. "It's Clark Gable's widow," he told me. "I guess I'll have to go over and say hello." I told him I'd pay the check and meet him outside the restaurant.

Some time later, he exited. He was shaking his head, apparently not wanting to believe what had just transpired.

"It seems," he told me, "her son died recently in Hawaii. And she's convinced that he was murdered." He shrugged. "You won't believe this. She wants me to ask Klugman to investigate the case."

In 1981, I got a call from Don Simpson, the president of production of Paramount Pictures. Enthusiastic is a mild description of Don's frenetic approach to a project. "We've got the rights to *The Joy of Sex*," he told me, then asked, "You're familiar with *The Joy of Sex*?" I said of course I was. Pretty much everybody in America was familiar with or Alex Comfort's textbook on lovemaking. In 1974, Brian McConnachie had written a parody called *The Job of Sex* which had become the biggest selling *National Lampoon* paperback of all time.

"Well," Simpson went on, "we've had the rights to the book for years, but nobody can figure out what to do with it. I mean, there's no story. But it's a hell of a title. Well, I was thinking last night, 'Why not *National Lampoon's Joy of Sex?*'"

I liked the idea at once. Ptak made a deal with Paramount, and I wrote a treatment about a young farm boy who comes to the city and, little by little, gets to learn about the joys of sex. Simpson, his associate Jeff Katzenberg, and their boss, Paramount chairman Michael Eisner, all approved the treatment and, once again, I called on John Hughes to write the script. He changed it so that the story started when the young man was a child.

We then stay with him until he's in his thirties. We go from his sheer horror at hearing his parent's screams of ecstasy as they make love in an adjoining room, to his first kiss in grade school, his first heavy petting in high school, his first sex in a bordello, his experience with the school slut, his first girl friend with whom he has frequent sexual relations, his fiancee who then becomes his wife, the women he cheats with, the divorce and reconciliation. It was, of course, all about sex, but like all the good *Lampoon* pieces on sex, it wasn't sordid or erotic. It was simply a very funny script that all of us, to some degree, could relate to.

By now, I was talking mostly to Katzenberg.

"I love it!" he enthused and then proceeded to give me forty pages of notes, suggestions, and changes.

Hughes and I went over them, threw out most and using a few, he rewrote the script. "OK," said Katzenberg, handing me another twenty pages of notes, "let's get a director."

While I was at Universal, I'd gotten friendly with Bob Zemeckis, a huge *Lampoon* fan who would drop by my office frequently to talk about articles in the magazine. Zemeckis, a

The Deltas of *Animal House*. Note Doug Kenney in his dork mode at the far right of the front row. Chris Miller with a haircut is next to him—1977. PHOTO COURTESY OF UNIVERSAL PICTURES

Doug Kenney, me, Chris Miller, and Ivan Reitman on the set of *Animal House*. The ominous vehicle behind us is the "Deathmobile," which tore up Faber College's Homecoming Parade in the final scenes of the film— 1977. PHOTO COURTESY OF UNIVERSAL PICTURES

On the *Animal House* set: (left to right) Tim Matheson, Stephen Furst, John Landis, James Daughton, Sarah Holcomb, and Kevin Bacon. Two Deltas (Matheson and Furst) and two Omegas (Daughton and Bacon)—1977. PHOTO COURTESY OF JOHN LANDIS

"Remain calm! All is well!" Kevin Bacon's final scene in *Animal House*—1977. PHOTO COURTESY OF UNIVERSAL PICTURES

Doug Kenney, John Belushi, and Chris Miller on the *Animal House* set—1977. PHOTO COURTESY OF UNIVERSAL PICTURES

The cast of National Lampoon's lone sitcom, "Delta House," plus their producer. Top row, left to right: Richard Seer (Pinto), Bruce McGill (D-Day), Josh Mostel (Blotto), Peter Fox (Otter). Bottom row, left to right: Michelle Pfeiffer (The Bombshell), Stephen Furst (Flounder), Jamie Widdoes (Hoover), and Wendy Goldman (Muffy)—1979. FROM AUTHOR'S COLLECTION

With P. J. O'Rourke at the *Animal House* opening. A suggestion of combat to come—1978. PHOTO BY PEDAR NESS

With Christie Brinkley at the opening of *Vacation*—1983. FROM AUTHOR'S COLLECTION

With Chevy Chase in the Italian Alps for *European Vacation*—1984. FROM AUTHOR'S COLLECTION

protege of Steven Spielberg's, had written two films with his partner, Bob Gale, and had directed both of them. The first, *I Wanna Hold Your Hand*, was about the Beatles' initial trip to America, the second was *Used Cars*, a satire, obviously, of the used-car business. The first movie was a flop, the second a very mild break-even. Both had low budgets, neither had any stars of note. I thought they were well directed and quite good. I proposed to Katzenberg that Zemeckis direct *The Joy of Sex*. A day later he called me. "Eisner won't hear of it," he told me. "He says Zemeckis can't direct and isn't funny."

Two weeks later I convinced Joe Dante, director of our aborted *Jaws* 3–*People* 0 project, to take the job. Dante was hesitant. He didn't like controversy, and he'd heard that "the guys at Paramount are difficult people to work for."

I assured him that I would insulate him from the studio. He reluctantly agreed. Next, we started looking for actors. There were four key roles, the male lead whose story this was, the girl friend who becomes his wife, the garrulous class bimbo, who actually initiates him into the true joys of sex, and the slick, egotistical gigolo to whom his wife goes for solace after she discovers that her husband has been cheating on her.

Dante and I were favoring Dennis Quaid and his then wife, P. J. Soles as costars. We liked Julie Brown for the female comedy lead and an equally unknown Jeff Goldblum as the self-adoring male escort who can't pass a mirror without a pause to admire himself.

The studio vacillated. They weren't sure about Quaid, didn't like Soles at all, kind of liked Brown and Goldblum but asked that we keep looking. We worked out of a large office on the Paramount lot. A few doors away, they were preparing *Grease* 2 which would introduce Michelle Pfeiffer to the big screen. We never ran into each other.

One day, however, I met another beautiful woman who was to become part of the *Lampoon* story. We were still looking for someone to play the role of the wife. At one casting session a magnificent-looking girl with long blonde hair, a deep California tan, and a charming smile burst into the room. We talked. She read some lines for us. We thanked her and she left. "Who is she again?" I asked the casting director Reuben Cannon. "She's Christie Brinkley, the top model in America," he told me. Christie wasn't strong enough for the role, but later I would remember her for still another film.

As the weeks went by the studio kept wavering on our casting decisions and the notes kept coming. Finally, one day, Dante came into my office looking very grave. "I-I-I'm sorry," he stammered apologetically, "but I'm gonna have to quit. I can't work with these guys." I couldn't get him to reconsider and he left.

A few days later, at John Ptak's recommendation, Bill Norton, who had directed the sequel to *American Graffiti*, was signed to replace Dante. Meanwhile, I was still holding out for Dennis Quaid for the lead. Finally, Katzenberg called and asked me to screen-test Quaid. If they liked the test, he had the role. We prepared for a week or so and then shot the screen test. Bill Norton directed it. I thought Quaid was charming and funny and looked great. Katzenberg called to tell me they didn't like the test. "We're passing on Quaid," he said, "and Norton's out, too. Eisner doesn't think he can direct comedy." I was shocked. Norton had actually failed Quaid's screen test. We argued but I got nowhere. A few days later, the picture was put on hold.

While all this was going on, I had given Katzenberg two projects to look at, a treatment on the adventures of Gerry Sussman's New York cabbie "Bernie X" and a short story by John Hughes that had appeared in a 1979 edition of the magazine, "Vacation '58." It was about a trip Hughes had taken to Disneyland with his family when he was a boy. There was, of course, no thought then that someday Katzenberg and Eisner would be running Disneyland.

Katzenberg liked the "Bernie X" idea but passed on "Vacation." I asked Sussman, John Weidman, and my son Andy, who had just started to work for the *Lampoon*, to write the "Bernie X" script. Once again I brought Bob Zemeckis into the mix. I reminded him that Eisner didn't like his work, but I would fight like hell to get him on as the movie's director. Meanwhile, he was put on, with Katzenberg's approval, as a fourth writer. Zemeckis worked with the other writers for a month or two, then left for Mexico to direct his first major film, *Romancing the Stone*.

A week after he left, Katzenberg called. "We've got problems," he told me. "Eisner says there is no way he will allow Zemeckis to direct the picture, and he wants him off the project." Once again, I argued. I asked to see Eisner. When I did, he dismissed the matter airily. "The guy can't direct comedy," he said, "forget it!"

I called Zemeckis and spoke to his wife. "I've got to talk to Bob," I said. "Do you have a phone number for him in Mexico?" "You can't reach him," she told me. "They're in the jungle. But I'm leaving for there tomorrow. Give me the message." Reluctantly, I told her what had happened with Eisner. She received it coolly.

I never spoke to Zemeckis again. Sometime later Jack Rapke, his agent at CAA, told me that Bob was angry with me for not calling him directly. He didn't stay angry with Eisner too long.

Romancing the Stone was a huge hit and some years later, now a major director, primarily of comedy, Zemeckis developed an idea for an interacting live and animated movie. Disney wanted it but Michael Eisner was now chairman of Disney, and Zemeckis was still burning from Eisner's snubs. Eisner knew how to swallow his pride when a buck was involved. He went to Zemeckis's house and apologized. Then, they made *Who Killed Roger Rabbit?*

"Bernie X" never got out of what is known in the trade as "development hell." Early in 1982, however, Katzenberg called to say they wanted Penny Marshall to direct *The Joy of Sex.* "Oh," I asked quite innocently, "does she direct?" "She's directed some TV," I was told, "and we're sure she can do it."

I met with Marshall. She didn't seem to be as "sure" as Katzenberg had been. "But," she told me, "my friends will visit the set daily and help me." I looked at her inquisitively. "Spielberg," she said, "Rob Reiner [her ex-husband]" and she tore off a litany of some of the best directors in the business. I called Katzenberg back. "Hey," I told him, "maybe she can do it." "I've got more news for you," he said. "I think John Belushi will do the picture."

I was delighted. On the few occasions I'd run into John in recent years, he'd shown me great affection. At a Blues Brothers concert at the Universal Amphitheater, he leaped over a barrier to greet me, encircling me in his arms with one of his Albanian bear hugs. It would be great working with him again. The studio had also come up with an interesting idea. John would play the character, not just as a man, but from infancy, allowing the audience to use its imagination and Belushi to exercise his enormous talents. It was a daring idea, one that could be carried off only by someone like Belushi who transcended reality anyway.

But John wasn't really sure he wanted to do the movie. He'd signed with Paramount to make a film he'd developed called *Dry Rot*, but the script had gone nowhere. The studio was passing on it and was offering him *The Joy of Sex* instead. John's drug habit had gotten enormously expensive. He had other offers, but this picture had a producer, a director, a supporting cast, and was ready to go. He'd get his money *now*.

On March 6, 1982, a few weeks after he agreed to do the movie and shortly before it was to go into production, John died. Two days after that the picture was canceled. The *Lampoon*, as contracted, was paid in full for both my services and the use of its name.

Two months later, Katzenberg called me again. "We're doing *The Joy of Sex*," he told me. "Our option on the title runs out at the end of June, and Alex Comfort won't renew it." I suggested we meet to discuss it. "No," he said, "I'm out of it. It's being turned over to Gary Nardino at Paramount TV. He wants to meet with you."

I met with Nardino, a pleasant man who proceeded to explain that they were making a low-budget movie which would be shot in five weeks. Martha Coolidge (who later directed *Rambling Rose* and *Lost in Yonkers*) had been signed to direct, and it would have a "no-name" ensemble cast. They also were not using the Hughes script but instead, one taking place in high school. They intended to use both my name and the *Lampoon* name on the picture. I said I would reserve any agreement on this matter until I saw a rough print. I saw a print of the picture late in June at the Paramount offices in New York.

Julian Weber and my sons Michael and Andy viewed it with me. Andy recalls the scene: "As we watched and as the movie became progressively worse, Michael and I, sitting behind you [Matty] became engrossed in your reactions. You'd watch an awful scene, then you'd bury your head in your hands or someone on the screen would utter some non-

sensical line, and you'd moan perceptibly. Finally, toward the
end of the film, you couldn't look, your head was lowered,
and your arms were wrapped around it to shield you from
what was going on. Meanwhile, throughout the movie, Julian
sat, transfixed, occasionally shaking his head in disbelief or
grimacing. When the film ended you didn't say a word. Julian
just uttered softly 'Oh, no!'"

Lampoon attorneys immediately notified Paramount that
since I hadn't approved the story or the director or the cast, as
I was entitled to do, they had no rights to use either my name
or that of the *National Lampoon* with the picture.

At the same time, I called Katzenberg. "I'm no longer
involved with this," he said. "Talk to Frank Mancuso."

It hadn't been announced, but Eisner and Katzenberg
were leaving and Mancuso would replace them. Mancuso
wanted $500,000 to take the names off the picture. My
lawyers assured me that if we sued, we'd get an injunction
against the names being used and would win the case. They
also estimated that our legal bills would be in the hundreds of
thousands of dollars. Once again I called Mancuso and we
negotiated a price. Finally, I sent him a check for $250,000.
The picture opened without the *Lampoon* name or mine on it
and closed a week later.

Meanwhile, Ptak had set up a breakfast with Mark
Canton, a new production executive at Warner Bros. He'd
worked on *Caddyshack* with Kenney and Ramis and loved the
Lampoon. I pitched him Hughes's "Vacation" story, then handed
him a copy of the issue in which the story had appeared. It
was the beginning of a long relationship. Mark is a man with
boundless energy and enthusiasm. Working with him became
one of the great pleasures I would have in the movie business.

Over the next couple of weeks, he convinced his bosses, Bob Daley, Terry Semel, and Bob Shapiro, that this indeed was a movie they should make and in the fall of 1982, we began production on *National Lampoon's Vacation*.

Katzenberg would come back into my life briefly soon after.

I had never been a fan of the Ted Mann-Todd Carroll "O. C. & Stiggs" stories, but, quite apparently, *Lampoon* readers liked them. Mann and Carroll wrote a book on the two characters and asked me to publish it under the *Lampoon* banner. I declined. Instead, we agreed, for the first time, to devote a complete issue of the magazine to only the one story.

Sales were average. Flushed by this moderation, the two then tried to persuade me that I should have them develop the story into a screenplay. I showed the issue to Warner Bros. where I was settled at the time, but they had no more enthusiasm for the project than I did. Mann and Carroll then asked me if they could shop the story to other producers. I told them to go right ahead but to remember that the *Lampoon* owned both the story and the O. C. and Stiggs characters since the writing had been done by staff writers for the magazine. Soon afterwards, they told me that the producer Lewis Allen wanted to proceed with the project.

A month or so later, John Ptak told me that Jeff Katzenberg had called him from Paramount. Sly Stallone had read an *O. C. & Stiggs* script that Mann and Carroll had adapted from their story and wanted to direct it. Paramount, anxious to keep Rambo happy, was equally eager to develop it. They were offering the *Lampoon* $400,000 for the story rights, ten percent down, and the rest if the movie was made plus a percentage of the profits. No use of the *Lampoon* name would be involved. I was delighted and more than amazed.

"What," I asked both John and myself, "could these people be seeing in this story that I can't see? I simply don't like it as a film."

An hour later, Katzenberg called me to tell me how much they liked the story. "Great!" I said.

An hour after that, Ptak called me back. He had yet to tell Paramount we would accept their offer. Meanwhile, Freddie Fields of MGM had called him. Mike Nichols, apparently an old friend of Lewis Allen's, was now in love with the story and wanted to direct it. MGM would move on it at once. They would give us $400,000 now, for the rights. No ten percent down, the entire amount, plus profit participation.

"What should I do?" Ptak asked. "Hey," I said, "$400,000 now is a lot better than ten percent now and the rest if they make the picture. Offer it to Katzenberg. If he passes, make the MGM deal."

Katzenberg passed. The deal with MGM was made, and we got the $400,000. Mann and Carroll were both excellent writers, but I still was convinced that this wasn't a movie. Mike Nichols dropped out of the project, and Robert Altman took over as director. Soon after they started shooting, he heard what we'd been paid for the rights and stormed into Freddie Fields's office demanding to know why we got more money than he was getting.

The picture opened and closed quickly. Mann told me he felt that Altman simply made it too esoteric, that it became vague and elusive. I told him once again that I never thought it would make a movie.

CHAPTER TWENTY

FINALLY, AFTER four years of false starts, pictures that I loved being canceled in preproduction, and pictures that I wasn't exactly enamored of being made and released to a public that didn't like them any more than I did, we were making a *Lampoon* movie that I felt certain would be our second major success.

Mark Canton and I, at the very beginning of our planning of *Vacation*, asked Harold Ramis to direct the film. Since *Caddyshack*, he'd appeared as an actor in several pictures including *Stripes* for Ivan Reitman and had written or rewritten several others. Harold is a very laid-back guy. He never seems to get excited and his first reaction to the offer was a bold and decisive—"Uh, well ... I don't ... mmm ... know. I'll have to think about it." We kept after him. He read the script and liked it. Like any good film maker, he started thinking about what he'd do with it and, finally, he agreed to direct it.

All three of us immediately concurred that Chevy Chase would be perfect as Clark Griswold. After a strong start, Chevy's film career had slowed down. His most recent films hadn't done well at the box office. He liked the script, and we all had known him for a long time, me since *Lemmings*, Harold since "The National Lampoon Radio Hour," and Mark since *Caddyshack*. So, immediately, there was a feeling of camaraderie. Now, he was set.

The story was about a hellacious cross-country trip the Griswold family takes to Walleyworld—Disneyland.

In Hughes's original story and in the first draft of the script he wrote, the girl the family meets on the road is a teenager, the same age as the Griswold boy, Rusty. It is he who is enchanted by her. One of Harold's first ideas was to change the girl to a woman. He described what he had in mind. "A beautiful woman with long flowing blonde hair and a deep California tan. And she would be driving an open-topped red sports car." "A Porche," I offered. "No, a Ferrari!" he countered. "And it would be Clark [Chevy], not Rusty, who is taken by her. She shakes him up, and, of course, nothing happens except that he acts like a lovesick jerk before he realizes he's a happily married man."

I loved the idea. "I know the girl for the role," I told him. "I auditioned her for *The Joy of Sex*. She's a model—the most famous model in the country." For the life of me, I couldn't remember her name. Finally, other people in our office started throwing out names. The second or third one mentioned was Christie Brinkley. "That's her!" I yelled excitedly.

There were a number of excellent actresses up for the role of Clark's wife Ellen, JoBeth Williams who had fared well in *Kramer vs. Kramer*, Dee Wallace, the mother in *E.T.*, Jessica Harper who had worked with Woody Allen, and Beverly D'Angelo who had been in *Hair* and *Every Which Way But Loose* with Clint Eastwood and had been lauded for her portrayal of Patsy Cline in *Coal Miner's Daughter*.

Beverly arrived at her audition wearing cowboy boots, a short skirt, and a low-cut blouse. She looked like anything but the long-married wife in a typical middle-American family, but when she read with Chevy, she immediately became Ellen Griswold. She was a fine actress, looked great, and was smart as hell. She would be the prototype for the young family matron of the eighties, good-looking, bright, and patiently long suffering. Clark Griswold would be attractive, good at his job, accident-prone, and frequently pigheaded and opinionated to the point of habitually screwing up everything. They were a great movie couple.

At a reading in New York, in our search for the Griswold son, Rusty, Anthony Michael Hall, a tow-headed fourteen year old with a mouth full of braces, walked in and in one reading got the part. I laid down one stipulation. He had to keep the braces for the movie. At the time, he was easily the best young actor I had seen. He was a kid with something few adult actors have, natural comedy timing and an ability to always be believable. Pretty little Dana Barron was quickly added as the daughter Audrey.

The script had wonderful roles for character actors. Harold came up with Randy Quaid for Ellen's hillbilly cousin, Eddie. I added Miriam Flynn who had worked for me in *Class Reunion* as Eddie's wife Catherine and Imogene Coca as Aunt Edna and Eddie Bracken, a major comedy star in the forties and fifties, as the theme park boss Roy Walley. For Coca, one of the greatest stars in television history, it was only her second movie. Bracken hadn't made a picture since 1953. Eugene Levy, one of Harold's pals from "SCTV," cameoed as an obnoxious car salesman and Brian Doyle-Murray, another Lampooner who had later joined "Saturday Night Live" would play the owner of a wilderness camp compound.

When John Hughes first wrote "Vacation '58" as a short story in 1979, I had told him, "If I can't sell this to a studio, I'll raise the money myself. But we're definitely going to make this movie." That may indeed have been wishful thinking with a goodly helping of bravado and bullshit thrown in, but I loved this movie for the very same reasons that audiences would love it. I related to it. It recalled not only frustrating car trips with my kids, but my own touring with my mother, father, and brother when I was a boy. We all agreed as we started to make the film that we stay as closely as possible to reality.

Several scenes have remained with people to this day when the subject of comedies comes up, notably the episode in which Aunt Edna dies and Clark places her upright, sitting in a chair on the roof of the station wagon, and the scene in which the dog is tied to the car and they are later stopped by a motorcycle cop who berates Clark for his (unintended) callousness. When the movie opened, we were flooded with letters from people who told us of tying a dog to a car with the same disastrous result, and more than a few letters from people who told us they traveled with an elderly relative who had passed away in the car.

Since *Vacation*, films Hughes has written, directed, or produced have grossed more than any moviemaker except Spielberg. None, in my most prejudiced opinion, had the nostalgia of *Vacation* or the memorably funny moments. Some, particularly *Home Alone*, would have much bigger box office grosses, but like most film comedies, they involved plots that had little sense of reality. It's an implausible stretch of the imagination to consider that you could fly to Europe and inadvertently leave your eight-year-old kid home alone. But the car trip in *Vacation* could have happened, and it did, in different ways, to all of us.

The shoot went well. There were no temper tantrums, no arguments, no heavy drinking, no discernible drugs. Everybody knew their lines and got to the set on time. Nobody bitched about the food, and everybody not only liked the director but the star. Chevy was a delight. He was free with his praise and generous in every way, always buying drinks, often picking up dinner tabs, and always pleasant and easy to be with. His wife Jayni was pregnant during the filming, and Chevy shuffled around her like a mother hen. The propmaster Bob Visciglia was the company clown, always providing laughter. The production manager, Bob Grand, knew where everything was and should be at all times.

Of course, there were moments. I was working in a makeshift office in a rural Holiday Inn in Colorado. Colorado, Arizona, and California would serve as the locales for filming the entire picture except for some second unit filming in Chicago and St. Louis. Even Cousin Eddie's Kansas farm was duplicated in Colorado.

One day, Ramis's car tore into the motel parking lot, and he dashed into my office, his usually tranquil face now ashen. "Imogene," he said, "I think she had a stroke." He explained that they'd been shooting a scene with Imogene, and she'd completely blanked out, couldn't remember her lines, her character's name, *her* name, or anything else. He'd shut down the set, and she was now in her motel room.

"We're going to have to replace her," he said.

I calmed him down and walked to her room. Her husband, the actor King Donovan, had put her to bed. He and I talked for a while, and he assured me that she was fine and it was just a momentary lapse. Soon, she walked out. She was wearing a robe at least three sizes too big for her tiny frame, and she had that famous pixie smile on her face. She whispered meekly, "I'm sorry." For the rest of the shoot, she didn't miss a minute of shooting or forget a line.

When we hired Christie Brinkley, she was making a million dollars a year as a model. Most of our filming was done outdoors, and we were on the road almost continually. All of her dialogue was shot indoors, and we needed to hoard indoor scenes in case of rain when you switch quickly from exterior to interior locations. That meant that Christie, whose part could have been shot in a week, had to stay with the troupe for the six weeks we filmed on the road before returning to Los Angeles. We were paying her twenty thousand for the entire film which meant it was costing *her* about fifteen thousand a week to be in the movie. She never complained. She was serious about becoming an actress.

On one rain day, we shot her cocktail lounge scene with Chevy. It's a scene where Chevy, after an argument with his wife, goes to the bar of the motel in which they're staying. He sits at the piano bar for a few moments (the piano player, an Italian count, was a Harpo Marx look-alike as well as being Beverly D'Angelo's husband) and then wanders into the lounge. There, to his unexpected delight, the ravishing Christie joins him. The conversation that follows is nearly all of Christie's dialogue in the film.

I arrived at the location shortly after the scene was shot to find Christie standing in the rain outside the motel with tears streaming down her face. "I was terrible!" she told me. I put my arms around her, which was not an onerous task, and calmed her. One of the assistant directors came by, and I asked him to get Harold. When he arrived, I said, "Harold, can I assume that if Christie's scene hadn't been good, you'd still be in there shooting it?" She looked at him inquisitively.

He smiled. "It was great," he said. "I was delighted with it."

She sighed and, unfortunately, I had to take my arms from around her.

Beverly D'Angelo had a nude scene in the picture. It was supposedly set in a bathroom shower. Instead, we shot it in a rectangular box in the middle of a gymnasium in Flagstaff, Arizona. Surrounded by director and crew, she arrived on the set, whipped off her robe, and naked from the waist up, stepped into her shower. I walked around the set to make sure that only people who were supposed to be there were.

Beverly had few inhibitions and appearing nude wasn't one of them, but one owes a nude actress at least the impression that this is for the "movie" and not the voyeur. As I walked, I suddenly noticed something. There, standing next to the camera, closer to Beverly even than the director, and enjoying himself immensely, was fourteen-year-old Anthony Michael Hall. I walked over to him and led him out of the gym. I laughed. "You want me to wind up on an Arizona prison farm for endangering the morals of a child?" I asked.

He grinned mischievously. "Wow," he enthused, "what a pair of bazongas!"

We wrapped in late fall. The production was under schedule and under budget.

The last scenes shot were set mostly at Roy Walley's house. The Griswolds had arrived at Walleyworld after their frightful trip only to find it closed for repairs. An incensed Clark finds out where Roy Walley lives and buys a gun—well, a BB gun that looks real. He then drags his protesting family to Walley's house, confronts him, demanding that the deserted park be opened. As this transpires, the police arrive and arrest the Griswolds, but Walley relents and promises he'll open the park for them. The end.

When we screened a rough cut of the picture with this ending, the audience who had loved the film until then, simply hated the final scenes. The reason was obvious: both they and the Griswolds had lived through hell to get to Walleyworld, and the audience never got to see the place.

We agreed. We had to rewrite the ending. Canton asked us to meet with Bob Daley and ask for the money to shoot the new scenes. Before we did, Hughes rewrote the offending ending. Now, they would go to the park. It would be closed. Clark would lose all sense of rationality. They would leave, buy the gun, and returning to the park, confront the two uniformed guards on duty. One would be taken with them as they boarded the various rides and had the time of their lives. Then, Roy Walley and the cops would show up.

We needed something else. We decided that we wanted a familiar face as the guard who goes on the rides with them. He would plainly hate amusement park entertainment. Harold asked Bill Murray who begged off. His second call was to John Candy who agreed to do it.

We went to Daley's office. As Bob and I chatted, I remember clearly that Harold was doing the *New York Times* crossword puzzle with a pen. I also remember thinking, as we talked with Harold seemingly oblivious of our conversation, that the only other person I'd seen do that was Henry Beard.

I told Bob what we wanted to do. I explained that we'd come in substantially under the film's nine million dollar budget. "How much will it cost?" he asked. I handed him Bob Grand's budget for the reshoot, "Five hundred thousand."

He didn't even look at the budget. He nodded, "OK." Harold and I shook hands with him and we walked out. As we did, I looked at the crossword puzzle. He'd finished it.

The movie opened to both critical acclaim and lines at the box office. Its final domestic box office gross was close to eighty million dollars. Video sales were huge and, to date, it has earned almost twenty-five million dollars from free and pay TV alone.

The picture once again made the *Lampoon* a factor in the film business. It resurrected Chevy's career, made Anthony Michael Hall a star, and Harold, never anxious to overwork, was turning down offers to direct at the rate of one a day.

Shortly after the picture opened I told Mark I had an idea for a sequel; the family wins a quiz show, gets a cheapo trip to Europe, runs into overfriendly Brits, nasty Parisians, and a whole assortment of other characters, and in the process they, and the audience, visit Buckingham Palace, the Louvre, the Vatican, the Austrian countryside, and the Swiss Alps. One day later, Hughes started to write the script.

In 1986, a Harris Poll asked American moviegoers to name their favorite comedies of all-time. *National Lampoon's Vacation* came in seventh, trailing such films as *M*A*S*H* and *Blazing Saddles*. In first place, by far, was *National Lampoon's Animal House*.

CHAPTER TWENTY-ONE

GERRY TAYLOR had returned to the magazine in 1979, but he and Julian agreed on very little and he left two years later. By 1984, Len Mogel had turned most of his responsibilities over to others and was concentrating on making more *Heavy Metal* movies. My daughter Julie who had been associate editor was now the editor of *Heavy Metal*, and that magazine was showing a profit after running in the red for several years. It would gradually, under her supervision, become more and more profitable.

The *Lampoon* magazine was losing money. Circulation was now down to 446,000 and more than 100,000 of that number came from Publishers Clearing House and similar subscription companies. Such plans provided numbers for advertisers but no income to speak of to the magazine. Advertising in 1984 was down $500,000 from the previous year. The company, for the third year in a row, would lose more than $500,000. The more than $1.3 million earned that year from films was keeping it afloat.

The editorial staff, as the *Rolling Stone* article had stated, was confused and indifferent.

We were to start preproduction on *European Vacation* in the summer. In the fall we'd be shooting in Europe for three months. I decided I had to do something about the magazine before I left. I told Julian that I was returning to New York for meetings with both the company executives and the editors. I wanted ideas and I wanted changes, and I let him know that if none were forthcoming, I was going to have to reclaim the direct operation of the magazine.

I arrived for the meetings, and neither group had any thoughts that involved change of any consequence. When we finished, I asked Julian to resign as president of the company and once again become the *Lampoon's* legal counsel. I decided that, after the movie wrapped, I would move back to New York to supervise the magazine and would run the film division from both coasts. I again met with the editorial and art staff and told them that I regretted this but that it was a time of desperation, and I was replacing all of them.

Larry "Ratso" Sloman, who had written several best-selling books, including the story of Bob Dylan's Rolling Thunder Review (he would some years later ghost the hugely successful Howard Stern book) and had years of magazine experience, was brought in as executive editor. Peter Kleinman, who had been art director of the magazine after Michael Gross, returned to replace Michael Grossman. My son Andy was on staff and my older son Michael, who'd left the music business some years before to be in charge of our film development in California, returned to New York to edit, write, do publicity, create special events, and get involved with as many other activities as possible.

Naturally, I knew that there would be eyebrows raised because all three of my children were now working for the company, but I felt certain that they could do the job. All three had known the *Lampoon* since we'd started it. All three were excellent writers. Julie had been working for the company since she was a teenager. She quit college because she missed the publishing business. When she took over the editorship of *Heavy Metal*, she gave it organization and direction and had brought in important new artists. Andy was simply funny. He had a knack for the absurd that had been missing since O'Donoghue and McConnachie. Michael was a connection with the *Lampoon*'s years that we hadn't had since O'Rourke's early days as editor-in-chief. In his close relationships with Kenney and Belushi and his years editing the "True Facts" section under Beard, he had made many good friends who had since drifted away from the magazine. As head of creative affairs he had a background in theater and film that would be invaluable.

As much as all of these things, I needed people who could be trusted and who wanted desperately for the magazine to succeed and would do whatever they could toward that end.

Kelly's statements to *Rolling Stone* and other publications, of course, had been no surprise. He'd stayed with the company this long despite his duplicities. It was the lack of direction and enthusiasm voiced in the *Rolling Stone* article that opened my eyes to the internal problems at the magazine. I knew that if we were going to recover from this steady erosion of readers and magazine revenues, new, dedicated people would have to get involved. And, goddammit! I figured, if my own kids didn't care, who would?

The first thing Michael did was to contact Ed Bluestone, Chris Miller, Ed Subitzky, and other original *Lampoon* contributors who had left the magazine. Then, we started cutting fat. In one year we reduced the company's overhead by $1.3 million. Since the second or third year of O'Rourke's editorship, the magazine had taken on a look and tone unlike the preceding years. It became more uniform and less daring. It had, as P. J. had always desired, longer articles, and, to my dismay, it had become not funnier but meaner. This continued in the Plunkett-Kelly years. Now, I asked for and got a return to the more robust humor of the seventies. I didn't want more tits, I wanted more laughter. And I got it. The magazine started to be funny again.

New writers and new features were introduced. Dave Hanson satirized a phenomena of the eighties, the "personal's" column. Nick Bakay introduced the first important new *Lampoon* character since Bernie X, the Evil Clown, a creation since ripped off in several horror flicks. Michael started writing "Drinking Tips and Other War Stories," a series of recollections of his barroom adventures. A 1987 readership study would name that feature as the second most popular in the magazine with the "O. C. & Stiggs" stories, which hadn't appeared in several years, as the favorite. Shary Flenniken's "Trots and Bonnie" remained the magazine's most popular comic strip. Film director John Waters and "down home" humorist Joe Bob Briggs were added to the list of regular contributors.

In 1985, the percentage of the number of magazines sold to the number distributed started to rise. We had dropped below 40 percent in the first four years of the eighties. All through the seventies, we had averaged sales in the sixtieth and seventieth percentiles. This is a very important figure for two reasons. One, a higher percentage sale cuts down on the number of unsold magazines and therefore the number you have to print, and two, by the eighties, magazine wholesalers were all computerized and if a magazine sold too few of the copies that were distributed, the computers automatically cut out smaller, less productive outlets. The increase in sales percentage was exciting. It spoke of renewed enthusiasm for the magazine at the newsstands.

John Hughes sent me the script for *European Vacation* in the summer of 1984. We expected it months earlier, but the studio had green-lighted the movie without a final script, and we were already in preproduction. I was scheduled to leave for Europe in August to start preparing for a start in October. I would return to Los Angeles for the filming of a few scenes on the Warners's lot and then fly back to London with the cast and crew and begin principal photography.

Harold Ramis had passed on directing the picture, telling me he didn't want to direct a sequel, even a sequel to a film he'd directed in the first place. My second choice was Amy Heckerling, who had directed only one film before, *Fast Times at Ridgemont High*. A delightful movie, funny and well-made, it was certainly not one of the insipid high school and college potboilers that Hollywood had been grinding out since *Animal House*. The studio agreed with my choice, but Amy wasn't sure she wanted the job. She hadn't worked with a major star before, and she'd heard Chevy could be difficult. As the star of the film, Chevy had to approve the choice of director, and he'd already okayed Amy. I assured her that they'd get along, telling her about the first *Vacation* and how it had been a wonderful experience for everybody and that, Chevy, in particular, had been great to work with. She accepted our offer.

Beverly D'Angelo immediately agreed to again be Ellen Griswold. Hughes had cast Anthony Michael Hall for *The Breakfast Club*, and he was unavailable for us. We decided to replace both kids, feeling that changing only one would have been jarring to the audience. It was a decision that I shared in making, but in retrospect, it didn't make too much sense. So, Dana Barron who was so right as Audrey in the first film, was left out. Amy recommended a splendid young actress named Dana Hill, whose performance in the Albert Finney film, *Shoot the Moon*, had made her that year's hot movie teenager. Michael Hall had been a most unusual and fortunate discovery in the first picture. Replacing him was more difficult. After endless auditions, a lanky sixteen year old named Jason Lively got the role.

When I read Hughes's script, I was dismayed. It was quite obvious that it had been written hurriedly. I knew that he'd been preparing several pictures that he not only would write but would direct; what he sent still needed a lot of work, unlike his usual submissions which had always been written with care. I called him and told him it needed a rewrite, and we had to have it in a hurry. He said it was impossible since he was leaving to start shooting *The Breakfast Club*.

I reminded him, not without anger, that he'd been paid $500,000 to write the script, that this was a *Lampoon* film and my film, and that he owed it to the studio, to the *Lampoon*, and to me, to give us a finished script. These were the first heated words he'd ever heard from me, and he responded only with an apology. "I'm sorry," he said softly, "but I'm committed to this other picture."

I've spoken to Hughes one more time since then. In 1985, he invited me to a screening of *The Breakfast Club*. I went alone and really liked it. Leaving my seat after the movie ended, I turned to walk up the aisle. Hughes suddenly was at my side, and I told him how much I enjoyed his film. He stopped and put both hands on my shoulders. "Whatever I am now or will be," he said, "is because of you."

I was startled. Appreciation wasn't exactly something that was spread around heavily in an industry where everybody who is successful thinks that success was preordained and accomplished without help. I answered probably with less tact than I should have used, but the experience with the *European*

Vacation script was still on my mind. "You won't remember that," I said. "Nobody does." I didn't mention the problem with the script nor did I have to. We shook hands and have never spoken since. I've called and written to him a few times. Once he called back but I was out. When I, in turn, called him back, he was unavailable.

After Hughes left the film, Amy, Mark Canton, and I discussed the need for a second draft. Amy suggested a veteran writer named Robert Klane who had made a splash a few years before with a movie called *Where's Poppa?* but had enjoyed little success since. We hired Klane and he added a few good scenes including a German slap-dance bit which begins with Chevy in Alpine shorts doing some clever dances and culminates in a free-for-all fight. It turned out to be one of the best scenes in the film, but the script still needed work and we were about to start shooting. We rewrote as we went along.

Initial filming on the Warners's lot went well except for one problem. In one of the opening scenes, Clark (Chevy) is shown using the video camera he'd bought for the trip. Beverly had complained about not getting enough to do in the first movie, so we wrote in a song for her to sing in their bathroom. As she flings off her robe, we see Clark film her nude from the waist up. They then proceed to make love off-camera.

The brief nudity was not gratuitous since in Europe the camera is stolen and Ellen (Beverly) anguishes that she appears naked on the film in it. Later in the picture, with everything else having gone wrong, they come upon a billboard for an Italian movie, *The Lady in the Bathroom*, and Ellen's photograph adorns the poster. Seeing Beverly nude in the bathroom scene was necessary. Without it, the porn movie gag would have far less impact.

Beverly asked if we could shoot the scene in Europe, claiming she'd not learned the lyrics. It never entered my mind that we'd have a problem with her about it. She'd been nude in the first *Vacation*, in *Hair*, and in other movies. I agreed we'd wait until Europe.

In Europe, we signed Eric Idle for a cameo as a put-upon Englishman who literally keeps on running into the Griswolds, accumulating one injury after another but never losing that incredible British need-to-be-polite. Robbie Coltrane, who has since appeared in a number of American comedies, did another cameo as a fellow resident in the cheap hotel the Griswold's stay at in London.

From the start, it was quite apparent that the filming of this picture would not be the same easy ride that we had on the first *Vacation*. We labored with the script, ran into assorted union problems in England, and Chevy was completely different. He was moody and often belligerent, especially to Amy whose fears now became a reality.

We argued a lot about the script, he, suggesting that it was a total family movie, sort of an Andy Hardy film. Me, reminding him that it was not the 1930s, that Andy Hardy wouldn't appeal to 1980s audiences, that the Hardy family would not have put a dead aunt on the roof of their car, and when Andy's dad, the beloved Judge Hardy, lost his temper, he didn't make his point with a stream of obscenities as Clark Griswold did, to the audiences' delight, in the first film.

In London, Beverly asked me to put the nude scene off until we arrived in Paris. Again, I agreed. In Paris, Chevy announced that he was absolutely against any nudity in the picture. Beverly suddenly agreed, telling me resolutely that she was "an actress, not a bimbo" and didn't have to take her clothes off in a movie. For the rest of the two-week stay in Paris, I refused to talk to her.

We built an overhang right off the Eiffel Tower to shoot action on its upper levels. At one point, Clark whips off a beret his son is complaining about and throws it out over the rail where it falls to the ground far below. An obnoxious little dog being held by an equally obnoxious French matron was to see the flying beret, leap out of his mistress' arms, and fly into space. Once again, an animal was "getting it" in a *Lampoon* movie; to wit: the horse who has the heart attack in *Animal House* and the dog tied to the station wagon in *Vacation*. We had one problem. The dog who was supposed to leap from the actress' arms to the off-camera hands of his trainer standing in the overhang, refused to jump. For an hour the trainer pleaded with the animal to jump to him. Members of the cast and crew and hundreds of tourists started urging him as well.

Finally, the actress pinched the dog hard. He yelped ... and jumped.

As we had done in London and would do in Rome, we filmed in and around the city's great landmarks. What we were shooting, we agreed, was a travelogue with a lot of comedy thrown in or, better yet, a comedy with a travelogue. Amy came up with a marvelously comedic scene at the Louvre, shot in high speed to emphasize the desperate dash tourists make through traditional visiting places, missing nearly everything they should savor because of a fear that they might miss something else. We kept rewriting the script, and Chevy kept complaining about it.

In Rome, Beverly rushed over to me, threw her arms around me and apologized. "I realize now," she told me, "that the nude scene is important to the plot." We were due back in London for three weeks after we wrapped in Italy. We decided we'd shoot the scene there.

In London, our home base in Europe, we started to wrap up little scenes that we'd shoot on sound stages rather than the real, or "practical," locations we'd mostly used to this point.

On the day we were to shoot Beverly's song-and-dance number, she changed her mind again and told me that there was no way she would do nudity. Chevy again agreed with her, and she refused to allow us to use a body double. I simply shook my head and walked away. A singer before she was an actress, and a very good singer, she did the scene perfectly. It was shot so you never saw her breasts. I sat off-camera somberly taking all this in. At one point she danced over, turned to me, smiled broadly, and whipped off the bathrobe she wore. There were two Band-Aids over her nipples. One said "fuck" and the other said "you." Then she kissed me on the forehead and danced back on camera.

It was a few days before we were to finish shooting in Europe, and we still didn't have an ending. None of us liked Hughes's, which was just sort of a fly-off into the skies, heading for home. We agreed we would each take a shot at writing a new one.

Chevy came up with the first, and he described it to Amy and me. The Griswolds would be home, all four of them sprawled on a couch in front of a roaring fire, and Clark would say, profoundly, "Gee, it's great to be home!"

There was a long pause as Amy and I waited for what was coming next, but there was nothing. That was it! We looked at each other, bewildered.

"Chevy," I said. "That's not funny. This is a comedy, we have to end with a laugh."

He was furious. He got up and stormed out of the room.

That evening we got together again. I described a scene I had written. The Griswolds again are at home. The kids are in their rooms, talking to friends telling them how horrible their trip was and making dates for parties, movies, etc. Ellen is on her phone, describing the trip to a friend and moaning that it was even worse than their drive to Walleyworld. Clark is downstairs feeling good to be home.

The doorbell rings. He opens the door and a man bursts in. Behind him come a photographer and several cronies. "Congratulations!" the first man shouts enthusiastically. "Mr. Griswold, you've won first prize in the Publishers Clearing House Sweepstakes, an all expense trip to the Great Wall of China for you and your family!!"

Clark is beside himself. "The Great Wall of China!" he screams in delight. "My favorite wall!" He turns to tell his wife and kids of their incredible luck, but they've heard it all and all three are standing on the stairs glaring at him. He pauses. Slowly, it sinks in. No more trips! He turns to the man and asks meekly, "What's second prize?" Fade.

Amy grinned enthusiastically. Chevy was glaring again. "I hate it!" he said emphatically.

Amy's version had the family flying to America. As they near the coastline they are delighted to see the Statue of Liberty. Chevy then leaves to go to the men's room and mistakenly barges into the cockpit, banging into the pilot who, in turn, slams the steering wheel causing the plane to dive and slice a hunk off the Statue of Liberty. As the plane flies off, we hear Rusty's voice saying, "Oh boy. The Griswolds are back!"

I was less than enthused. I had long been leery of this kind of escape from reality. Chevy, however, not anxious to please me at this point, agreed to shoot this version. I argued but he wouldn't budge. And that's how the picture ended.

The movie opened hugely and grossed more than seventy million dollars at U.S. and Canadian box offices. Once again it became immensely popular on pay TV and in video.

Shortly after the opening, a news story was released stating that Chevy had entered the Betty Ford Clinic for addiction to prescription medicines for back problems he'd suffered since his many pratfalls on "Saturday Night Live." There is no question in my mind that this drug use caused the difficulties on *European Vacation*.

A few years later, when *Christmas Vacation* was shot, he was the same cooperative and warm person he'd been on the first *Vacation*. Beverly and I remained friends. I've always been a staunch admirer of hers. Whatever her reasons for not doing the nude scene, they remain her reasons. She has since been nude in several films. Would it have helped the movie? I firmly believe that it would have, but actors can sometimes be very difficult to understand and impossible to explain. A producer friend once said to me, "A terrible thing happened on the set today. My leading lady had a tantrum—and I understood why."

Years later, comparing the difficulties on the shoot with childbirth, Amy Heckerling said to me, "I'd rather go through three weeks of intense labor than live through another *European Vacation*."

Six months or so after *European Vacation* opened, my marriage ended. Soon, I started dating for the first time in more than thirty years. It was a strange feeling. For someone used to being sure and secure and in charge, it was like being a boy all over again. "One thing for sure," I told myself and anyone who'd listen, "I'd never consider getting married again."

CHAPTER TWENTY-TWO

IN 1977, AN unknown Methodist pastor from a small town in Mississippi announced to the world that he and his followers had organized "to fight filth in the media." His first effort to attract attention was a campaign called "turn the television off week." "The strategy of so much network planning," he said, "is to appeal to the purient interest of man and not to spend money for quality programming." The statement was not without a morsel of truth, but Donald Wildmon did not explain then nor has he revealed since why he or anyone else is qualified to tell us what we can watch or read.

In 1978, he announced his first boycott of television advertisers or programs he had designated as those that should be forced off the air. To supplement this, a handful of underlings staged demonstrations outside Sears stores in several parts of the country. The boycott worked. Sears canceled its commercials on "Three's Company" and "Charlie's Angels," and, as meaningful to Wildmon, the press started covering his campaigns and spelling his name right. Flushed by the attention he was getting, he ran for a seat in the Mississippi House of Representatives but finished a distant third, getting only 921 votes or 15 percent of the total votes cast.

His group was called the National Foundation for Decency, as if decency was something you could build a memorial to. Now, with a boost from Jerry Falwell's Moral

Majority, he segued into the Coalition for Better Television. He officially named himself to head what he described as an alliance of two hundred organizations with, he claimed, a combined membership of more than three million people. It was, he announced, a membership sworn to back boycotts of advertisers of offending programs.

Although no scrutiny of his claims of popular support ever showed even a fraction of the membership numbers he frequently quoted, the television networks didn't even attempt to answer him until some years into this campaign, once again proving the effectiveness of the big lie.

Then, in 1981, four years and not a few victims later, a poll commissioned by ABC revealed that 64 percent of those surveyed believed that the popularity of a program should be the sole factor in determining what was on television. One point three percent said they would consider backing a boycott. The poll also showed that Wildmon and his good friend Falwell had little support among Evangelical Christians and that even members of the Moral Majority opposed efforts to force their opinions on others.

But the threats kept coming, and in 1981 the chairman of Proctor and Gamble, a company spending $500 million a year on television, more than any other sponsor, announced that fifty television shows had been taken off their advertising schedules. He denied that this had been done under pressure from Wildmon's group but did say, in a disgraceful speech to the Academy of Television Arts and Sciences, "We think the coalition is expressing very important and broadly held views. We are listening very carefully to what they say, and I urge you to do the same."

Wildmon promptly boasted of his arrangement with Proctor and Gamble. Now, he really went at it. With another newfound ally, right-wing gadfly Phyllis Schlafly, aboard and with Falwell more firmly in his corner than ever, he attacked dozens of shows for references to abortion, sex outside of marriage, and for violence and profanity. Among his targets were "All In The Family," "Taxi" and "WKRP In Cincinnati," three of the longest-running shows in the history of television.

Then, in a total display of arrogance, he decided to take on one of the networks and laid down a litany of rules for the National Broadcasting Company. Aside from cleaning up their act morally, he wanted NBC to start "portraying life as it is lived by Christians with Christian characters and values." And as kind of an aside, "no more portraying business executives as crooks and con men."

In essence, NBC told him to get lost. He went to their advertisers and threatened a boycott of their products if they didn't cancel their schedules on NBC. This time, he was ignored. In the announcement of their third quarter of 1982, NBC parent, RCA, reported an increase in earnings of $152.4 million over the previous year when there had been no boycott and the company had shown a loss.

Soon after, the Coalition for Better Television faded from sight. But Wildmon, having, latched on to a good thing, kept promoting his cause. He came up with yet another partner, one as publicity hungry and into demagoguery as he was, Ed Meese, Ronald Reagan's attorney general. Now, Wildmon actually participated in preparing letters for the Meese Commission, a right-wing committee hurriedly organized, ostensibly, to fight pornography. If the networks were too tough—they decided—how about magazines?

And so it was on April 10, 1986, the Southland Corporation announced that it was pulling *Playboy* and *Penthouse* from its 4,500 7-Eleven stores and was recommending to 3,600 franchise-owned 7-Elevens that they get rid of them as well. Immediately, forty other supermarket and drug store chains announced that they, too, were dropping the country's two leading men's magazines. By August, more than 17,000 stores had banned the two publications. A flurry of "book burnings" ensued, and many outlets stopped selling rock-and-roll magazines, *Cosmopolitan*, and even the swimsuit issue of *Sports Illustrated*.

Wildmon had scored a direct hit, and he and his pal Ed Meese could smell the blood.

At the *Lampoon*, things had been looking pretty good. The new editorial and art staff had, for the first time in years, brought back a sense of rowdy, good fun. And Chris Miller was back as were Shary Flenniken, Ed Bluestone, and Ed Subitzky, M. K. Brown and B. K. Taylor whose "Timberland Tales" was right up there with "Trots and Bonnie" in reader popularity. The advertising department signed long-term contracts with Camels, Lowenbrau, Miller, Winston, Budweiser, CBS, Fox Video, and other major advertisers.

The theme of the June 1986 issue was horror and fantasy. The cover was a spectacular painting of a beautiful female devil. Among the articles in the issue were "Veepshow: The Haunting of George Bush" by George Barkin, a parody of the horror comics that were so popular at the time; "Tragedyland," a sort of Disneyland chamber of horrors; a very funny short story called "Cosmo Live," about a totally inept (another Schwarzenegger look-alike) alien who arrives from another planet and proceeds to screw up everything he touches. And "Sixty Seconds," Andy Simmons's eerie dream sequence about what races through a man's mind minutes before he's going to crash to his death. This was a piece we would also use as a sketch in our musical, *Class of '86.* It was a good issue. There was one more feature in the issue, "Baby in a Blender."

Peter Kleinman brought up the idea at an editorial meeting. The line was based on a series of old gags like "Polish" and "lawyer" jokes. His idea was to have the cover of the horror issue exhibit a baby in a blender. I rejected it immediately. The rest of the staff liked it and opted for it as a double-page spread inside the magazine. I turned that down, too. I certainly didn't think that a picture showing a baby in a blender was funny. It's not that, for a moment, I thought that anyone would suspect that it was being suggested that anyone should put a baby in a blender. It was simply not funny! The editorial staff, including my two sons, disagreed with me. Kleinman pleaded that I reconsider. I was adamant.

The next day, Kleinman and Larry Sloman, who was now executive editor, came into my office and again asked me to let them do the spread. For reasons I cannot recall, I did. On May 15, the June issue reached subscribers and the newsstands. We got a number of congratulatory calls about "Sixty Seconds" and about a very funny article by Dave Hanson who would soon be asked to join the staff. It was called "Thirty Three Uses For A Dead Yuppie." Among the suggestions were "Make a pate out of his liver," "Take him to brunch and position the body so you can beat him to the tax-deductible receipt," and "Use his feet to stomp domestic grapes." Several poster companies asked about making it into a *Lampoon* poster as we'd done with "Deteriorata" years before and, more recently, with a feature called "The Nerd." An independent film producer called about "Cosmo Live," but we'd already decided we'd pitch that to the studios ourselves. (We did, without success.)

There seemed to be no reaction to the "Baby in a Blender."

Around the first of June, our advertisers started canceling their contracts. We discovered that the Wildmon consortium had written to every one of them, included a picture of the "Baby in a Blender," and notified them that if they continued advertising in the *Lampoon*, a boycott of their products would be organized. Down the side of the Wildmon letterhead was a list of prominent churchmen, including the head of the Salvation Army, who supposedly endorsed these threats.

We were not NBC. National advertisers cannot live without the major networks. They sure as hell could live without the *National Lampoon*. The Wildmon attacks, only a few months earlier, had cost *Playboy* and *Penthouse* millions in advertising and circulation; losses from which neither magazine has recovered. The immediate loss for the *Lampoon* was well over a million dollars or two thirds of our 1985 net advertising sales. There was no defense—the advertisers and agencies didn't want to debate. They summed it up succinctly, "We don't want to get involved." I felt like Czechoslovakia after receiving a similar message from Neville Chamberlain.

A week later, our distributor notified us that the company-owned 7-Eleven stores would no longer sell our magazine. Other cancellations would follow.

While all this was going on, we'd started assembling a new stage review, *National Lampoon's Class of '86*. Dave Hanson wrote a sketch about the making of a douche commercial that was possibly the funniest in the history of *Lampoon* revues, and Andy's short story, "Sixty Seconds," transferred to the stage beautifully. Bumpass was back and a young actress named Veanne Cox was as talented a comedienne as we'd seen since Gilda Radner.

Add to all of this the death of my thirty-year marriage, it was little wonder I was taking both Valium and Halcion to stay calm.

ITEM: REMEMBERING MATTY FOX, A MAN WITH A PLAN.

In 1952, the Diners' Club was two years old. Its growth had been phenomenal. People were catching on to this new credit card craze. So far, the card was being used only in the U.S. and Canada, but we were about to open up the foreign market. Al Bloomingdale had recently become president of the company, but the company's chairman, Ralph Schneider, ran the show. One day, Schneider told me that Bloomingdale had asked him to meet with a man named Matty Fox in New York. Fox, the nephew of the founder of Twentieth-Century Fox, was known as a wheeler-dealer, a guy with dreams and a lot of nerve if not an enormous history of success. Schneider agreed to meet Fox at the Copa Lounge, the spacious bar area of what was then the city's best known nightclub. He asked me to join him.

Fox was all energy. He told us how exciting the world of credit cards was to him and that he felt the future was unlimited. Then, he told us his plan. He would take over operation of the Diners' Club. Using his contacts, he would franchise Diners' Club to every nation on earth. Schneider and I started to look at each other, wondering if we'd missed something. And then Fox triumphantly threw in the kicker. "And you!" he said, with so much enthusiasm that I thought he would shatter at any moment, "you—will get the American franchise!" He sat back, smiled proudly, and waited for our reaction. Schneider had trouble clearing his

throat for a moment or two, then he spoke. "You mean," he
asked softly, "you're giving us a franchise in our own company?" Fox nodded. I asked the waiter for the check.

For sheer chutzpah, I had not met anyone like Matty Fox until
1985 when a man named Michael Wolff let it be known
around town that he was taking over the *National Lampoon*.
We'd heard this rumor for several days when Wolff finally
called Julian Weber and asked if we'd meet with him and some
of his associates. A meeting was set. Meanwhile, Julian tried to
check him out. All he could come up with was that he was a
free-lance magazine writer. We could find no background in
editing or in running a company, much less a company which
at this point was largely dependent on its activities in the
entertainment business.

At the meeting, he introduced his associates, one a
partner in a small Wall Street investment firm, the other, a
former publishing executive, who were acting as consultants
and were apparently close personal friends of his. Wolff
wanted control of our company. His associates would arrange
for an infusion of capital into the *Lampoon*, and he, Wolff,
would take over with all current management leaving.

I was stunned. The name "Matty Fox-Matty Fox" kept
flashing in my brain. I tried not to get angry. "Have you ever
run a publishing company before?" I asked. "No." he said.
"Have you ever edited a national magazine?" Again the answer
was negative. Now, I found it more difficult to stay calm.
"What makes you think," I asked, "that you can do a better job
than we can? Your idea of putting money into the company
sounds fine, but the wrong management can blow every dime
in a hurry, and how do we, or how does anybody, know that
you're not the wrong management?"

A friend had once commented, "In the eighties we entered the stupid zone. People who knew nothing about running a business but had access to money took over public companies and ran them into the ground."

Whether Wolff and his friends could raise the money and whether, if they could, he would have run the company well, are questions for which we'll never have answers. The idea that they were asking for control of a company that they had no ownership in made continued discussions seem useless.

In 1989, Wolff would reappear. I had sold my interest in the company, and he wrote a biting article in a soon-to-be-defunct magazine called *Manhattan Inc.*, edited by Clay Felker, who has a long history of being involved with magazines that eventually go out of business. In the article, Wolff quoted Sean Kelly. "Goddamn it," Kelly had said when he heard I was actually not only getting paid for my stock but was getting a rather decent severance deal. "Goddamn it!"

The article went on to ridicule me for passing on the Wolff (his) deal and to put down my efforts for the company in general. He repeated a Thom Mount quote in Hendra's book which had minimized my contributions to *Animal House* and which had since been called "untrue and absurd" by Mount as well as by the writers of the screenplay and Reitman, my coproducer. Wolff described *Heavy Metal* magazine as "a loser" (it wasn't) and in a flourish of vitriol, described me as having "no sense of humor. *None.*" He went on. Not only was I "the least likely person to run the *Lampoon*" but "everybody" associated with the magazine had, according to Wolff, always hated me.

Kelly was quoted again, several times, and, as I read, I remembered thinking during our discussions several years earlier that some of the things Wolff had been saying were familiar. He had been Kelly's friend, even then.

Years later, when I spoke to him while I was preparing this book, Wolff hemmed and hawed, then told me, yes, Kelly had been his friend. He still thought that his proposal to acquire the magazine in 1986 was valid and would have been good for our stockholders. Again, I asked him if at the time he'd had any experience running a magazine. "*New Times Magazine*," he said. "I was involved with that." "What did you do there?" I asked, recalling that, like *Manhattan, Inc.*, *New Times* was a short-lived publication that was neither especially popular or particularly original. "I was a writer," he replied softly.

We spoke for a while, and I told him what had been on my mind since his article.

I had, of course, considered his attacks on me in the article vicious and personal. I also said that it was obvious that the tone of the article was as nasty as it was because I had turned down his offer. Flustered, he suggested that during my next trip to New York we "get together and bury the hatchet."

ITEM: ANCIENT FRENCH THEATRICAL ANECDOTE

A famous middle-aged Parisian actor was appearing in a play that had been savagely reviewed by a very popular newspaper columnist. The critic had been particularly rough in denigrating the star's performance and had included some references to his middle-age paunch and bags under his eyes. A few nights later the actor was in the men's room of a restaurant in Paris when the critic walked in. The actor turned his back on him at once. The critic was flustered. "I'm sorry if I was too harsh," he said. "Perhaps I was cruel." He held out his hand. "Please accept my apology." The actor looked at him disdainfully, ignoring the hand. "Next time," he said, "say nasty things about me in the men's room and apologize in the press."

Advertising sales for 1987, the year most drastically affected by the boycott, were $319,100. In 1985, before the boycott, they'd been five times that amount. In 1987, revenues from newsstand and subscription sales totaled $2 million. In 1985, they'd been $4 million.

Once again, we had to do something drastic. In November 1986, the *Lampoon* became a bimonthly. We increased the number of pages and raised the cover price from $2 to $3.95. Since there was virtually no national advertising, we cut out all our unprofitable subscription plans. Average circulation in 1987 was 254,000. As recently as 1985, it had been 450,000.

The *Class of '86* opened at the Village Gate in early summer and, as planned, played there for three months. The reviews were mostly good. The *New York Post* critic, Clive Barnes, however, called it "sophomoric" and, once again, it was suggested that the performers were better than the material. The *New York Times* liked it, as did the *Daily News*. The show had been presold to Showtime and Paramount Home Video, insuring profit. The Showtime sale had meant there would be no touring company since it was to be shown on the cable network in the fall. When it was, reviews in both *TV Guide* and *People* magazine lauded the production.

Total company revenues in 1987, which included income from movies and theater, were down $3.3 million, but costs and expenses were down $4.2 million after more drastic cost cutting. In 1987, for the first time in years, and despite the continuing effects of the boycott, the company showed a profit before a special entry for a one-time loss. As part of our paring overhead, we moved our offices at 635 Madison Avenue to Soho, where at the Avenue of the Americas and Spring Street, we relocated in space not much bigger than the tiny offices we'd started in twenty years before.

By 1988, Wildmon's influence began to abate along with Meese's and the popularity of the Reagan administration. We would never get 7-Eleven back, but many other outlets changed their minds, and national advertisers, mostly the beer and cigarette companies, drifted back in.

The boycott had cost us hundreds of thousands of readers and millions in advertising. Now, we were into our third return from the grave.

Wildmon is still around, with a lot of effort and a little bite, but his efforts are apparently benefiting someone. In 1988, he was at it again. His newly founded American Family Association filed their first tax return, showing income of $5,228,505. *TV Guide* reported in 1992 that, two years earlier, he had received a salary of $101,159 and a tax-free housing allowance of $14,400. One of his closest friends and allies over the years was Charles Keating, Jr., who founded Citizens for Decent Literature. Keating once warned that Bermuda shorts were immoral and declared Hugh Hefner to be "a greater threat to America than Socialism."

In the 1980s, Keating moved his group to Phoenix and grew enormously wealthy in crooked real estate and banking schemes, awakening memories that Wildmon had once insisted that NBC stop criticizing shady American businessmen. Keating's "citizens" group, which in 1986 revealed that two of its directors had shared salaries from the "nonprofit" venture of more than $300,000, continued to flourish until 1989 when, as anyone who even glances at a newspaper or TV set knows, Keating was arrested for defrauding thousands of primarily elderly investors out of many millions of dollars, much of which was spent on a lavish lifestyle for him and his family.

With Keating in jail, his campaign for higher morals collapsed, but Wildmon hired the two well-paid Keating henchmen, and they went to work for his AFA, again at elegant salaries. Talk about throwing pearls before the swine.

In 1992, the American Family Association announced that its budget for the year was seven million dollars.

CHAPTER TWENTY-THREE

BY 1987, THE new editorial team of the *Lampoon* was turning out issues that had the bite I'd been looking for. Bluestone was writing the best satire of his career, and a cartoonist named Buddy Hickerson had suddenly become popular to a degree reminiscent of Vaughn Bode. The June cover was graced by a painting of the recently departed Liberace with a sparsely dressed young woman in his arms as, rifle slung over one shoulder, he moves through a jungle thicket in macho-Rambo style. Featured in the issue was the illustrated "last will and testament" of Liberace by Ratso and Andy in which the pianist leaves all his worldly goods to an assortment of strange bedfellows and finally reveals that he and Ella Fitzgerald had fathered a son named Michael to whom he bequeaths his entire wardrobe. A smiling Michael Jackson is then shown in Liberace-Jackson-like sartorial splendor.

There was also a short story by Chris Miller and Bluestone's marvelous "How To Be Offensive at Weddings," "... Funerals," also, a Joe Bob Briggs story called "How I Invented the Titty Bar" which, for several years, Michael Simmons urged Joe Bob to turn into a screenplay only to be told that sadly he had no time for anything else in addition to his cable-movie hosting chores, newspaper column, books, and numerous other activities.

As usual, Shary was there as were M. K. Brown and Rodriguez's crazed detective-in-an-iron-lung and a wonderful side-by-side comparison of Thomas Jefferson and Ronald Reagan which noted such landmark accomplishments as, "Jefferson—founded the University of Virginia. Reagan—abolished free higher education in California, cut federal aid to education."

The October issue had a cover by Gahan Wilson, his first in years. There was another short story by Chris Miller, "Famous Last Words" by Bluestone, and, among an assortment of other goodies, a parody of Ted Turner's new technique for colorizing classic black-and-white movies in which the world's most memorable black-and-white paintings and photographs were colored. Included were da Vinci's "Vitruvian Man," Durer's "Hands In Prayer," the unforgettable photo of the Hindenburg disaster, and even the rising of the flag at Iwo Jima. It was *Lampoon* satire at its very best.

I wrote the editorial in the issue that, tongue imbedded firmly in cheek, asked Jerry Falwell to tell Donald Wildmon what great guys we were and call off his boycott. I ended: "We challenge you—Jerry—speak up! Tell him (and those advertisers who ran like hell in the face of the ground swell of approximately sixty-two letters) that we're part of the American Dream; that we have the right to be funny and, not infrequently, to irritate.

"And Jerry, if you don't speak up....

"We forgive you anyway."

ITEM: TAKING OVER TIME-LIFE

It's 1986 and we've not yet been a target for take-over attempts. Feeling ignored while American business, thrashing about in a feeding frenzy, devotes itself to swallowing each other, we decide to do something about it. The front-page story of the day has Ted Turner's young cable company trying to take over giant CBS and offering stockholders huge gobs of garbage in exchange for their stock. We dash off a letter to Time-Life notifying them that we are raiding their company and intend to take over. We explain further that we have little money and only some stock that we can spare, but that we're thinking of things we can give them in exchange for control of their billion-dollar company.

Notorious for their lack of humor, Time-Life does not reply to our letter which we then release to the nation's press. A guy from the Wall Street Journal calls to thank us "for brightening up an otherwise dimly lit day." Not offended that neither he nor Time-Life nor anyone else is taking us seriously, we decide on a frontal attack. The board of directors of our company will trek off to the Time-Life Building in an attempt to confront the chairman of that company with our threats. Of course, a photographer will photograph us as we leave our building, march along the streets, and arrive at our points of attack.

We start at Fifty-ninth Street and Madison Avenue. When we pass Fifty-fourth Street and Avenue of the Americas, we are spotted by an old friend, Tony Thomopoulos, the former president of ABC. He waves and smiles. Noting the photographer, he asks, "Where are you going?" I shrug. "We're taking over Time-Life." A puzzled look creases his face. "Oh?" he says. And we walk off.

At the Time-Life Building, we are asked to leave. The event is recorded for the pages of the Lampoon.

Story in Daily Variety on December 1, 1986:
LAMPOON NIXES MERGER OFFER

National Lampoon, Inc. has rejected a friendly offer from Vestron, Inc. to acquire through a merger, all of the Lampoon's outstanding shares, saying Vestron's offer, while above the stock's current market value, is "far short of what National Lampoon believes is the value of its company."

Asked if Vestron would make a new friendly offer, or perhaps attempt an unfriendly takeover, a Vestron spokesman said all options are being considered.

Vestron offered to pay four dollars a share for the out-standing 1,600,000 shares, making the deal worth about $6,400,000. As of Wednesday, the stock was being quoted at 3 1/8 bid, up 1/8.

Vestron declined to comment on reasons it's interested in acquiring Lampoon, though there would appear to be some natural video crossovers between the humor publica-tion-production company and the indie vidprogram supplier.

The key in the story was "friendly." Primarily in the video business, Vestron would later produce several films including the highly successful *Dirty Dancing*. The company's chairman Austin Furst had called me on a matter of "great importance and urgency." We met the following afternoon in his company's New York offices in a midtown hotel. With him was the president of his company, Strauss Zelnick, a young businessman who had apparently devised the agenda for the meeting and had planned the proposed take-over.

My son Michael was with me. As soon as we sat down, Zelnick asked if we wanted a drink. While he was getting them, Furst, a large, imposing man, reached out and handed me a letter. "My lawyer says I have to give you this in writing," he told me. The letter stated that Vestron wished to acquire the *Lampoon* and would offer the stockholders four dollars a share for their holdings. I tossed it on the floor and looked at them. Zelnick was now standing in front of us, a drink in each hand. I was furious.

"What ever happened to, 'Hey, are you interested in discussing a deal?'" I asked. Furst retreated. Zelnick offered the drinks which we ignored.

"Listen," I said, "this may be your style of doing business in your yuppie world but it's not mine. We've never even thought about being acquired, but if we did, it wouldn't be for four bucks a share, and it wouldn't be like this!" Michael and I stood up and turned to leave. Zelnick, who was still holding the drinks, said to us, rather meekly, "You're required to report this offer to your board of directors." We left. It was not a "friendly" offer or a "friendly" meeting.

The *Lampoon* board dismissed the offer summarily. A few years later, Vestron was to become one of the first of the eighties baby-boom companies to go through a major bankruptcy. Zelnick was rewarded sometime later for having steered Vestron to failure by being named president of Twentieth-Century Fox.

As noted, the story appeared in the film trade journals. It also appeared prominently in the *Wall Street Journal* and in other newspapers around the country. When it did, we started to get calls.

A group headed by the former president of Golden West Broadcasting, Anthony Cassara, arrived with an offer of $6.25 a share, more that 50 percent above the Vestron offer. Hours later, another syndicate, this headed by Mark Shanker, a

274 "IF YOU DON'T BUY THIS BOOK,

former executive of the film and video company Nelson Entertainment upped the offer to $6.75. And then Thom Mount called and asked if he could see me.

A year or so after *Animal House*, Mount had succeeded Ned Tanen as president of the film division at Universal Studios. Not too long after that he'd been replaced by the next man on the totem pole, Sean Daniel. Now, Mount was doing what all former studio heads do while waiting to be named head of another studio, producing. He'd done well with the Kevin Costner—Tim Robbins baseball film *Bull Durham* but had lost a fortune (his investors') on a Roman Polanski bomb called *The Pirate*. Now, he wanted to acquire the *National Lampoon*, presumably had the backing, and was prepared to offer $7 a share.

When, in the next day's newspapers, that offer was announced, Shanker upped his bid to $7.10 per share plus a seventy-five cent warrant for each *Lampoon* outstanding warrant. Cassara and his associate, lawyer George Vandeman, beseeched me to take their offer. In addition to the more than $12 million needed to purchase the stock, they said they would raise an additional $85 million for the development, financing, and production of twelve *National Lampoon* films as well as pump money into the publishing business.

The frenzy of the bids and the calls from the press continued. The Cassara group raised their offer to $7.25 a share plus one dollar for each warrant. Mount, like Vestron, dropped out. Shanker went to $7.50. Cassara matched the deal.

By this time, we'd drawn a report on everyone who was courting us. The Cassara group looked the best by far. They were backed by Furman, Selz, a well-known investment banking firm, and had bought television stations in the past for even bigger numbers than were being discussed here.

On December 12, less than two weeks after Vestron had made its initial move, we accepted the Cassara deal. In the process, we'd incur hundreds of thousands of dollars in bills for legal services. The deal made sense in every way. The company needed financing to shore up its publishing division and to develop new movies and even finance moderately budgeted *Lampoon* films. Cassara wanted the current management to stay, so everybody's job, including mine, was safe. And, of course, the stockholders would be bought out at an excellent price for their ownership in the company. It was more than a "friendly" deal, it was totally simpatico.

The buyers spent months arranging to put the money together. Vandeman had assured us that the money was in place and that the deal would be closed in sixty days. We started to get antsy but were constantly reassured.

Late in May, he notified us that they'd been unable to raise the capital they needed. The other offers we had passed on to accept theirs were gone. As a condition of the purchase, we had been on hold for nearly six months, unable to enter into any new contracts or do anything that might discernibly indicate change. On May 25, 1986, we announced that the acquisition had been terminated. The price of *Lampoon* stock, which had risen from three and a quarter to seven on the strength of the deal, would drop to two and a quarter by year-end.

The expense of the merger, notably the one-time legal costs, would be the difference between profit and loss in 1987.

Something else had happened in 1986. Len Mogel retired.

Len and I had worked together since 1951 when I was a very young New York press agent and he a slightly older printing salesman. In addition to doing publicity, I was learning to be a marketing man on the job at the Diners' Club, edging for the first time into advertising and direct mail. One of the first things I'd done was to start publishing a small newsletter called the "Diners' Club News" which was inserted in the bills going to members.

Mogel came calling one day, and I gave his company the printing of the "News." A few months later I had a notion. "You know," I suggested to Len, "if you went out and sold advertising to restaurants and other places handling the Diners' Club card, we could have a bigger newsletter, and you would be selling us more printing." I also agreed to pay him a commission on each ad he sold. Soon, he left the printing business and for sixteen years he would run the advertising and production end of the magazine which I edited while still directing the company's sales and marketing. By 1953, I had left the publicity business, the "Diners' Club News" became the *Diners' Club Magazine*, and within five years it had a circulation of well more than a million, featured prominent writers, and was the most influential travel and dining magazine of its time. By 1960, it was making a profit of three million dollars a year. In 1963, we changed the name to *Signature*.

When, in 1967, I decided to leave the Diners' Club, Mogel came with me, and we started the company that was to become National Lampoon, Inc..

Over the years he wrote numerous textbooks on publishing and started to prefer teaching to the frenetic life of magazine publishing, especially *National Lampoon* magazine publishing. When he left, he moved to California where he still writes and teaches.

A strange thing happened at the magazine in 1987 and 1988. People were working together and enjoying it. They actually liked each other.

Something happened in my personal life, too. For nearly two years after my marriage ended, I dated a number of different women. Always, I maintained my firm belief that I would never again get seriously involved. In 1987, I met a transplanted Canadian by the name of Patti Browne. Since this was Hollywood, it was not extraordinary that we were introduced at a birthday party for a 150-pound Rhodesian Ridgeback named Banker, owned by an actress named Kathy Baumann. I was fascinated by Patti at once. She was beautiful, smart, and charming. She was the most honest person I'd ever known. She said exactly what she thought and yet was uncommonly kind and thoughtful. Wow! I was in love! Like me, she has just ended a marriage and like me, professed no interest in getting married again. We dated very casually for nearly a year, both reassuring each other and ourselves that we didn't want to get serious. Patti had a long background in the movie business, and I asked her to join me at National Lampoon Films. At first, she demurred, then she became my associate.

In early 1990, we were married at the Beverly Hills home of our good friends, Helen and Marvin Meyer. It was a lovely, simple garden wedding.

Later that year, Kate Bradley Simmons joined this new family grouping. At three, she is already totally in charge.

In August 1987, we sold the television rights of the name *National Lampoon* to the Barris Company for one million dollars. The deal was for five years and would include profit participation for the *Lampoon* on all shows produced under the agreement. It also gave us a strong selling partner for TV projects we might develop. We had not been on television since 1979 and in the period since, had produced only two specials for cable networks and a couple of pilots. We had not exactly been thriving in the television business. Everybody agreed, this was a helluva deal for us.

In 1988, we started to prepare for the magazine's twentieth anniversary due in 1990. Fox Broadcasting agreed to air a ninety-minute tribute to the *Lampoon* on our anniversary date in April of that year. But we weren't going to have the usual dreary parade of platitudes and backslapping. Our plan was to have people like Bill Murray, Chevy Chase, and others filmed at their homes or, better yet, while on movie sets, trying in any way possible to avoid any further affiliation with the *Lampoon*. We would mix this with reenactments of various sketches and songs from *Lampoon* shows, film clips, and a never before shown tape, or at least parts of the tape that could be shown on television, from *Lemmings*.

We had another idea. We'd form yet-another touring company and travel it around the country to mark the anniversary. Our plan was to start touring the show in 1989 and culminate it soon after the birthday. We met with Nissan's advertising people, and they agreed to completely underwrite such a venture. The William Morris Agency eagerly agreed to book the tour. And, of course, we'd feature the best material in the twenty-year history.

All this activity was stimulating interest in the *Lampoon* all over again. We were well into our third comeback.

I spent all of 1987 and '88 traveling between the two coasts. At Warner Bros., we were developing numerous properties but producing none. My relationship with Mark Canton, now head of film production, continued to be close, but we couldn't get out of "development hell."

In 1987, John Ptak had come to me with an interesting proposal that became one of the deals put on hold because of the prospective merger with the Cassara group. A French-

Canadian company, FilmAccord, run by a personable Frenchman named Michel Roy and financed by the huge European bank, Credit Lyonnais, made us an offer to form a company called National Lampoon Films to develop and produce comedies. FilmAccord, via the bank, would finance everything. We would produce and the *Lampoon* and FilmAccord would be equal partners. At this point, Credit Lyonnais had already started funding several FilmAccord films (not comedies).

I liked Michel. He was loquacious and flamboyant—and he had access to all this money. We made the deal.

Credit Lyonnais had insisted that before we start producing anything, we make a deal with a distributor. I suggested Warner Bros. I had worked with them since the first *Vacation*, and the relationship had been mutually profitable. Terry Semel, Warner's president, had assured me, some years before, that they'd be interested in distributing *Lampoon* films if we ever went the independent route, but Ptak had a different idea. "Why be a little fish in a big pond," he reasoned, not ashamed to employ that old bromide, "when you can be a big shot somewhere else." He wasn't ashamed to mix a metaphor either, but his suggestion did make sense and he had a small "pond" in mind. Bernie Brillstein, who made a fortune managing Belushi, Aykroyd, Lorne Michaels, and other stars, writers, and producers, had just been named to head Lorimar, and they were forming a film distribution network. They would welcome a deal with National Lampoon Films.

For six months, deal memos went back and forth, and meetings went on and on, then, Lorimar collapsed. Brillstein went back to the management business, and we still had no distributor, which meant no production money from Credit Lyonnais.

Eventually, Lorimar was bought by—Terry Semel at Warner Bros. But before that, Ptak, still adhering to his "small pond" theory, brought us to MGM. Once the most powerful of all film studios, MGM had virtually been out of business for years. Now, under the management of Alan Ladd, Jr., and with substantial European financing supposedly in place, it was attempting to regain its traditional position among the giants.

While we were negotiating with MGM, Credit Lyonnais put up additional monies for development, and in a few months we were ready to go with our first production, *National Lampoon's Family Dies*. I had no taste for horror spoofs or overly broad comedy after *Class Reunion*, but this script by English director Piers Ashworth changed my mind. Michel Roy shared my enthusiasm for it.

It had been brought to us by a young producer named Brad Wyman and the actor Emilio Estevez whose concept the film was. It was agreed, I would produce the film; they would be executive producers; and Brad would be my right-hand man. The story was about a sweet, lonely, slightly demented young man who accidentally kills his mother and then visits her grave daily. Eventually, he turns grave robber and brings home an entire family plus the family dog—all very dead—to stay with him. Thanks to the magic of the movies, they all come alive. The rest is pure bedlam.

MGM liked the script, but once again, the negotiations were dragging on. By mid-1988, there was still no deal. And then, like Lorimar, MGM just fell apart.

Ladd left and MGM settled back into the netherworld. He was to return some years later and briefly took over the company with the financial backing of—Credit Lyonnais, eventually being replaced by our old Paramount nemesis, Frank Mancuso. Somewhere in there, helping to put it all together, was John Ptak who had moved from the William Morris Agency to CAA, the entertainment industry powerhouse.

National Lampoon Films was still scrambling for a distributor late in 1988 when I got a call from Canton at Warner Bros. We met the next day. John Hughes had written a third *Vacation* script, *Christmas Vacation*. Chevy had already seen it and was eager to do it. Since I'd already been cut out of the early stages of what had always been my project, I waited for what was coming next. "Hughes wants to produce it himself," Mark told me. "This in no way affects our deal with you except that you'd be executive producer. You get the same money as if you were producing, and the *Lampoon* gets the contracted fee for use of its name."

There was nothing for me to say. The fees added up to three quarters of a million dollars and, of course, there were the profits that would likely accrue from another *Vacation* movie. Mark assured me sadly that if I refused to go along with this, Hughes would pull the script. No script. No Chevy. No movie. I told him to go ahead and make the movie. He asked me if I would visit the set regularly once shooting began in 1989. Hughes, he felt, would surely disappear once the pre-production casting and selection of director and crew was finished. And, Mark added, he would feel good knowing that in some way I had a presence during the shooting of the film. I said I would.

I have never quite been able to figure out the reason for Hughes's animosity to me. This was surely a slap in the face. I had brought him into the film business by the hand. The only problem we ever had was about the clearly unfinished script he turned in for *European Vacation*. Certainly, we could have produced this picture together. I had never been an executive producer before. Usually that title goes to the guy who puts the money together or the star's manager or the director's girl friend. I had always been a hands-on producer, involved with just about every key decision in the making of a film. Now we were discussing my "visiting" for the second sequel to a picture that I had nurtured from the beginning, brought to the studio, and produced in every conceivable way. I didn't blame Canton or Warner Bros. The picture would be a surefire winner, and Hughes, by now, was the most important comedy writer and director in the film business.

The next year, Warners would put a Hughes picture into turnaround (release it for production elsewhere) because of a disagreement with him over the budget. The film wound up at Fox and became the biggest grossing comedy of all time, and it is estimated that Hughes earned more than forty million dollars on it. It was, of course, *Home Alone*.

In the December 1988 issue of the *Lampoon*, Lance Contrucci, a gifted parodist, did a take on Tom Wolfe's best seller, Contrucci's being called "The Bonfires of the Banalities." Gerry Sussman's painstaking parody of the Yellow Pages was so precise and satirical that it could well have been a book of it' own.

And Sloman had fun with Hugh Hefner's latest romantic liaison, with the by-then-spurned lady actually posing for the *Lampoon* cover. Will Durst wrote "Remembering Reagan's Best Years—Somebody Has To," and Rick Meyerowitz did one of his series of caricatures for another feature, "Bye Bye Bozo." Reagan was leaving office, and we were wondering if Bush would be nearly as funny.

Southern Comfort, Newport, Camels, and other national advertisers were back and, except for 7-Eleven-owned stores, most of the retail outlets who had banned us during the Wildmon boycott, were carrying us again.

ITEM: MY GOD! WE'VE KILLED A CHICKEN!

We had a run-in with MTV over a television commercial we ran in which a housewife talked of her love of the Lampoon while chopping up a chicken for dinner. When they stopped running the ad because they considered it "distasteful," we released the following statement which was picked up widely by the press: "In television's world of illicit love affairs, under-the-cover romps, bikini-clad pitch people, rock videos choreographed with whips, chains and leather, lying politicians, overstated commercials, overpaid athletes, mediocre talents, hard sell and soft porn, we have had our commercial pulled because we showed a housewife chopping a dead, plucked chicken."

This, of course, was the network that would later feature "Beavis and Butthead."

We decided to do another show, a Broadway musical. Michael Simmons came up with an idea. "It's 2076 and America is about to celebrate its tricentennial. And in song and dance and sketches, we look back at the past three hundred years, including, of course, the eighty-six or so we haven't lived yet."

We all loved it. Nelle Nugent, a veteran Broadway producer, was a friend. I told her the plan and the proposed theme. She was equally enthused and a few weeks later brought Jujamsu, a major Broadway theater operator and backer of plays, onto the scene. They would put up the money. Nelle would run the business end. I would produce, and Michael and other members of the staff and regular contributors would write it.

With Mogel gone, George Agoglia, who had worked for me as a bookkeeper at the Diners' Club, was doing the projections. Just before Christmas of 1988, he finished his forecast for 1989. His previous prognostications had been dead-on. Now he told me that he estimated that the company would earn just under three quarters of a million dollars for 1989. He projected further a 50 percent increase in advertising sales and an additional 20 percent jump in circulation. For the first time since 1981, he indicated, the publishing division would be in the black. The advertising projections were easy since many contracts for 1989 ads were already in the house. The circulation increases actually came from our distributing company and were based on our having been welcomed back at many retail outlets.

Comeback number one came with *Animal House* in 1978.

Comeback number two, with the new staff and austere cutbacks in 1984.

Comeback number three, back from the ashes of the sordid Wildmon affair, from "Baby in the Blender," and from the diversions and costs of the aborted mergers, was definitely underway. In a way, it almost felt like the old days were back.

In 1988, an industry study by the Market Research Institute had revealed some interesting facts about *Lampoon* readers. First of all, there were, at this point, about 2 million of them. Advertisers were paying to reach only the 250,000 who bought the magazine and not the pass-along audience, those who shared it with the purchaser, so they were getting a free bonus of readership of 1.75 million. Then, and these were the most surprising figures unearthed, the average age of the reader was 27.8 which indicated that a lot of people who read the magazine in its early years remained with it, and their average income was $37,000 a year. Both these figures were up considerably from surveys taken in the seventies. It was not, as had been bandied about in the press, a kid's magazine. The results of the study were stunning and, once again, advertising agencies started paying attention to the *Lampoon*.

By February 1989, shortly before the eventual sale of my stock, the *Lampoon* had not been assaulted since Wildmon. The Reagan years were gone, Bush was just kind of hapless, and most people were beginning to get the idea that, hey, free speech and freedom of the press and the right to ridicule or put down people and ideas aren't such a bad things after all. Right-wing ministers were going to jail or being caught in motel rooms with hookers or with their hands in the cash register, so, it seemed they didn't have much time for a magazine which continued to emphasize life's little absurdities.

That very month, the *Lampoon* published an article by Nick Bakay called "Diarrhetics." It was a most unflattering satire of the late L. Ron Hubbard's popular cult-philosophy Scientology. The gist of it was that those who joined this group had to surrender their money, their independence, and their common sense. With five pages jammed with reviews of books by Hubbard like *Suck Them Dry* and *Your Money Can Kill You*, "interviews" with such Scientology followers as John Travolta and Karen Black, and tests, advice, and charts, which all pretty well suggested that "these people are after your money," the piece was, let us say, less than favorable.

What happened over the next two months was in some ways unparalleled even in the "let's kill these guys" life of the *National Lampoon*. Private investigators started checking on the editors, speaking to former employees, and dropping suggestions that the editors were involved in drug trafficking, money laundering, and pornography (there we go again).

Andy Simmons soon realized that when he walked his dog he was being trailed by two burly men—yes—in trench coats. It was all right out of a spy novel. Now, they were knocking on his neighbors' doors asking about his habits and suggesting that he was in deep trouble, that it was possible he was involved in drug rackets and worse. Their comments were so absurd that the neighbors immediately repeated them to Andy.

The stalkers finally confronted Andy in his apartment. He immediately called his brother Michael who arrived simultaneously with the return of the phone to its perch. The men identified themselves as private investigators hired by a Los Angeles law firm to investigate the *Lampoon*. One then said he had proof that Michael had a drinking problem. "Incredible!" Michael answered. "I've been writing about it in the *Lampoon* for two years. ["Drinking Tips."] How'd you find out?" The discussion was cut short when Andy decided to walk his dog, and all four men left the apartment. In the *Lampoon* article he wrote some months later, Michael described what happened next.

"Andy subsequently took his fifteen-year-old schnauzer, Phineas, for a walk. Minutes before, these two foot soldiers had told Andy that while they themselves were not violent men, there were those who were so bothered by what the *National Lampoon* had printed that some wouldn't mind seeing Phineas cut in half. When Andy and Phineas hit the street, our Nazis-for-hire were waiting with cameras in hand. Somewhere in the bowels of a tall building of a world-famous cult are photographs of my brother with dogshit in a pooper-scooper and a huge smile on his face."

Some research later filled us in on the two men who were apparently part of a goon squad hired by the cult to intimi-date members of the press who write or might write disparaging articles about their movement. One, it turned out, was Eugene M. Ingram who, according to newspaper reports, had been kicked off the L.A. police force for various shady activities, including allegedly running a house of prostitution.

In an investigative story in 1990, the *Los Angeles Times* reported that this type of harassment was regular policy when dealing with reporters and other critics of Scientology.

Hubbard's wife and ten other Scientologists had been jailed in the seventies for bugging and burglarizing U.S. government agencies that were looking into their activities. Once when they were put on trial, one of their private detectives investigated the sex life of the judge, then leaked rumors to a Washington columnist who printed them. Soon after, the judge resigned from the case.

L. Ron Hubbard's writings have been the inspiration for this type of activity. "Never," he wrote, "agree to an investigation of Scientology. Only agree to an investigation of the attackers ... start feeding lurid evidence on the attacker to the press. Don't submit."

A British lawmaker in a report to his government observed, "Anyone whose attitude is such as Mr. Hubbard displays cannot be too surprised that the world treats him with suspicion rather than affection."

They were never heard from at the *Lampoon* again, but only a few months later we would laugh about it and think, "Wouldn't it have been funny if they started terrorizing Grodnik and Matheson?"

CHAPTER TWENTY-FOUR

SINCE THE mid-eighties the *Lampoon* had been attracting some unlikely investors. In 1988, I was the largest single stockholder with approximately 12 percent of the stock or slightly more than 126,000 shares. The second largest owner of *Lampoon* stock was the Des Moines General Hospital which owned more than 100,000 shares and, according to its representative, Dennis Barsky, was being advised in its investments by the Wall Street guru Warren Buffet. The third largest individual holder of stock was another midwesterner, an investor from Elkhorn, Nebraska, who also intimated that he relied heavily on Buffet before making decisions. His name was Alan Parsow, and at one point he owned close to 80,000 shares in the company. Neither before they appeared or since had any of us ever heard from Buffet, and there is no record that he ever owned any stock in the company. It was clear, however, that the most notorious Wall Street name of the eighties *was* very much involved with the company. Drexel-Burnham, soon to disappear in a blaze of greed and deception, by 1988, represented more than 30 percent of the outstanding stock in the *National Lampoon*.

George Agoglia and I spoke daily when I was in Los Angeles, and in further discussions, he reaffirmed his forecast of profits for 1989. The third *Vacation* movie alone would mean substantial income, and as usual, royalties from *Animal*

House and the earlier *Vacation* pictures would be in six figures. As he had predicted earlier, magazine circulation and advertising sales were going up and overhead was going down.

Just before New Year's, Tim Matheson, Otter in *Animal House*, called me. On the phone, he introduced me to Dan Grodnik who he described as his partner. They then told me that they had accumulated nearly 100,000 shares in the company over the past months, and, more than that, they were now holding proxies for the stock owned by the Des Moines General Hospital and Alan Parsow and others and, in total, represented approximately 22 percent of the *Lampoon*'s stock.

I was stunned. They went on to say that they would be demanding three seats on the board of directors and wanted to be elected copresidents of the company. They assured me that they wanted me to stay as chairman and chief executive officer.

When I hung up, I called our lawyers and set up a meeting, then I called Dennis Barsky at Des Moines General to be told that he had left the hospital days before. I called Alan Parsow with whom I'd always had a pleasant relationship. He confirmed that he had given Grodnik and Matheson his proxy, then he explained. The "Co-Bros," as they would come to be known for their need to share titles and everything else, were being guided by—David Batchelder.

Batchelder had been T. Boone Picken's chief take-over strategist. Pickens was, of course, one of the dominant corporate raiders of the time. Batchelder had planned the entire scenario for Grodnik and Matheson. It was he who had called the hospital and apparently assured them that the move would mean huge profits on their investment in the *Lampoon* and who then called Parsow. Parsow needed little persuasion. When you're sitting out there in Elkhorn, a call from the guy who headed T. Boone Pickens brain trust is such a kick for your ego that you'll agree to anything. Parsow, with no idea whether the two guys had ever run a company, knew anything about publishing, or even had ever produced a successful movie (the business they purported to be in at the time) just said, "yes" and turned over his votes.

So, this was a take-over. My next call was to Bob Becker, the broker at Drexel-Burnham who represented most of the investors there holding *Lampoon* stock. He hadn't heard from Batchelder. "Look," he assured me, "we recommended this stock because we liked its management. We think the company can come back, and if it does, it'll be because you made it happen. I can tell you unequivocally, if there's a proxy fight, we're with you."

I breathed more easily. With the Drexel stock, my own, my children's, and the support of other employees and friends who owned stock, I could now count on a majority. Grodnik and Matheson called back. They asked for a meeting to which they would bring Batchelder. We met in New York and talked for hours. To honor the substantial holdings they represented, I agreed to give them three seats on a seven-man board of directors. The other seats were held by me, my son Michael, George Agoglia, and Howard Jurofsky, a longtime company executive. The four-to-three edge meant that control of the company stayed with me. I turned down their request for a copresidency, reminding them that it seemed to me that they brought nothing to that job (cojobs) that would benefit the company. It was agreed that Alan Parsow would be their selection as the third member of the board. We would present the new slate to the stockholders at the earliest possible time.

By now the press around the country had picked up the story and described it as an "unfriendly" take-over attempt. I tried to deny such stories but on January 17, Grodnik and

Matheson filed papers with the Securities and Exchange Commission indicating that they would eventually become copresidents. My answer to the press was that it had been agreed that they would serve as advisors but that neither I nor the board had agreed that they would be officers of the company. I had carefully stated that to them and in press announcements.

We were like two dogs each standing the length of a leash away from each other and snarling. Unlike the Cassara deal which seemed to have the right ingredients—namely— people of supposed stature and backers with deep pockets, this one was all wrong. They talked of raising money for the company, but that would come after they gained entry. Their own involvement only added salaries and expenses and confusion to a company that needed restraint and competence. Like Michael Wolff, a few years earlier, they brought no background in business to the table. Their manner and lack of savvy would, I knew, only result in constant problems with me. I stood my ground. If they wanted to fight, I'd fight.

Then, sometime in late February, they called to tell me that Drexel-Burnham had agreed to support them in their demands for a copresidency. Later the same day I spoke to Becker who told me that he and his son, also a Drexel broker, had flown to Los Angeles the previous weekend and had spent an entire day with Grodnik and Matheson. They were impressed and were convinced that they could make important contributions to the company. He would, he said further, continue to support me as chairman.

I hung up, astounded. What could they have possibly seen in these two guys that could have impressed them? Matheson had been one of the stars of one successful movie, *Animal House*, then had a less-than-spectacular ten years or so in a string of failed or totally mediocre films and TV shows. When I'd asked him, he'd admitted he had no prior business experience. Grodnik's background was even less impressive. A film producer, his best-known feature had been *Mad* magazine's attempt to follow *Animal House* with something called *Up The Academy*. It had failed miserably at the box office and critically as well.

When the news stories were appearing almost daily on their proposed take-over, Mark Canton, president of Warner Bros., asked me, "How could you get involved with those guys, a failed movie actor and a 'meerskite?'" A meerskite can loosely be interpreted from Yiddish to mean, a weird, little loser.

But, of course, there were two things: Batchelder had to have set up the Becker meeting and been there, and both Batchelder and his credentials *were* impressive. He was glib and smart and successful, and he was pushing these guys. And secondly, there was Matheson's charm. Matheson had been so good as Otter because he *was* Otter. He was good-looking, and he came across as being a genuinely sweet guy and a smart guy. He was neither sweet nor terribly smart. He had been smart enough to come up with Batchelder who was to be paid heavily by the company once they took over, but he wasn't smart enough to know that a business should be run by people who know what they're doing.

A week after Drexel's defection, I decided that fighting any longer would hurt both the company and me. But I wasn't interested in being chairman of the board of a company that could be controlled by other people, and certainly with a majority of the stockholders now in their corner, a change in the makeup of the board in their favor was inevitable. I met with Grodnik and Matheson at a restaurant called Le Dome on Sunset Boulevard in West Hollywood. It was four o'clock in the afternoon, and we were the only customers in the place. We drank bottled water and talked. I told them that I wasn't interested in staying with the *Lampoon* under these circumstances. I had an employment contract which ran for another five years, but I was willing to leave and turn the management of the company over to them if they agreed to terms I had prepared, terms not as imposing as those in my contract.

First, they had to buy my 126,000 shares of *Lampoon* stock at $7 a share. The market price that day was around $5.25 a share. And they'd have to buy out the 33,000 stock options I held, at the difference between my option price and the market price.

Next, I wanted a four-year consulting agreement—a normal procedure involving a chief executive officer of a public company, much less the founding officer. This was a year less than my contract with the company called for.

Third, I wanted an office and secretary and the company car I was presently driving for the four years I was to consult. This was in my employment contract. Along with this, they would continue my medical insurance.

It was to be agreed further that I would produce all *Lampoon* films then in development as well as any sequels to films already produced. This meant that I would produce the upcoming *Christmas Vacation*. And from here on in, I, and not the company, would be paid directly by a studio for my producing or executive producing services.

Lastly, but a must, two-year employment agreements had to be extended to Agoglia, Jurofsky, the company treasurer Walter Garibaldi, and my son Michael, all officers of the company. I did not ask for contracts for any of the editors, including my son Andy and my daughter Julie.

I agreed not to compete with the magazine during the term of the agreement and to be available for consultation.

The "Co-Bros," who would soon name themselves cochairmen and copresidents as well as cochief executive officers, had read my employment agreement and knew that what I was asking for, except for the buyout of my stock and the contracts for the executives, was covered in that agreement and that it would hold up in court should they decide to battle for and win control of the company. This would be an easy, painless way for them, and it meant that I would tell the world that I had prompted their buying me out, which was true in a way comparable to someone saying, "I give up!" while being beaten to a pulp. The take-over stigma would not be there.

They agreed to everything I asked for, but I left the restaurant with a sick, empty feeling. I felt that I had betrayed myself by trying to be practical. I had just made millions of dollars, and it was the worst day of my life in business. As I drove through the streets, I wanted to call the deal off, to fight, even just to lose, but I didn't.

Anyone in the film business with the kind of success I'd had as a producer would have made tens of millions of dollars on such successes. I'd earned only my salary plus a modest annual bonus. Ivan Reitman, my coproducer on *Animal House*, had made millions on the picture.

Aside from producing the movies, I'd founded the company and run it since its inception. I'd also been the editor of *Weight Watchers Magazine* and *Liberty*, did all the hiring and firing and executive decision making (outside of advertising and production) on the *Lampoon*, and for five years was that magazine's editor-in-chief. I'd made the decisions to go into theater and into the movies and produced nearly all of the shows and films. When the company had been on the verge of bankruptcy, I'd called on my personal relationship with Steve Ross to keep it afloat.

If, over the next four years, the new management would pay me the balance of the money they owed me, it would mean that I earned less than $120,000 a year in addition to the salaries I drew over the twenty-two-year span. There wasn't one complaint from the stockholders or any suggestion in the press at the time that the deal was particularly "sweet."

Only Sean Kelly and his cries of anguish would be heard in Michael Wolff's article.

"You know," John Weidman said to me recently, "Sean and Tony were just bitter. They ragged about Henry and Doug getting all that money as much as Sean did when you sold control of the company. Look at it this way, these were guys who were in the core years of their careers at the *Lampoon*, and, like most people, they wanted to get rich. It had nothing to do with you but with the frustration and discontent that while people around them were making millions, they never would."

I left a group filled with uncertainty at the magazine, including my own kids, despite the contracts I'd insisted on for the executives. Grodnik and Matheson met with everyone and assured them that "millions" would be pumped into the magazine to resuscitate it. Larry Sloman was made the top editor to replace me. Agoglia was still in charge of the New York office, but they would rely heavily on Julian Weber for advice and Howard Jurofsky, who was always a strong and loyal management man. Agoglia started thinking about retiring well before his two-year contract expired.

By July, a little more than three months after they took over, the "Co-Bros" started looking for a new editor. They also gave themselves a salary—a "cosalary"—of $300,000 dollars a year. It was well in excess of the salary I had been drawing as chairman, president, editor-in-chief, and producer after twenty-two years with the company. The "cosalary" was supposedly being split by the two but, apparently, the time on the job wasn't. Matheson continued his acting career, and even Grodnik would complain about his long absences.

I called them regularly, offering to fulfill my end of the deal and consult, but they'd quite obviously decided that my advice was unnecessary.

And then things—bad things—started to happen.

The plans for the twentieth anniversary celebration collapsed when Fox called off the ninety-minute tribute they'd been excited about only months earlier.

Nissan said that they'd only been interested in backing a touring show if the man who'd produced *Lemmings* and *Animal House* was involved. I was willing, but Grodnik and Matheson would have no part of it.

Michael Simmons left and the stage show he'd conceived, *National Lampoon's Tricentennial*, just evaporated.

Michael, who'd been an officer of the company and was one of those given two-year contracts, was dismissed by communique. He arrived at work one morning, opened his office door, and found a letter on the floor. It was from the "Co-Bros" notifying him that his services were no longer required. He sued and the case was eventually settled.

A few months after Michael's firing, my son Andy opened his door to discover a similar message.

My daughter Julie, who literally produced the *Heavy Metal* editorial package by herself, stayed with the company for several years, leaving that magazine shortly after it was sold.

As soon as Grodnik and Matheson took over, they decided that the Barris television deal was no good and that

they'd either figure out a way to end the relationship or nego-
tiate a deal with Barris to buy back the five-year contract that
would expire in 1992.

They also decided that I'd made a big mistake with the
FilmAccord deal and notified that company that they were
breaking the agreement. Backed by Credit Lyonnais and
already having invested time and money in developing
Lampoon product, FilmAccord immediately sued, claiming millions in damages.

Their search for a new editor-in-chief wasn't going well
either. Prospective choices would meet with Grodnik and
Matheson and quickly decide they didn't want the job.

Meanwhile, Dave Hanson who, with Andy Simmons,
had been the most prolific and funniest writer on the *Lampoon*
in years, quit and joined the newly formed Comedy Channel.

But the worst thing that was happening was what was not
happening. Batchelder, who'd assured Grodnik and Matheson
that there would be new funding once they took over the
company, either couldn't or didn't want to come up with more
money. Now, he and his proteges started bickering over the
sizeable fees he'd been promised.

George Agoglia's projections for the year had indicated a
healthy profit for 1989, but those projections did not foresee
the additional salary for two new executives plus the expenses
involved in their traveling to New York from their base in Los
Angeles and substantial fees for Batchelder. Mostly, it did not
figure on money wasted on bad ideas and bad vibrations.
People who'd been doing business with the *Lampoon* for years
suddenly decided they'd rather not continue the relationship.

In the fiscal year 1989, losses were $1.5 million. The pre-
vious three years had been difficult, but the total loss for those
years was just about the same as the Grodnik-Matheson man-

agement had lost in the one year. The first quarter of 1989 had been under my management and had shown a profit of $300,000. So the loss for the nine months of the new management had even been greater, approximately $1.8 million. Agoglia, with all the facts and figures now available for 1989, confirmed that, without question, the year, had it continued under the original management and with the same overhead, would have shown a profit.

It was inconceivable to him, and to me, that the *Lampoon*, with the smallest staff in its history, housed in low rent quarters, and with its highest sales in several years, should lose money.

CHAPTER TWENTY-FIVE

ONE CHANGE Warners asked me to make for *Christmas Vacation* was in production credits. Hughes was insisting on "A John Hughes Production" which would replace my usual contracted credit, "A Matty Simmons Production." I agreed immediately. I have never understood the desperate need in the film industry to have multiple credits. If you get a "Produced by" credit, why would you need "A Matty Simmons Production" as well? I had accepted the two credits on previous pictures because it was the way things were done but I could never figure out why both were necessary. Now, directors are also getting two credits, "Directed by" and "A Film by," as though they might not be noticed with merely one.

On the set, I felt like the bride's father at a wedding—not much to do but walk around and chat. If the actors had problems, I tried to help them. If they had an attack of nerves, I reassured them. I made suggestions to the director, Jeremiah Chechik, and some to Chevy who—like he was during the filming of the first *Vacation*—was easy to work with and always willing to listen. As far as I was concerned, the problems we'd had on *European Vacation* happened because, as I've said, both of us had been going through difficult personal times.

I had little authority on *Christmas Vacation*, but no one seemed to have any and none seemed particularly needed. It was the second sequel to a hit film, and the two stars were

301

totally familiar and comfortable with their roles. It, unlike the first two *Vacations*, was basically shot at the studio in L.A. so everyone was home and relaxed.

The supporting cast was comprised of mostly veteran actors who were thoroughly professional, knew their lines, and were always ready and on time. Chechik was a pleasant fellow shooting his first theatrical movie, but with an imposing background in commercials and a wealth of knowledge about film.

It was the easiest shoot ever, if not the most scintillating.

It didn't have the excitement or camaraderie of the first *Vacation* or the challenge of the second. It was simply by the numbers, and it went without a hitch.

Hughes was never, to the best of my knowledge, on the set. His right-hand man at the time, Tom Jacobson, was in charge. Jacobson would, soon after the film opened, become head of production at Twentieth-Century Fox. His wife, Susan Arnold, had worked as a casting director on the first *Vacation* and she and I were friends. He was cordial to me during the *Christmas Vacation* shoot, but there was none of the usual kinship of two people making a movie together. It was quite apparent that Hughes had spoken.

Hughes not showing up on the set of a movie he was producing astounded me. My own approach to producing always has been to "be there," on the set or attending to the film's business constantly. John's lack of attentiveness has had rather unusual and conflicting results. Many of his movies, obviously, have done very well, but they've done well because he's a marvelous screenwriter and his ear captures nuances and humor that escape most people until they see it on the screen. He's also produced quite a few duds, but most moviemakers have had their share of those, and I'm sure his success ratio, as far as box office is concerned, ranks with anyone.

What I feel Hughes's movies don't have, with exceptions, is sophistication or wit for anyone over twelve. They're actually kind of kid-dumb. I refer to a sophistication and wit which he could provide. He's not incapable of making a really good movie for adults, but he's turned himself into a mini-studio, grinding out three or four films a year, all of which he writes and for the most part, no longer directs and simply does not supervise on a day-to-day basis. Many of the best things in a movie are not in the original script but come from a daily relationship with the movie while it's being filmed. Lines and scenes and nuances are added by an actor, a director, or a producer on the set.

"A producer," John Ptak feels, "is often the guy with the dream. The guy who comes up with the story, shepherds it through development, then picks the director [with studio approval, my friends], and, with him, casts the movie. He then stands around nervously and watches and advises and comforts and worries and he kibitzes, adding lines here and thoughts there."

Hughes succeeds in the early stages and, it would seem, fails in the latter. Walter Matthau who starred in Hughes's *Dennis the Menace*, says, "He acts sometimes like Howard Hughes. He's hard to reach. I asked him once, 'How come you don't come around more often?' He said, 'Well, if things are going okay, I don't want to fuck them up.'" A colorful, if not exactly honest answer. The truth is that Hughes is busy working on his next six pictures while one or two are being shot. What happens is a sameness of plot—many of his films seem to be revised versions of earlier ones—and the lack of the intelligence and wit that we saw in some of his earlier scripts, notably *Vacation*, *The Breakfast Club*, and *Trains, Planes and Automobiles* but haven't seen much of in his busy recent years.

One wonders how good a movie this hugely talented man could create if he gave one his undivided attention. John Hughes can literally make any movie he wants. In that respect he is possibly even more powerful a moviemaker than Spielberg or Reitman, whose films generally are in a higher budget range and who do not write their own scripts. It is doubtful any studio will make the mistake Warners made when they put *Home Alone* into turnaround, although more recently his movies have either been only moderately successful or moderately unsuccessful, including a sequel to *Home Alone* which was an unabashed rewrite of the first film.

Christmas Vacation opened just before Thanksgiving of 1989 and grossed twelve million dollars over its first weekend. It was the number one picture at the box office for several weeks and ran strongly into January, finally grossing more than seventy million dollars at domestic box offices.

It was, as expected, a success. My own reaction to it was ambivalent. I wanted it to succeed because it was my movie or at least an offshoot of my movies, and because, more practically, its success obviously meant money for me. What bothered me about the picture was that, unlike *European Vacation*, which had been an original—if a somewhat often troubled original—in that it had the same lead characters but a new plot and new jokes, *Christmas* had been, as *Home Alone* 2 would be, a rewrite of the first film, set at Christmas instead of on the road

Unlike either of the first two movies, it had few big moments you'd remember well after you'd seen the movie. I felt that the most memorable scene in the picture was the one in which Chevy is locked in his attic, and after some Chaplin-like encounters with some faulty carpentry, he comes upon some home movies from his youth and a projector. His reactions, as he remembers years gone by, was Chevy at his best and first-rate movie making.

Christmas Vacation probably had more good reviews than the other *Vacation* movies. Almost nobody disliked it. A few critics had treated the earlier films poorly. Of course, nobody called it a "classic" either, and that was said or inferred by many about the first movie and a number of reviewers had enthused about the strong satire in the second.

During the filming of *Christmas*, I renewed my friendship with Randy Quaid who played Cousin Eddie. I told Randy about an idea I had for a spin-off to be called *Cousin Eddie* in which his character would lose the farm to a mortgage company and travel west in his dilapidated van with all his kids and the mutt Snots. Eddie would then battle upward mobility, and from a failure in Kansas, he'd become a success in Los Angeles.

He loved the idea. A month later, I pitched it to Bruce Berman, a bright, likable guy who had replaced Mark Canton at Warner Bros. He was equally enthusiastic, and we started developing a screenplay. Working with Rob Guralnick, Warner executive vice-president, we assigned Kevin Curran, then with "Married With Children," and Jeff Martin, a writer-producer with "The Simpsons," to write the script.

At the magazine, things were in a turmoil. George Agoglia was managing the day-to-day operations of the company with Howard Jurofsky in charge of production and distribution. Julian Weber, whose voice at the *Lampoon* had been heard only about legal matters since he left as president of the company in 1985, was Grodnik and Matheson's eyes and ears in New York as they continued to spend most of their time in Los Angeles or, in Matheson's case, on movie and television locations. With Andy Simmons gone, Ratso Sloman was now in total command of the editorial of the magazine. Sloman remembers the "Co-Bros" sadly.

"The funniest thing about them," he recalls, "was the way they set up their office. Two identical desks, identical chairs, phones. When I wrote them memos, I would put Grodnik's name first, then, on the next memo put Matheson's name first. At their request, we also alternated their names on the masthead, so the June issue would say 'Co-Publishers, Daniel Grodnik and Tim Matheson' and in the July issue that order would be reversed.

"I think they really did have good intentions to keep the magazine iconoclastic and antiestablishment. They understood, like the prior management, that the magazine was the core of the company and that all other things—the movies, whatever—orbited around it. It was vital to keep the *Lampoon* magazine alive and honest. They always struck me as being sincere, if inexperienced.

"I think they were totally misled by Batchelder and other financial guys who promised them financing but never came through."

Howard Jurofsky says, "The less than two years with Grodnik and Matheson was one disaster after another. They meant well. They simply had no business experience, and they tried to make extravagant changes without the money to support those changes. They hired a new publisher, Michael Carr, a good man with good ideas and good contacts, but he couldn't do anything without financial support, and they had no money."

In my own way, I tried to help. I agreed to delay payments due me from the company for months and on the few occasions we met, I tried to advise them. Once, I suggested that one of the most tangible things they could offer the company was Tim's celebrity and personality. I proposed that Tim make calls with the new publisher to such key accounts as Budweiser and Miller. Michael Carr had agreed with me that such visits would enhance their chances of getting stronger advertising contracts considerably, but Matheson dismissed it, saying he was too busy.

At no time in the first year did they seem to lose either their confidence or their swagger. They were always certain, it appeared, that they could come into this twenty-two-year-old company and solve all of its problems with solutions they'd not yet come up with and never would.

In his *Manhattan, Inc.* article, Michael Wolff described an interview he had with them in the late spring of 1989. "'We have a dream,' says Matheson, sitting in a Central Park South hotel room with Grodnik. The actor's face is tempered by a businessman's suit and by the earnestness with which he speaks about his vision of an entertainment conglomerate.

"'We want to be to comedy what MTV is to music,' the partners say in virtual unison. [A few weeks later, MTV, as well as HBO, would beat them to the punch by announcing plans for all-comedy cable networks.] They speak of comedy clubs and touring companies.

"'The *Lampoon* is just one aspect of what we have in mind,' Matheson says. 'We have big plans,' says Grodnik. 'We'd like to get some hard assets, too.' 'Like a film library,' Matheson says. 'And real estate,' adds Grodnik. Matheson laughs. 'I hope we're not going to stop here.' Grodnik shakes his head vigorously. 'We want to be Gulf and Lampoon.'"

They did have plans. They wanted to organize a new film and television department with established executives in those industries. They wanted to bring the magazine back to a monthly publication. They wanted to delve into the morning cartoon shows, forgetting or perhaps not realizing that few people would let small children anywhere in the vicinity of something bearing the *Lampoon* name. They wanted to set up a comedy board of directors to advise and consent on comedy projects; a board comprising "*Lampoon* celebrity alumni and new comedy stars." It soon became apparent that nobody was interested in joining them on such a board.

Late in 1989, Ratso Sloman told them he'd have to leave or take an extended leave of absence to write a book on the life of his late friend, Abbie Hoffman. Ratso had obviously been aware that they were trying to replace him but had been philosophical about it. Now, he'd signed a lucrative book deal, and he needed time off. They asked him to wait until they could find someone.

Meanwhile, the worst had happened. Batchelder wasn't coming through. The deal to buy me out and take over the company had made no sense at all because of their lack of knowledge about publishing and the business world in general. The only semblance of intelligent thought anyone might have had in going along with the take-over was the presence of Batchelder and his assurances that major financing was on hand. In later years, Alan Parsow explained why he sided with them against me. "It was like voting for Clinton over Bush. People didn't vote for Clinton, they voted against Bush. I just felt it was time for a change." If, indeed, he felt that way, dissatisfaction was never expressed earlier or at the time they had come in, asking only to be copresidents. Parsow, like the Beckers and Tim and Dan themselves, had originally said they wanted me to remain as chief executive officer and had already accepted minority representation on the board. I forced a break by refusing the officerships and salaries they wanted. There is no doubt in my mind or Weber's or Jurofsky's or Sloman's or anyone on the scene at the time that this had been Batchelder's take-over.

Batchelder wasn't backing up his assurances of the inflow of capital, which, incidentally, he had made to me as well, since I was to be the company's largest creditor because of my consulting agreement.

On New Year's Day 1990, Matheson and Grodnik had a company that was rapidly running out of money, and they hadn't implemented one change other than to elevate overhead to a scale where bankruptcy was up ahead jutting out from behind a rock.

"Hey," Grodnik said to me in a very confidential tone at a meeting at the *Lampoon* office in Los Angeles, "we're gonna be okay. We have a new friend, Mike Milken."

CHAPTER TWENTY-SIX

THE REACTION of the press to the *Lampoon* and its new management, which was now faltering and sputtering, was amazing. They attacked it like so many scavengers snapping at a dying animal. Even more interestingly, the most vicious attacks came from magazines themselves about to die. Like *Manhattan Inc.*, a magazine called 7 *Days*, which would soon go out of business, published a bitter article about Grodnik and Matheson and, for good measure, did a "job" on me, calling me everything from a "panderer" to a "cheapskate."

In the article, Grodnik and Matheson discussed the plans which had so excited Parsow and Becker; they would publish the magazine, produce films and TV, license products. They spoke of comedy clubs and trading cards. "We're gonna do things for a change," they declared, as though a company that published successful magazines and produced hit shows and blockbuster movies had been sleepwalking.

The 7-*Days* writer described the Co-Bros search for a new editor-in-chief as a Marx Brothers' set piece and suggested that Tony Hendra was the front-runner for the job. Was I losing it, I thought, as I read the article, or hadn't Tony been the editor of the magazine after Henry Beard left and before O'Rourke? Hadn't he been replaced because the magazine had been lurching and heaving under his editorship?

Hadn't deadlines been missed regularly, and hadn't it simply become more bitter and less funny during those years?

Nobody seemed to want the job. Why? Grodnik had the answer. "They're all wimps. A lot of people have turned us down," he said in a newspaper interview. "People who don't have guts or vision."

Spy, itself not exactly an ongoing success in the magazine business, in April 1990 summed up the publishing industry's general reaction to the *Lampoon's* new management and their never-ending search. "It's becoming less and less likely that any *National Lampoon* renaissance will occur under the dawdling stewardship of the thoroughly producerish Dan Grodnik and ingratiating actor Tim Matheson. ... [They've] required a year to locate a human being willing to be their editor." The article went on to excerpt a memo from *Lampoon* publisher Michael Carr to his bosses in which he revealed that the magazine was $90,000 in arrears to newsstand dealers and had similar problems with the printer and paper suppliers. He begged for operating capital. For the first time in its history, the *Lampoon* was not paying its bills.

To add to their many miseries, a Grodnik and Matheson coproduced film *Blind Fury* had opened and promptly closed at theaters around the country. The *L.A. Times* reviewed it thusly, "*Blind Fury* is a numbskull, cornball action comedy....a slovenly bash-a-thon." Other reviews were even harsher.

Grodnik was infuriated at the suggestion that they were lost souls. "We're not at sea, and we're not the Marx Brothers," he told a reporter. "You know what? We know what we don't know. Henry Kravis can come in and buy R. J. Reynolds, and he doesn't have to know how to run a cigarette company."

The difference was, of course, that Kravis had the money and influence and smarts to hire experienced people who did know how to run a cigarette company.

Instead, Grodnik and Matheson hired Billy Kimball.

By 1990, Tim and Dan, now referred to as "Tan and Dim" around the *Lampoon* offices, had moved to break the FilmAccord contract and were talking about buying out the Barris television deal. They were prepared to return $500,000 to Barris if they could find the $500,000.

I urged them to reconsider both moves, reminding them that the Barris deal would expire in 1992 and that in the two and a half years Barris had held the rights to the name for television, they'd done absolutely nothing. "Let it expire," I said. "Then you can get it back for nothing." "But what if they pick up the option?" the Co-Bros asked. "Great," I shrugged. "Then they have to pay you another million."

To this day, I have no idea why Barris paid a million dollars for something and then just let that something sit there, but that's just one more thing about Hollywood and the entertainment business that mystifies me. Certainly, if the *Lampoon* were to get yet another million from Barris, it would have been one more gift—a payment for something which was never meaningful before I had left the company and had been less meaningful since. The Co-Bros disagreed with me—once again they said I was being shortsighted.

I had made the FilmAccord deal mostly because of the domination of the film industry by the major studios. I have enjoyed good relationships with most of the major motion picture companies. Any project I submit to them is read immediately and attended to by an important executive who is part of the decision-making process. But producing movies is a heartbreaking business, and it's more heart-breaking when you have no part in the decision as to whether a film should be made.

There are seven companies that basically control the industry. Their decisions can bring great rewards, as in *Animal*

House or the *Vacation* pictures, a year or so of emptiness, as in *Class Reunion*, or total frustration when you can't get a picture made that you feel is worthy, as in *Jaws 3* or *The Joy of Sex*.

The *Lampoon* developed a dozen screen comedies at Universal and Warner Bros. that still sit, unused, in filing cabinets. I desperately wanted to have more to say about what gets made and what doesn't. I'd felt the only way the *Lampoon* could be a major factor in the film business was if we could finance our own films and make our own decisions as to which movies we'd make, or at least share those decisions. When John Ptak had brought the FilmAccord and Credit Lyonnais deal to me, I'd jumped at it. Ptak, a shrewd deal-maker, felt as strongly that this was a way for us to go. It offered unlimited financing to develop and produce and a partner who liked what we were doing and was easy to work with. It looked like real freedom and a real voice.

We'd made mistakes. The Lorimar and MGM distribution negotiations had wasted almost two years and then, an action movie FilmAccord had produced was deemed unreleasable and the bank decided they wanted to rethink that relationship. But now, they were ready to go again—and Grodnik and Matheson wanted out of the contract.

They had no other deal in place. Once again, this agreement, if it didn't work out in a year or so, would simply expire, but they were in a desperate hurry to go nowhere. When their lawyers notified FilmAccord that they were breaking the contract, FilmAccord immediately had filed the breach of contract suit, asking for, among other things, the $2.2 million they claimed to have already invested in National Lampoon Films.

With the twentieth anniversary having come and gone without a television show, without celebration of any kind except a tribute in the magazine, the talk now was about a twenty-fifth anniversary. Marketing consultant Whitten Pell, who had brought Nissan to the table when I was planning the twentieth anniversary, came up with other national advertisers who wanted to talk, but Pell told me no one at the new *Lampoon* seemed ready to pursue it. The advertisers dropped out and so did he.

Early in 1990, Grodnik and Matheson made a decision about the new editor. Billy Kimball had been an editor on the *Harvard Lampoon*—the Co-Bros thought they were home free. Aside from this time on his college humor magazine, he had no experience in publishing, but, reasoned Tim and Dan, "remember Kenney and Beard—no publishing experience except the *Harvard Lampoon*."

To paraphrase. I knew Beard and Kenney—and Billy Kimball was no Beard and Kenney.

And Beard and Kenney worked under people who had been in publishing for many years. Kimball would be led by Grodnik and Matheson who hadn't even been on their own college humor magazines.

Kimball had all the arrogance and assuredness that a Harvard education provides. He would not work with Agoglia or Jurofsky who between them had perhaps forty years of publishing experience. He ignored Sloman who was now a lame-duck editor anxious to leave and start writing his book but was more than willing to advise and help wherever he could.

Kimball insisted on communicating only with the cochairmen, copresidents, cochief executive officers, and copublishers—all of whom were Grodnik and Matheson. He told them he'd need months to prepare before he could take over. Reluctantly, Sloman agreed to stay longer, and Kimball started charting his budgets and editorial plans and interviewing a support staff. Perhaps unknown to Grodnik and Matheson, he also continued as a writer-performer on the newly formed Comedy Channel.

What astounded everyone most at the *Lampoon* was that Kimball who had never before been an editor of a "grown-up" magazine, signed a contract for $135,000 a year plus perks. A fanciful salary at a time like this?

By early summer of 1990, Kimball, in a memo, outlined his plans and his budget. Apparently, he expected to be in charge of everything from the editorial package to deciding what time the receptionist went to lunch. He would supervise *Heavy Metal* as well as the *Lampoon*. At the time, *Heavy Metal* was showing a substantial profit.

Kimball proposed a monthly "outside" editorial budget (it would return to being a monthly publication) of $110,000 a month. This did not include salaries and other "in-house" expenses. It was $66,000 a month more than the budget at the time which was the highest in the history of the magazine.

He asked that the current editorial staff all be replaced, which would have meant there would be no one on hand who had any relationship with any of the current or past contributors.

He described the noneditorial staff as "lazy and ineffi-cient" and insisted that he would not "involve the editorial staff in a fruitless mission to cover up their inadequacies." He also expected the senior managers (obviously Agoglia and Jurofsky) to bring office problems to him and not to discuss them directly with Grodnik and Matheson.

He ended with three paragraphs describing his pre-scribed instructions as to the eating schedule of the recep-tionist and other members of the support staff.

The memo was quickly circulated around the office. In Los Angeles even Grodnik and Matheson blanched. In New

York, Agoglia sold his last stock holdings in the company and submitted a date for his retirement. Howard Jurofsky, without question, the most dedicated worker in the company's history, a "company man" who was expert in production, distribution, and subscription fulfillment, was apoplectic.

The gall of this totally untested young man who literally had one credential, a college humor magazine, was simply astonishing to all. In addition to Andy Simmons and Dave Hanson, several art directors had left. The magazine which once averaged a tenure among its editors of more than six years and had had some (O'Rourke, Sussman, Kelly, Hendra) who stayed with the magazine for more than ten, was now a revolving door with editors coming but mostly going. Money woes were getting even greater. By now Michael Milken, with problems of his own, was no longer discussed.

In April of 1990, Grodnik and Matheson came up with at least a partial solution. They stopped paying the money they owed me.

Of course, in all fairness, I wasn't alone. They had defaulted on the second Warners' loan, and Warners had promptly deducted the monies owed them from settlements due on magazine sales. They were well in arrears to the printer and paper companies. Many contributors hadn't been paid in months. I was informed, however, that they continued to draw their own $300,000-a-year salary.

My contract required that we submit to arbitration should there be a dispute, so we turned our case over to the required board and waited for an arbitration hearing.

The disparagement of the magazine and its management continued in the press as word got around that bills weren't being paid. Then, in the summer of 1990, we were told that the *Lampoon* was merging with a video software company called J-2 Communications. J-2 stood for Jim Jimirro, "J" twice.

That company had gone public in 1988 and had had three years of minor success with combined earnings for the years from 1988 through 1990 of about $1.2 million. Jimirro had been president of the Disney Cable Channel, leaving when Michael Eisner and the new regime came in. Why an underwriter took them public with no particular assets other than Jimirro's past relationship to Disney remains a mystery to many to this day, but in the summer of 1990, J-2 had millions in cash on hand from the underwriting and a sudden awareness that it could not compete in the video business with the major studios who controlled nearly all of the important motion pictures and, naturally, fed them into their own video companies.

J-2 had enjoyed some success with a comedy video called *Dorf on Golf* which featured Tim Conway as sort of a "Toulouse-Lautrec" in knickers and golf cap, but Conway had decided, after a couple of videos, to move elsewhere. J-2 had to do something either to generate more videos with a potential for sale or move into another business.

In the *Lampoon* Jimirro saw an answer to both needs. *Animal House* and the *Vacation* pictures, he rationalized, proved that the *Lampoon* name had great appeal in the marketplace. Producing *Lampoon* comedy videos would be a natural. More importantly, with one agreement, he would be Jim Jimirro, film producer, publisher, and chief executive officer of one of the best-known names in the entertainment and publishing worlds. He started negotiating.

Grodnik and Matheson came to the table with nothing. They were "hungrier" than I'd been twenty years earlier. Either they made the deal or the company would go into bankruptcy, probably reverting to my management since I was, by far, the principal creditor. The company, which had been valued on the open market at $8 million the day I had sold my shares, was acquired by J-2 about eighteen months later for $4.7 million in stock and warrants, which would prove just about worthless in a little more than a year.

"The warrants are the key," Alan Parsow told me at the time. "They're going to be worth a lot of money."

I shook my head in disbelief. Once again, the fact that new management hadn't an inkling about either publishing or the motion picture business was being ignored.

Dan and Tim had given themselves long-term employment contracts. Jimirro asked that they be canceled and declared he would reevaluate their relationship to the company once he took over. In desperation, they agreed; anxious, one supposes, to get their hands on that J-2 stock which had soared to two and seven-eighths on disclosure of the deal and the warrants which their friend Parsow seemed to think would someday be of great value. But what could they have done? It was the deal or nothing, so they agreed to the deal.

Before he would complete the merger, Jimirro insisted that, as the principal creditor, I renegotiate my deal. He had to cut down the overhead, he said. He was prepared to put millions into the *Lampoon*, but everybody would have to sacrifice.

It sounded logical and fair. Patti and I had recently married and were expecting a baby. I had no desire to get embroiled in a bankruptcy. If this guy could save the *Lampoon*, I was with him.

The company owed me $750,000 payable over three years. I agreed to take it over six years.

I also agreed to waive all the ancillary perks that had been in my buyout contract: car, secretary, medical plans, expenses, everything, with the understanding that if the company should again default on the payments owed me, all of these things would come due as though they had always existed.

I asked for two other things: a lien on the movie royalties paid to the *Lampoon* for *Animal House* and *Vacation* should there be a default and payment of the monies the Grodnik-Matheson management hadn't paid me over the recent months. We signed the deal that summer.

In a *Variety* article covering the merger, shortly before it was completed, Jimirro revealed that he "planned to incorporate the humor mag's widely recognized name into a line of original [video] programs lensed for around $1 million each. 'I believe in marketing, and know how to market a product,' he said further. 'That's where success lies.'"

He also said he planned to retain the team of Tim Matheson and Dan Grodnik. "The J-2 deal provides us with funding and support of a major company," Matheson declared in the article, generously elevating tiny J-2 to "major company status." "Jim Jimirro is known for his business acumen," he added with a further flourish of generosity.

The story also noted that Billy Kimball would soon take the reins of the magazine.

The article ended with the announcement that two stockholders had filed for a class-action suit, complaining that the deal did not reflect the company's value.

J-2 and Grodnik-Matheson signed a deal that summer, and Jimirro took over the *Lampoon* in the fall of 1990.

He immediately made two decisive moves to improve the company's fortunes. He fired Grodnik and Matheson as "Co-Bros" of the *Lampoon* and increased his own salary from $250,000 to $350,000 a year.

He did something else. He fired Billy Kimball who after months on the job was still developing plans and was yet to edit an issue. In a statement to the press, Jimirro said that "Kimball was hired despite having no experience as an editor." He also revealed that the search for a new editor was already underway.

And he paid the delinquent bills and paid me up to date, to boot. Soon afterward, he hired a new editor. Recommended by Sloman, George Barkin had been a contributor to the *Lampoon* for five years. Brother of the actress Ellen Barkin, he tried, but quite simply was neither a humorist nor a strong editor, and the magazine just got duller and duller.

The "class action" suit was dropped.

But it was Jimirro who quickly proved that the "Co-Bros" weren't the only guys who could go astray in a world they did not know.

Like Grodnik and Matheson, Jimirro didn't like the Barris deal, and like them, he was prepared to buy out the balance of the contract. At one of our few meetings, I urged him to reconsider just as I did with his predecessors. It was 1991. In a little over a year, I reasoned, the agreement would end. If Barris, now called the Guber-Peters Company, wanted to renew, they would have to ante up another million dollars. In the more than three and a half years that they'd held the rights to the *Lampoon* name, they had done absolutely nothing with it. It was illogical to think that they'd renew, and if they did, that would mean the *Lampoon* had cleared $2 million for rights to something we'd made almost nothing from in twenty-one years.

Jimirro disregarded my advice and paid $500,000 to Guber-Peters, effectively buying them out of the remaining eighteen months of the contract.

In the years that followed there was no *Lampoon* TV programming.

Jimirro also agreed with Grodnik-Matheson's disdain for
the FilmAccord-Credit Lyonnais deal.

The original agreement with FilmAccord was a fifty-fifty
partnership. The *Lampoon* provided the name and the creative
input, and FilmAccord invested or got others to invest in the
day-to-day business operations, development, and, finally, in
the production. It seemed to me to have been an excellent
move. Jimirro at first insisted it was a lousy deal, then a year
later, after continuous attempts at solving what was an impasse
that was running up legal bills and keeping the name dormant,
John Ptak brought in a distributor, New Line; the bank was
back in the action and a new deal was cut.

When I read the new agreement, I shook my head in disbelief. The deal that my successors had held out for and had
spent tens of thousands in legal bills on was not as favorable
for the *Lampoon* as the original which I had made and which
had been in place. They actually renegotiated a lesser deal for
themselves. Now, FilmAccord, which under the new terms
only raised the money and had no management responsibilities, was getting a bigger slice of the pie than the *Lampoon*.

Jimirro's plans for the *Lampoon* were as grandiose as
Grodnik and Matheson's had been. On one occasion, he
showed me a giant graph listing as many as fifty businesses for
which he planned to license the *Lampoon* name. He was
turning it into a bargain-basement licensing spree. I was particularly struck by *Lampoon* comedy cruises. Cruises are basically supported by people past fifty. The *Lampoon*, conversely,
is especially meaningful to people younger than, let's say,
thirty-five with a lot of eighteen and twenty-twos thrown in.
They do not go on cruises.

He had other ideas: comedy clubs, merchandising (for years the *Lampoon* sold T-shirts, jackets, etc. but there was never successful in-store merchandising). And, of course, theater and the original video programming plan which never materialized.

In February of 1992, desperate for cash, J-2 sold *Heavy Metal* magazine for $500,000, the same amount they'd paid to Barris. The magazine had earned more than $360,000 in 1988, and would earn as much or more in 1989. It was sold at a times/earnings ratio of less than one-and-a-half-to-one. We had purchased the minority stock in the *Lampoon* in 1975 for fifteen times earnings. Without changing a thing, the purchaser, Kevin Eastman, the creator of Ninja Turtles, earned his money back in a little more than a year.

What was perhaps most mind-boggling was Jimirro's constant involvement with litigation. He seemed to always be suing or being sued.

Over the years, the Grodnik-Matheson-Jimirro triumvirate had, I am told, more than a dozen outside law firms handling assorted lawsuits. In addition, to the best of my recollection, J-2 had, over a three-year period, four or five different in-house counsels, a number of whom left under angry circumstances.

My son Michael's suit was settled after nearly three years of litigation when the lawyer representing the *Lampoon* in New York dropped out of the case because his bills had not been paid. The suit could have been settled years earlier and saved the company tens of thousands of dollars.

My own legal bills, in dealing with the two managements, have been well into six figures. One can only surmise that *Lampoon* legal costs in handling my actions and the others the new owners caused were many, many times more.

In addition, by contract, the *Lampoon* will have to reimburse me for my legal costs should my suit prevail.

In the five years since the company has been under new management, legal bills for litigation far exceed the total for the company's previous twenty-two years.

Like so many other things they did, Grodnik-Matheson-Jimirro, the three horsemen of the preposterous, ignored existing contracts and bills, regularly ran up legal bills and then settled for less than they had or could have negotiated in the first place.

The overall impression had been, as already stated, that the Marx Brothers were running the store, and things hadn't changed when Jimirro took over. In the publishing industry in New York and the film business in Los Angeles, the *Lampoon*, once respected in both communities, had become a running joke.

In J-2's annual statement dated July 31, 1991, the now-merged companies lost $2.7 million.

Barkin would leave and two bright, young, junior editors on staff, Sam Johnson and Chris Marcil, would edit the magazine and do a decent job until it ceased regular publication early in 1992. Howard Jurofsky, who had managed the New York operation for Grodnik and Matheson after Agoglia retired and then for a while for J-2, left to join the new *Heavy Metal* team as did treasurer Walter Garibaldi. My daughter Julie also stayed with *Heavy Metal*, then left after a disagreement with Eastman. That magazine remains profitable.

Another issue of the *Lampoon* was not published until March of 1993 when Ratso Sloman was rehired to put together an issue to keep the *Harvard Lampoon* franchise intact. That agreement requires the publishing of at least one issue a year.

In 1992, the *Lampoon* once again stopped paying its bills, and J-2 notified all creditors that it would pay a small amount on each dollar owed to clear up their debt. Jimirro warned, if creditors didn't agree to such a settlement, he'd put the *Lampoon* into bankruptcy. Most of the creditors, owed relatively small amounts of money, went along with the threat and took the lesser payment. I told him, more or less, what I told Austin Furst in 1986 and what I probably should have told Grodnik and Matheson in 1989, "FUCK OFF!"

I sued the *Lampoon* and J-2 for all monies due me plus legal costs.

J-2 cut losses for the year ended July 31, 1992, to $1.202 million.

For the nine months ended April 30, 1993, J-2 announced a loss of $1.148 million. The assets of the National Lampoon, Inc. were taken out of that corporation and handed over to J-2 in an attempt to provide corporate insulation which they apparently hoped would short circuit my lawsuit. According to their forms filed with the SEC, "this [foreclosure] would leave National Lampoon with no remaining assets."

J-2's video business doesn't seem to be in much better shape than the *Lampoon* magazine. The only active part of the entire company seems to be the licensing of the *Lampoon* name. The New Line deal, a leftover from the FilmAccord-Credit Lyonnais-National Lampoon company formed six years ago, and the royalties from *Animal House* and the *Vacation* pictures, seem to be keeping them afloat. To the best of my knowledge, the Grodnik-Matheson-Jimirro managements have produced virtually no income on their own and have succeeded only in reducing the magazine to a once-a-year publication.

In the Milken and Boesky trials, the defense characterized their kind of recklessness as victimless crimes. I can attest
to the fact that they are not. The take-over of companies led
by people like Milken and Boesky and David Batchelder and
endorsed by people like Drexel-Burnham's Bob Becker and
Elkhorn, Nebraska's Alan Parsow, had, in the case of the
Lampoon, many victims:

Dozens of employees—

Printing and paper companies who exist on magazines
that are published—

Stockholders—

and, people like me who devote their lives to something they
care deeply for. Henry Beard could take his money and leave
the *Lampoon* without looking back. I could not do that. I was
taken from it, kicking and screaming. It was the last sick joke.

EPILOGUE

IT'S LATE IN 1993 as I write these words. My days and nights are primarily occupied with writing and developing films and with our daughter, Kate, who was three in September and is already a California girl with a light golden tan and swimming form better than mine. My lawsuit against Jim Jimirro and J-2 Communications and the *National Lampoon* for well over a million dollars has been settled for less than that amount. My decision to accept less being based mostly on the company's dwindling fortunes and the ongoing cost of pursuing such litigation.

Since I left the *Lampoon*, I have produced (executive produced) one film, *National Lampoon's Christmas Vacation*. Another project I developed at Warner Bros., *Cousin Eddie*, is now being rewritten there under my supervision. It's a script that the production mavens at Warners are quite excited about. The rewrite is being done to accommodate a star. We shall see. I have other scripts hanging in the balance in various places—some look like they might flower. We shall see about these, too.

A third sequel to *Vacation* was put on hold when Chevy and the studio couldn't agree on a variety of things that might still be worked out. Again, we have the rudiments that everybody involved—including Chevy—really likes. It would be something of a Swiss Family Griswold, with the hapless clan being shipwrecked in the South Seas.

I've toyed with the idea of going back into the magazine business—I've always loved the rush to deadlines and the freedom you have with a magazine that you don't have with a movie, the constant activity, all day, all week, all year. In the movie business, a producer's work while a film is actually being shot is somewhat akin, excitement-wise, to watching grass grow. I've also thought about putting together another theatrical revue—another undertaking that keeps you in motion at all times.

The *Lampoon*, under J-2's aegis, has been even less active. The film, *National Lampoon's Loaded Weapon*, which required little involvement by J-2 executives, was moderately successful, primarily because it opened well thanks to the *Lampoon* name. As part of the three picture deal with FilmAccord, Credit Lyonnais, and New Line, it will soon be followed by yet-another *Lampoon* picture which will again presumably not be written, directed, or produced by anyone who has ever been part of the *Lampoon* family.

In July of 1993, a *Lampoon* revue opened with virtually no hoopla, at a small nightclub theater in Pasadena. "The wit is mostly innocuous and sitting through [it] feels a bit like watching your neighbors perform charades," wrote *L.A. Weekly's* critic. Innocuous!? Charades!?—Can this be a *Lampoon* show?

In December, *Christmas Vacation* and *E.T.* competed against each other on prime-time television with the *Lampoon* film pulling down much higher ratings.

The *Lampoon* is now, according to its latest issue, published in December 1993, resuming bimonthly publication. The issue, in front of me as I write this, is not even a pale imitation of the original *Lampoon*, circa 1970-1988.

It would appear that they've finally killed the dog.

The successes of John Hughes, Ivan Reitman, Chevy Chase, Harold Ramis, Michelle Pfeiffer, P. J. O'Rourke, Michael O'Donoghue, and Bill Murray have already been chronicled on these pages and virtually everywhere else.

Karen Allen, Tom Hulce, Peter Riegert, Stephen Furst, and Kevin Bacon—all of whom made their screen debuts in *Animal House*—have been heard from regularly since.

Michael Gross now produces films under the Ivan Reitman banner, including *Beethoven*, *Twins*, *Kindergarten Cop*, *Dave*, and others.

Jeff Greenfield is an ABC political correspondent seen and heard regularly on "Nightline" and on the evening news.

John Weidman won a Tony Award for the book of *Pacific Overtures* and rescripted *Anything Goes* for Broadway and a national tour.

Lucy Fisher (an adopted *Lampoon* family member) is an executive vice-president at Warner Bros. Peter Ivers was murdered in his apartment during a burglary.

Michael Tolkin was nominated for an Oscar for his script (adapted from his novel) of *The Player*. Stephen Tolkin wrote the original HBO film, *Daybreak*.

Gilda Radner died on May 20, 1989.

Larry Sloman wrote the Abbie Hoffman biography and the autobiography of Howard Stern, *Private Parts*, which became a number one best-seller. Going from being an editor of the *Lampoon* to being Howard Stern's biographer must be something like switching from sirloin to Spam.

Harold Chamberlain, who brought us to the *Harvard Lampoon*, left Warners in the seventies and died a few years later.

Brian Doyle-Murray is one of the busier film character actors.

Chris Guest writes, acts, and directs, his most recent directorial effort being HBO's *The Attack of the Fifty-Foot Woman*.

Janis Hirsch, Wendy Goldman, and Peter Kaminsky are much-in-demand TV producers. Kevin Curran was producer and head writer of "Married With Children." He now has his own NBC sitcom "It's a Good Life." Michael Reiss and Al Jean were the producers of "The Simpsons" and now have their own show, "The Critic."

When I called David Batchelder at his office in Orange County, the phone had been disconnected, which is not to say he isn't still out there like a fox in a hen house.

Meat Loaf, years after the success of "Bat Out Of Hell," and nearly twenty years after he replaced John Belushi in *The National Lampoon Show*, revisited the spotlight with the hugely successful "Bat Out Of Hell II" album. Once again the music was written by former *Lampoon* musical director Jim Steinman.

Ted Mann is currently producing the TV show "NYPD Blue," perhaps the most heralded new dramatic program in years.

Former *Lampoon* contributor Larry David created and produces "Seinfeld."

Casey Silver, who worked in TV development for the *Lampoon* in the early eighties, is now president of Universal Pictures.

Rodger Bumpass, as reported earlier, does voice-overs for commercials and animated films.

Judy Belushi remarried, has a son, and lives happily on Martha's Vineyard.

Tom Leopold, a *Lampoon* writer and actor, most recently was the story editor and producer of "Seinfeld" and before that, of "Cheers." Fred Graver was a producer of "Cheers."

Chris Miller just sold a script to Columbia and has a cookbook coming out soon.

Graham Loving died in Aspen, Colorado, in September of 1986.

Emily Prager is a successful author and columnist.

John Michael Higgins, featured in *The Class of '86*, has had the title role in the play "Jeffrey" for the last year, garnering enthusiastic reviews.

Paul Shaffer, a composer, musician and actor on the "National Lampoon Radio Hour" and on several *Lampoon* comedy albums, notably, "Goodbye Pop," is doing the same for David Letterman—for more money.

Brian McConnachie, Danny Abelson, Bruce McCall, John Boni, Tim Crouse, Ellis Weiner, Ed Bluestone, Anne Beatts, Tod Carroll, and Henry Beard continue to write magazine articles, screenplays, and (Henry and Bruce) successful books and for television. Mitch Markowitz wrote *Good Morning Vietnam*.

Gerry Taylor is the publisher of *Spy*.

Bob Tischler who went from sound engineer to producer of the *Lampoon* radio show, is the supervising producer of the TV show "Empty Nest."

John Bendel, who edited the *Lampoon's* "True Facts" column for more than a decade, is an editor of a New Jersey daily.

Sean Kelly and Tony Hendra, I am told, dissolved their friendship after a disagreement about a book they were to write together. Hendra, now the editor of *Spy*, whose *Lampoon* satires of religion, particularly his own, drew so much wrath, I hear goes to church every Sunday with his new family. Kelly, author of the book *Fart*, now writes for a children's TV show.

Len Mogel writes books on publishing and lectures at colleges.

Tim Matheson has apparently retired from the business world and still stars, mostly in made for TV movies. Dan Grodnik is "around."

Stu Kreisman and Chris Cleuss, *Lampoon* writers throughout the seventies, produced TV's "Night Court."

Contributor John Podhoretz is a prominent political columnist. He wrote speeches for Ronald Reagan during his last years in the White House.

Former *Lampoon* board member and investor Alan Parsow, once as ecstatic about the J-2 deal as he was about the Grodnik-Matheson incursion, now says of Jimirro, "It appears that his reputation exceeded his abilities" and, about Jimirro's problems, "It's not like he didn't deserve them." Parsow still invests in the stock market.

Parsow, who has never, to the best of my knowledge, admitted to losing money on an investment, now also says that he got out of the J-2 stock, which he got in exchange for his *Lampoon* holdings, "without a loss." If so, it was an escape worthy of Houdini considering that the stock has been virtually dormant for years. The warrants, as has been said, would be meaningful only if the current price of the stock, at the very least, quadrupled. I suspect that no forecaster on Wall Street is expecting that to happen in the foreseeable future. Certainly, the Drexel investors brought into the *Lampoon* by Bob Becker and his sons and used as the voting block to take control of the company, lost a great deal of money. One Philadelphia-based investor, a former Becker client who still holds a large number of J-2 shares and warrants, estimates that his paper losses have been more than a quarter of a million dollars. At the time of the take-over, he was in profit for about the same amount, a half million dollar swing.

Joe Bob Briggs does everything.

Richard Belzer, Gilbert Gottfried, and Will Durst perform everywhere except at bar mitzvahs.

Nick Bakay and Dave Hanson wrote and produced for the Comedy Channel. Hanson is now writing for David Letterman.

Former editors Chris Marcil and Sam Johnson are writing for "Beavis and Butthead," which makes about as much sense as a one-time *Lampoon* contributor writing speeches for Ronald Reagan.

Paul Krassner, who wrote for the *Lampoon* on and off for nearly twenty years, still lives and still edits *The Realist* and is still angry and funny. His recent book, *Confessions of a Raving, Unconfined Nut,* attests to that.

Gerry Sussman, as noted, died, as did Mara MacAfee, perhaps the greatest of all of the *Lampoon* cover and poster artists.

Robert Hoffman, I hear, still sells soda.

I am told, George W. S. Trow has left the *New Yorker* and recently wrote a two-hundred-dollar coffee table book.

Chris Cerf is at Random House and many other places and is still the most affable of all ex-Lampooners, which is something like being the only Tibetan in Nigeria.

Julian Weber has his own law practice.

One-time editor Les Firestein is executive producer of Fox TV's "In Living Color."

Julie Simmons, like her father, is contemplating a return to publishing but, meanwhile, is concentrating on more vital matters like her kids and teaching art at a local grade school in faraway New Jersey.

Michael Simmons has been music supervisor and contractor on several major films and is currently writing an authorized biography of a legendary rock group and a screenplay.

Andy Simmons is the editor of *Cracked,* the young men's humor magazine.

Shary Flenniken continues her successful cartooning career as do Drew Friedman, Frank Springer, Sam Gross, Buddy Hickerson, Rodriguez, Jeff Wong, Randy Jones, and many of the other *Lampoon* artists. Gahan Wilson is developing an animated film for Stephen Spielberg's Amblin Productions. B. K. Taylor, who created the classic "Timberland Tales" and "The Appletons" for the *Lampoon* for years, now writes for the TV comedy "Home Improvement."

Why did the *Lampoon* work? In his review of *Animal House*, critic Roger Ebert wrote, "The movie is vulgar, raunchy, ribald and occasionally scatological. [It] is funny for some of the same reasons the *National Lampoon* is funny; because it finds some kind of precarious balance between insanity and accuracy, between cheerfully wretched excess and an ability to reproduce the most revealing nuances of human behavior."

Good enough. When you got right down to it, however, it was the laughter that counted.

Two of my favorite maxims have long been:

"The biggest liar in the world is, 'they say.'"

and

"The greatest cause of stomach disorder is the thought, 'What if?'"

Well...they say...

what if,

those *Lampoon* movies that were going to have been made but never were had been made? For example, what if Universal hadn't canceled *Jaws 3–People 0*?

the purchase of the minority stock had been under less onerous terms?

we'd gotten a distributor and Credit Lyonnais had financed the production of National Lampoon films?

Austin Furst, Strauss Zelnick, Tony Cassara, George Vandeman, Thom Mount, and the other would-be acquirers had somehow been unable to find our phone number?

Belushi hadn't died and we'd made *The Joy of Sex*?

Kenney had lived and we'd made more movies together as we'd planned?

Matheson and Grodnik had stayed with acting in and coproducing bad movies instead of being co-kings of industry?

we'd come back—again?

Special thanks to Michael O'Donoghue, Harold Ramis, Ted Mann, Chris Cerf, Judy Belushi, Janis Hirsch, Gerald Taylor, Julian Weber, Michael Gross, Chris Miller, Ned Tanen, John Landis, Kevin Curran, Rodger Bumpass, Wendy Goldman, Stephen Furst, Marvin Meyer, Todd Bonder, Michael Simmons, Andy Simmons, and especially Julie Simmons-Lynch; all of whom helped me remember the way it was.

January 1994